The Routledge Intermediate Chinese Reader

The Routledge Intermediate Chinese Reader is a comprehensive reader designed to provide varied, stimulating, and up-to-date reading material for learners of Chinese at the intermediate level.

The Chinese Reader provides a bridge between basic literacy skills and the ability to read whole novels and newspapers in Chinese. It consists of 40 readings, graded on the basis of complexity of vocabulary, grammar, and syntax. These readings present a range of different text types representative of modern Chinese popular writing that will inspire students to continue reading independently in Chinese.

It is ideal for learners who already possess a knowledge of essential grammar and vocabulary and who wish to expand their knowledge of the language through contextualized reading material.

Key features include:

- extracts from newspaper and internet articles
- vocabulary annotation next to the reading paragraphs for quick reference
- short grammar explanations of any complicated structures
- comprehension and discussion questions
- notes on culture and idioms
- text structure maps to aid comprehension
- full glossary at the back and answer key for reading questions
- a companion website containing audio files and electronic vocabulary flashcards.

Suitable for both class use and independent study, *The Routledge Intermediate Chinese Reader* is an essential tool for facilitating vocabulary learning and increasing reading proficiency.

Helen H. Shen is Associate Professor of Chinese at the University of Iowa, USA.

Yunong Zhou is Lecturer in Chinese at the University of Pennsylvania, USA.

Xiaoyuan Zhao is Lecturer in Chinese at the University of Iowa, USA.

ROUTLEDGE MODERN LANGUAGE READERS

Series Editor: Itesh Sachdev
School of Oriental and African Studies, University of London

Routledge Modern Language Readers provide the intermediate language learner with a selection of readings that give a broad representation of modern writing in the target language.

Each reader contains approximately 20 readings graded in order of difficulty to allow the learner to grow with the book and to acquire the necessary skills to continue reading independently.

Suitable for both class use and independent study, *Routledge Modern Language Readers* are an essential tool for increasing language proficiency and reading comprehension skills.

Available:

Chinese
Turkish
Welsh

Forthcoming:

Arabic
Brazilian Portuguese
Dutch
Hindi
Japanese
Korean
Polish
Russian
Yiddish

The Routledge Intermediate Chinese Reader

Helen H. Shen, Yunong Zhou, and Xiaoyuan Zhao

Routledge
Taylor & Francis Group

LONDON AND NEW YORK

First published 2013
by Routledge
2 Park Square, Milton Park, Abingdon, Oxon OX14 4RN

Simultaneously published in the USA and Canada
by Routledge
711 Third Avenue, New York, NY 10017

Routledge is an imprint of the Taylor & Francis Group, an informa business

British Library Cataloguing in Publication Data
A catalogue record for this book is available from the British Library

Library of Congress Cataloging in Publication Data
Shen, Helen H.
  The Routledge Intermediate Chinese Reader / Helen H. Shen, Yunong Zhou, and
Xiaoyuan Zhao.
    pages cm. – (Routledge Modern Language Readers)
  Includes bibliographical references and index.
    1. Chinese language–Readers.   2. Chinese language–Textbooks for foreign speakers–
English.   I. Shen, Helen H., editor of compilation.   II. Title.
  PL1115.S54 2013
  495.1'86421–dc23
                                                                                    2012046305

ISBN: 978-0-415-63635-3 (hbk)
ISBN: 978-0-415-63636-0 (pbk)
ISBN: 978-0-203-49436-3 (ebk)

Typeset in Scala
by Graphicraft Limited, Hong Kong

Printed and bound in Great Britain by
TJ International Ltd, Padstow, Cornwall

目录

Contents

Preface

The Routledge Intermediate Chinese Reader textbook is suitable for college or high school Chinese learners who have completed 15 to 18 credit hours in Chinese study. It is intended to be used either as a textbook course of extensive reading to supplement the intensive reading textbook lessons or as part of the weekly reading homework for learners to complete independently. It is also suitable for self-study learners of equivalent level.

The goal

The main goal of providing this extensive reading textbook is to reinforce and expand vocabulary knowledge, stimulate reading interests, improve reading comprehension skills, and gain knowledge of Chinese society and culture through reading. The selection of reading materials in this textbook follows three principles of compiling an extensive reading textbook: 1) the reading materials are easier than those for intensive reading so that learners can increase their reading speed to improve reading fluency; 2) the content covers a variety of topics so that learners can choose what they want to read about; 3) the materials are interesting and informative so learners are reading for pleasure, for information, and for a general understanding of the text.

Pedagogical measures for chapter design

Guided by the goal and purpose of intensive reading instruction, the chapter design of this textbook is in line with the following pedagogical measures.

Accelerating automaticity of word recognition and expanding vocabulary

It is widely accepted by Chinese scholars that knowledge of roughly 9,000 commonly occurring words is essential in order for an individual to be able to read Chinese newspapers and magazines with some dictionary help. For intermediate learners, our instructional goal is to acquire vocabulary knowledge of around 5,000 words (not characters). Therefore, this textbook ensures that learners are exposed to the frequency range of 5,000 words by using *ChineseTA* software to control the difficulty level of vocabulary in each chapter. (This software is an integrated computer software program which enables teachers to create, adjust, and evaluate their teaching materials (for more information please visit http://www.svlanguage.com/ChineseTA%20Feature.htm).) Each chapter is designed to take into consideration both intentional and incidental vocabulary learning.

Fostering reading interests, positive reading attitude, and good reading habits

The topics selected for this textbook are based on a survey of intermediate students in US universities. In order to support intensive reading, we also incorporate popular topics from various intermediate textbooks (for intensive reading) on the market. The chapter design strives for attractive presentation in terms of both content and layout to keep learners focused on their reading tasks.

Improving global/general reading comprehension of the reading lessons

In order to keep learners focused on what is being read without being frustrated by unfamiliar words, grammar, or cultural content, we provide each chapter with annotations for new words, notes on culture and grammar, and reading comprehension questions. Answer keys for the reading questions are provided for learners' convenience during self-study.

Developing and reinforcing good reading skills and strategies

We strive for a variety of important reading skills, which build from gaining the main idea to making predictions based on available information. We also emphasize reading fluency development by designing reading lessons that involve a certain degree of challenge but that learners can undertake with some effort. We intend to foster good reading strategies on the part of students by including exercises that call for vocabulary and background knowledge preparation prior to reading and an overall reading-performance check following the reading.

Broadening knowledge of Chinese society and increasing cultural awareness

Chapters are structured according to cultural themes. In order to increase learners' cultural awareness, we include chapters that describe Chinese and Western observations of cultural differences from comparative perspectives.

Chapter organization and structure of the textbook

Organization of each chapter

Each chapter consists of two short reading texts, 阅读A (Reading A) and 阅读B (Reading B), with a focused cultural theme. Reading A is designed as the major reading lesson, and Reading B is designed to support Reading A. Reading A includes the following sections:

1   *Warm-up exercises.* This is designed for directing learners' attention to certain key words in the text, to activate learners' background knowledge, and to stimulate learners' reading interests.

2   *Reading text.* We provide annotation to the possibly unfamiliar words alongside the text so that learners can check word meanings easily and without interruption of their sentence comprehension during reading.

3   *Culture/idiom notes.* The notes on culture and idioms help learners' understand traditional and modern culture as well as the local culture the text conveys. We also provide notes for the idioms that reflect Chinese language culture.

4   *Grammar/language points.* This section provides translation and explanation for important sentence structures, patterns, or structural words in the text using plain language to aid comprehension.

5   *Reading comprehension.* This section provides various questions to guide reading comprehension. In addition to traditional closed and open-ended questions, we provide exercises in completing a text structure map to help learners understand how the text is constructed and what main points the author is trying to convey. Following the text structure map exercise, we provide discussion questions that allow learners to relate the reading content to their personal life, to apply learned knowledge to real-life situations, and to foster their critical thinking abilities.

Reading B adopts an organizational structure similar to that of Reading A, but with a reduced number of exercises (the warm-up and text structure map exercises are excluded). Because learners will already have learned Reading A, we would expect them to have acquired the necessary knowledge and skills to explore Reading B with more autonomy.

Structure of the whole textbook

The whole book includes 20 chapters. At the end of the textbook, we provide an answer key for the exercises in each chapter, including answers for some of the open-ended questions. The answers for open-ended questions are not intended to serve as standard answers for the questions; rather, they are there to provide samples or references on how to answer the questions. The vocabulary for the chapters is provided in two glossaries: one is in Pinyin, and the other in English.

In addition, we provide a companion website for the textbook: http://www.uiowa.edu/intermediatechinesereader. The website provides audio files for all reading texts, which will help learners to establish a connection between each character and its pronunciation. For readers' convenience, both simplified and traditional character versions of lesson texts are provided along with the audio files. We also provide links to the online dictionary so that readers can check any new words that may not be listed in the vocabulary annotation. The website also provides links to relevant DVD clips to supply background knowledge for understanding the chapter content.

We would like to thank Dai Yang 戴阳 from Thomas Jefferson University in the United States for his technical assistance in completing the glossaries for this textbook.

Acknowledgments

The texts used in this textbook were mainly selected from the online versions of Chinese newspapers. The authors of this textbook have made considerable modifications to the selected materials from the newspapers to fit the learning level. One article is from the internet with permission from the author. The rest have been written by the authors of this textbook. While the authors and publishers have made every effort to contact related newspapers and individuals for the material used in this textbook, they would be grateful to hear from any they were unable to contact. Meanwhile, the authors and the publisher of this textbook would like to thank the following newspapers and individuals for their contributions:

网络来源： http://world.people.com.cn/GB/157278/17041651.html
原载中国日报网2012年2月7日 作者：不详 责任编辑：杨牧 有删改

网络来源： http://www.chinadaily.com.cn/hqzg/2007-12/11/content_6313452.htm
原载《中国日报》2007年12月11日 文：Patrick Whiteley 编译：张博 有删改

网络来源： http://overseas.cn.yahoo.com/ypen/20111019/647174_5.html
原载《健康时报》2011年10月19日 文：记者 薛京、吴尧、杨波 有删改

网络来源： http://overseas.cn.yahoo.com/ypen/20111019/647174_1.html
原载《健康时报》2011年10月19日 文：记者 薛京 吴尧 杨波 有删改

网络来源： http://sjb.qlwb.com.cn/html/2011-04/26/content_117801.htm?div=-1
原载《齐鲁晚报》2011年4月26日 文：记者 李飞 实习生 任辉 徐青 有删改

网络来源： http://jrzb.zjol.com.cn/html/2010-07/03/content_436874.htm?div=-1
原载《今日早报》2010年7月3日 文：通讯员 李莹 记者 陈宇浩 有删改

网络来源： http://daily.cnnb.com.cn/nbwb/html/2011-09/06/content_360827.htm
原载《宁波晚报》2011年9月6日 文/整理：记者 白蓓

网络来源： http://wanghdingq.blog.163.com/blog/static/87928592007558142763/
作者：五月采萧 有删改

网络来源： http://www.ycwb.com/ePaper/xkb/html/2012-02/06/content_1313900.htm
原载《新快报》2012年2月6日 文：苏文翰 有删改

网络来源： http://epaper.yangtse.com/yzwb/2008-10/21/content_11819549.htm
原载《扬子晚报》2008年10月21日 文：林墨瞳 有删改

网络来源： http://www.ycwb.com/ePaper/jyzk/html/2012-04/13/content_1368200.htm
原载《羊城晚报-家园周刊》2012年4月13日 文：易彪 有删改

网络来源： http://paper.people.com.cn/rmrbhwb/html/2009-03/21/content_215711.htm
原载《人民日报海外版》2009年3月21日 文：记者 林琳 有删改

网络来源：http://www.gdchrc.com/art/ArticleShow.aspx? ArticleID=7733
原载《新民晚报》2006年11月25日 文：邢燕 有删改

网络来源：http://www.fesco.com.cn/210/2009_10_10/1_210_25690_0_1255167121968.html
原载《新民晚报》2005年7月25日 文：向阳生涯职业规划中心 有删改

网络来源：http://cjmp.cnhan.com/cjrb/html/2011-01/31/content_4753071.htm
原载《长江日报》2011年1月31日 文：记者 李少峰 通讯员 陶铭东 有删改

网络来源：http://news.163.com/11/1019/07/7GN9AM6E00014AED.html
原载《四川日报》2011年10月19日 文：吴璟 有删改

网络来源：http://www.zmdnews.cn/Info.aspx?ModelId=1&Id=323270
原载《天中晚报》2011年2月9日 文：记者 朱晔 有删改

网络来源：http://www.cefla.org/news_view.jsp?nid=217
原载《西安晚报》2008年3月5日 文：记者 李洋 有删改

网络来源：http://edu.gmw.cn/2012-01/19/content_3415846.htm
原载《扬子晚报》2012年1月19日 作者：榛果 有删节

网络来源：http://epaper.nfdaily.cn/html/2012-02/24/content_7060348.htm
原载《南方日报》2012年2月24日 文：记者 吴敏 实习生 江艳博 有删改

网络来源：http://www.morningpost.com.cn/fukan/rwgc/2012-01-26/279312.shtml
原载《北京晨报》2012年1月27日 文：记者 周怀宗

网络来源：http://www.gmw.cn/01shsb/1999-06/26/GB/1021%5ESH1-2636.HTM
原载《生活时报》1999年6月26日 文：巩俐 有删改
作者：成龙 有删改。

网络来源之一：http://sjb.qlwb.com.cn/qlwb/content/20111230/ArticelK24002FM.htm
网络来源之二：http://www.zaobao.com/special/newspapers/2001/06/wzqxb070601.html
原载之一《齐鲁晚报》2011年12月30日 文：记者 赵松刚 有删改
原载之二《温州侨乡报》2001年6月7日 文：记者 陈小敏 有删改

网络来源：http://sprbszb.chinajilin.com.cn/html/2012-03/19/content_2500005.htm
原载《四平日报》2012年3月19日 文：新华社记者 许晓青 于希旖 有删改

网络来源：http://xinmin.news365.com.cn/lycs/201112/t20111220_3209085.htm
原载《新民晚报》2011年12月20日 文：刘蔚报 有删改

网络来源：http://news.sciencenet.cn/sbhtmlnews/2009/12/227008.html
原载《科学时报》2009年12月17日 文：记者 李芸 有删改

网络来源：http://zqb.cyol.com/html/2011-01/21/nw.D110000zgqnb_20110121_2-03.htm
原载《中国青年报》2011年1月21日 文：李剑平 有删改

网络来源：http://zqb.cyol.com/html/2011-12/06/nw.D110000zgqnb_20111206_1-11.htm
原载《中国青年报》2011年12月6日 文：记者 方奕晗 有删改

网络来源：http://www.fawan.com/Article/gghz/2012/03/14/134052149034.html
原载《法制晚报》2012年3月14日 文：张鑫 有删改

网络来源之一：http://epaper.tianjinwe.com/mrxb/mrxb/2010-03/09/content_23157.htm
网络来源之二：http://epaper.tianjinwe.com/mrxb/mrxb/2010-03/30/content_37369.htm
原载之一《每日新报》2010年3月9日 文：记者 张莹 门莉娜 见习记者 苑冰
有删改
原载之二《每日新报》2010年3月30日 文：记者 张莹 门莉娜 见习记者 苑冰
有删改

网络来源：http://news.xinhuanet.com/society/2012-04/28/c_123050673.htm
原载《人民日报》海外版2012年4月28日 文：新华社记者孙浩 郭曼桐 有删改

网络来源：http://www.yznews.com.cn/yzwzt/2011-08/11/content_3687972.htm
        原载《扬州日报》2011年8月11日　文：何瑞琳　有删改
网络来源：http://www.zmdnews.cn/Info.aspx?ModelId=1&Id=237313
        原载《天中晚报》2008年12月29日　文：华安　有删改
网络来源：http://www.chinanews.com/gn/2011/06-28/3142054.shtml
        原载中国新闻网2011年6月28日　文：中新社记者　刘舒凌　有删改
网络来源：http://news.cnr.cn/gnxw/201109/t20110903_508455005_1.shtml
        原载中国广播网2011年9月3日　责编：时晨　有删改

List of terms

adj. = adjective 形容词
adv. = adverb 副词
ci. = colloquial idiom 俗语
cm. = compound measuring word 复合量词
conj. = conjunction 连词
m. = measuring word 量词
n. = noun 名词
np. = noun phrase 名词词组
phr. = phrase 词组
pn. = proper noun 专有名词
pr. = pronoun 代词
prep. = preposition 介词
v. = verb 动词
vc. = verb complement 动补式词
vo. = verb object 动宾式词
simple sentence = a sentence that contains only one subject and one predicate
compound sentence = a sentence that contains two or more simple sentences

第一课　校园文化

Chapter 1　Campus culture

课文导入 Introduction

　　中国的校园文化、学习生活有自己的传统和特色，跟西方的校园文化相比有很多不同的方面。但随着全球化时代的到来，国与国之间的相互影响，我们发现，中国的校园文化也在不断变化。

生词注释 Vocabulary

1. 导入【dǎo rù】導入 vc. 一 introduce to

2. 全球化【quán qiú huà】v.; n. globalize; globalization

3. 不断【bú duàn】不斷 adv. uninterruptedly, continuously, constantly

阅读 A: 不同的中美校园文化 Differences between campus culture in China and America

读前准备 Warm-up

一、对错题 True or false? (Answer the questions based on the situation in your country.)

1　（　）学生在学校里可以叫老师的名字。
2　（　）高中跟大学一样是四年。
3　（　）每门课的成绩有A、B、C、D和F这几种。
4　（　）在读高中时，老师不允许男生和女生谈恋爱。
5　（　）申请大学的时候得请老师写推荐信。

课文 Reading

中美文化的不同，教育体制的不同，也形成了校园文化的差别。那么中美校园文化有哪些差别？我们来看看如下几个方面：

一、师生关系：在中国，师生之间的关系比较正式。举例来说，我在中国读高中的时候，没有学生会在学校里直呼老师的名字。但在美国，许多老师认为学生直呼他们的名字，是理所当然的。多数的学生不只是把老师视为指导者，更把他们当成自己的朋友。

二、学制：中国大部分的孩子都在7岁左右上学。小学六年，初中三年，高中三年，大学四年。美国不一样，一般来说，美国的小学包括幼儿园，而中国把幼儿园算作学前教育。因此美国的小学一共是六年，包括幼儿园。美国的很多学区，初中是从七年级到八年级，高中跟大学一样，采取四年制。

三、计分方式：中国的计分方式最常见的是数字计分，60分及格，100分满分。一般来说，90分以上被评为优秀。而美国，除了用数字计分外，学生在期末每门课程的成绩都是用A、B、C、D来分等级的。A表示最高的等级，D是最低等级，F代表不及格。同时也还会出现A+或者A-这样的计分方式。

四、男女关系：在中国的校园，要是男女朋友过分亲热，在公共场所接吻等，如果被学校行政人员发现，是会受到口头警告的。很多高中对待学生的"早恋"现象是非常严格的。在中国，男生和女生在老师面前，一定要保持距离。在美国，男生、女生的交往开放多了，根本不会受到严厉的处分。

五、报考大学：中国的学生在报考大学的时候，只要有高考*成绩就可以了。在美国，既要有一份良好的个人简历又要请老师写推荐信，得准备很多资料来说明自己除了学习以外，在其他方面也很优秀。当然，SAT考试成绩是每个人都必须的。

生词注释 Vocabulary

1. 体制【tǐ zhì】體制 n. system, organization

2. 呼【hū】v. exhale, cry out, call

3. 理所当然【lǐ suǒ dāng rán】理所當然 take for granted; it goes without saying（成语）

4. 幼儿园【yòu ér yuán】幼兒園 n. kindergarten, nursery

5. 学区【xué qū】學區 n. school district

6. 及格【jí gé】v.; n. pass a test or examination; a pass grade

7. 优秀【yōu xiù】優秀 adj. excellent, outstanding

8. 接吻【jiē wěn】vo. kiss, give a kiss

9. 行政【xíng zhèng】n. administration

10. 发现【fā xiàn】發現 v.; n. notice, find out, discover; discovery

11. 警告【jǐng gào】v.; n. warn; warning

12. 处分【chǔ fèn】處分 v.; n. take disciplinary action against, punish; punishment

13. 推荐【tuī jiàn】推薦 v.; n. recommend; recommendation

六、大学的选择：中国的高考生填报大学<u>志愿</u>，只能按本人志愿，<u>依次</u>填三所大学，<u>申请者</u>只能被一所大学录取。在美国，你能同时被好几所大学录取，然后<u>挑选</u>一所自己最喜欢的大学。我觉得美国的做法比较合理，因为你可以申请多所大学，最后决定哪一所是你想去的。

(785字)

作者：不详　责任编辑：杨牧　有删改

原载中国日报网2012年2月7日

网络来源：http://world.people.com.cn/GB/157278/17041651.html

14. 志愿【zhì yuàn】志願 v.; n. volunteer to do something; wish, will

15. 依次【yī cì】v.; adv. progress in proper order; sequentially

16. 申请【shēn qǐng】申請 v.; n. apply for, make an official request; application

17. 挑选【tiāo xuǎn】挑選 v. pick, choose, select

文化/熟语注释 Culture/idiom notes

*高考【gāokǎo】高考的全称是"高等学校全国统一招生考试"，这是高中毕业生为了进入大学必须参加的入学考试。高考成绩直接决定着考生能否进入大学及进入哪类大学。

高考 is the acronym for the "National Colleges and Universities Entrance Examination." This examination is required for all high school graduates who wish to continue their education at a college or university. The test result is used directly to determine whether the student can be admitted to a college/university and to which type of college/university.

语法/语言点注释 Grammar/language points

1 把 ...... 视为 ......; regard ... as ...

多数的学生不只是<u>把</u>老师<u>视为</u>指导者，更把他们当成自己的朋友。
Most students regard their teachers less as mentors and more as friends.

In this compound sentence, 把 is used to introduce the object of the sentence. That is, the object of the sentence is fronted and placed before the verb (predicate) for the purpose of emphasizing how the object is treated.

Example:

许多中国人把春节视为合家团聚、拜访亲友的一个最好时机。
Many Chinese regard the Spring Festival as an opportunity for a family reunion and for visiting relatives and friends.

2 只要 ...... 就 ......; as long as ...

中国的学生在报考大学的时候，<u>只要</u>有高考成绩<u>就</u>可以了。
In China, students can get into college as long as their entrance exam score meets requirements.

This structure is used to express that a certain result occurs if a certain condition is met. 只要 is used in the first simple sentence to introduce a condition and the adverb 就 in the second simple sentence to indicate a result.

Example:

"有志者事竟成"这句话的意思是，只要坚持下去，就一定能成功的。
The idiom "where there's a will, there's a way" means that a person who sticks to her goals will surely succeed.

阅读理解 Comprehension

一、填空题 Fill in the blanks with a corresponding item based on your understanding of the chapter.

中国的校园文化	美国的校园文化
	学生可以直呼老师的名字
中国的高中是三年制	
	男生、女生的交往很开放
报考大学只要有高考成绩就行了	
	能同时被好几所大学录取

二、翻译题 Translate the following sentences into English.

1   在中国，很多高中对待学生的"早恋"现象是非常严格的。

2   在美国，男生、女生的交往开放多了，根本不会受到严厉的处分。

根据提示完成课文结构图 Complete the text structure map according to the clues provided

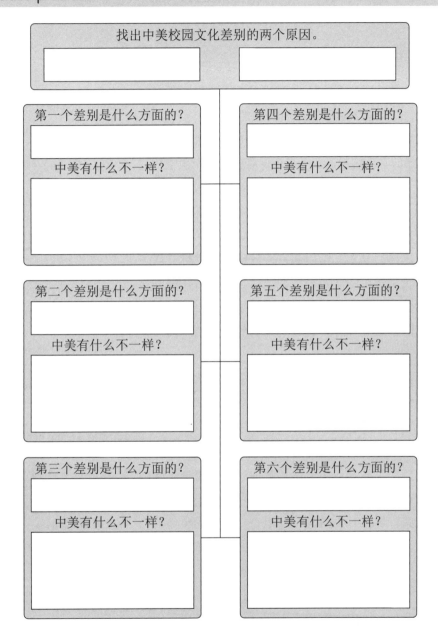

找出中美校园文化差别的两个原因。

第一个差别是什么方面的?

中美有什么不一样?

第二个差别是什么方面的?

中美有什么不一样?

第三个差别是什么方面的?

中美有什么不一样?

第四个差别是什么方面的?

中美有什么不一样?

第五个差别是什么方面的?

中美有什么不一样?

第六个差别是什么方面的?

中美有什么不一样?

讨论 Discussion

1   你觉得自己更愿意在美国的学校上学,还是在中国的学校上学?为什么?
2   你对中学生"早恋"现象有什么看法?你认为学校应该严厉一些,还是应该给学生自由,允许男生、女生公开交往?

阅读 B: 中学生的生活在变化 Changes in the lives of middle school students

课文 Reading	生词注释 Vocabulary

课文 Reading

在一位外籍员工的眼中，中国的中学校园生活正在发生着变化。下面是该外籍员工告诉我的故事。

从我的窗户望下去可以看到一个学校的操场和校园。每天早上激昂的音乐响起，一千多个穿着校服的学生整整齐齐在操场上列队准备做早操*。一个老师拿着大喇叭喊着节拍"一、二、三、四、五、六……"，两千只手臂同时举起又放下，校服的蓝色和白色交替着，构成一幅忙碌的画面。在这样的早上，学校通常会放国歌，举行升旗仪式。那些负责升旗的学生经常在课后努力练习，因为要在音乐响起的一刻漂亮地把国旗升起来是需要下功夫的。但是，除了这些以外，我也观察到他们生活中的另一面。

午休通常是热热闹闹的。男生们都去打篮球，有时候老师也会加入进来一起玩。女生们喜欢扎堆聊天，也有些女生手挽手大笑着走过，校园里没有不合群的人。

最有趣的是每天放学铃声响过后这里发生的变化。学生一走出校门，就获得了自由和解放。一个男生把颜色鲜艳的背心套在校服外面，还戴上一顶"强盗帽"，遮住一只眼睛。男孩、女孩们一起走着，甜蜜的小情侣们随处可见，这在校园内是被明令禁止的。在黄昏的车站旁，学生们聚集在一起，并不打算搭车回家。

一辆自行车横在了路中间，一个漂亮女生熟练地坐上男朋友的车后座，向大家挥手告别。孩子们发出了银铃般的笑声。这个十六岁的女孩优雅地坐在自行车后座上。两只手紧紧抓住男朋友的上衣，一直到下车才会松开。当然并不是为了保持平衡，只是一个用来掩饰在公共场合表达爱意的借口罢了。

生词注释 Vocabulary

1. 外籍【wài jí】n. foreign national, non-local resident

2. 激昂【jī'áng】adj. excited and indignant

3. 列队【liè duì】列隊 vo. line up, form into lines

4. 喇叭【lǎ ba】n. brass wind instrument, trumpet

5. 节拍【jié pāi】節拍 n. time, beat, tempo

6. 交替【jiāo tì】v.; adv. supersede; alternately

7. 扎堆【zhā duī】vo. gather sb/sth round

8. 挽【wǎn】v. draw, pull, retrieve

9. 合群【hé qún】vo.; adj. get along well with others, fit in; gregarious

10. 强盗【qiáng dào】強盜 n. bandit, robber

11. 遮住【zhē zhù】v. shut up, blot out

12. 情侣【qíng lǚ】情侶 n. sweethearts, lovers

13. 明令禁止【míng lìng jìn zhǐ】prohibit by explicit order（成语）

14. 横【héng】横 v.; adj. cross; horizontal

15. 优雅【yōu yǎ】優雅 adj. beautiful and elegant, graceful

16. 掩饰【yǎn shì】掩飾 v.; n. cover up, conceal; dissimulation

孩子们是快乐的，我从中已经能够看见中国的未来了。是的，当我第一次看到学校里的活动，我只看到了中国的"<u>老一套</u>"：做操、唱国歌、升旗，但那是我初始印象中的中国校园。随着我更多的观察，整个<u>集体</u>变回了各具特色的"<u>个体</u>"，他们<u>精彩</u>的生活在我面前一一展现。

17. 老一套【lǎo yí tào】n. conventional (things), conventionality

18. 集体【jí tǐ】集體 n. collective team, collectivity

19. 个体【gè tǐ】個體 n. individuality

20. 精彩【jīng cǎi】adj. brilliant, splendid, wonderful

(725字)

文：Patrick Whiteley　编译：张博　有删改
原载《中国日报》2007年12月11日
网络来源：

http://www.chinadaily.com.cn/hqzg/2007-12/11/content_6313452.htm

文化/熟语注释 Culture/idiom notes

　　*做早操【zuòzǎocāo】做早操指的是做广播体操。广播体操是一种徒手操。1951年11月24日，中华全国体育总会公布和推行第一套广播体操，从12月1日开始在中央人民广播电台播出体操口令和配乐。从此，从小学到大学，早晨或课间做广播体操是每个学生必须参加的体育活动。到目前为止，广播体操依然是中国校园最普及的健身活动。

The "morning exercise" refers to a kind of freehand gymnastic exercises accompanied by set radio music. On November 24, 1951, the All-China Sports Federation announced the first set of freehand exercises and then started broadcasting the instruction and accompanying music on the Central People's Radio Station from December 1. Since then freehand gymnastic exercises have become a sports activity for all students from elementary school through to college in China. Students are required to do the exercises in the morning or between classes. Even now freehand gymnastic exercises are still the most popular fitness exercise in Chinese schools and colleges.

语法/语言点注释 Grammar/language points

1 ......般的......; ... like ...

孩子们发出了银铃<u>般的</u>笑声。
The kids broke into a burst of sweet giggles that sounded like the ringing of silver bells.

The word 般 in this sentence is used as a particle attaching to the noun 银铃, meaning "similar to" or "like."

Example:

> 秋天来临的时候，树叶变颜色了，从我家的窗户望出去处处是油画般的色彩，美极了。
>
> When autumn comes, the leaves start to change color; the view through the window of my house is beautiful, with colors like oil paints everywhere I look.

2 只是 ...... 罢了 ...... ; (it) is just . . . (nothing more)

> 当然并不是为了保持平衡，只是一个用来掩饰在公共场合表达爱意的借口罢了。
>
> Of course, holding on tightly to the rider is not just for balance [on a bicycle], but to disguise an expression of love in public (. . . nothing more).

The word 罢了 is a particle used at the end of the sentence to express a tone of "that's all" or "nothing more." It is often used together with 不过、无非 or 只是.

Example:

> 其实你一直生活在幸福中，只是你没意识到罢了！
>
> You have always been living a happy life; it is just that you haven't realized it yet! (That's all.)

3 当 ...... （的时候） ...... ; when . . .

> 当我第一次看到学校里的活动，我只看到了中国的"老一套"：做操、唱国歌、升旗，但那是我初始印象中的中国校园。
>
> When I first saw school activities in China, I saw the old-fashioned ones: doing morning exercise; singing the national anthem when the flag was raised. However, that was only my first impression of Chinese schools.

The word 当 here indicates a certain time in the past, meaning "when/at the time of." Usually, it is used together with 的时候. However, 的时候 is often omitted in a colloquial situation.

Example:

> 当篮球比赛进入第二场(的时候)，我们队一位主力球员不小心受伤了。
>
> When the basketball game reached the second quarter, one key player in our team accidentally got injured.

阅读理解 Comprehension

一、选择题 Multiple-choice questions.

1   根据课文内容，这个学校早上的校园内可以看到哪些情景？

   a) 做早操   b) 跑步   c) 放国歌   d) 举行升旗仪式

2   根据课文内容，这个学校中午的时候是怎样的？

   a) 很热闹   b) 老师们都在办公室休息   c) 男生打篮球   d) 女生聊天

3   根据课文内容，这个学校放学以后是怎样的？

    a) 学生留在学校做功课　　　b) 男生、女生自由地交往
    c) 学生在穿戴上有了变化　　　d) 大家都骑自行车回家

二、填空题 Fill in the blanks, choosing from the words provided.

    观察　　　看　　　展现　　　望　　　见

1   从我的窗户＿＿＿＿下去可以看到一个学校的操场和校园。
2   除了这些以外，我也＿＿＿＿到他们生活中的另一面。
3   男孩、女孩们一起走着，甜蜜的小情侣们随处可＿＿＿＿。
4   他们精彩的生活在我面前一一＿＿＿＿。

第二课　在中国医院看病

Chapter 2　In a Chinese hospital

课文导入 Introduction	生词注释 Vocabulary
《健康时报》记者采访了几位在中国看过病的外国朋友，请他们谈谈在中国医院看病的经历。一位外国朋友看了中医，他对中医的印象好吗？另一位外国朋友对中国的医院和医生<u>满意</u>吗？我们来读一读他们各自不同的看病经历。	1. 满意【mǎn yì】满意 v.; n. satisfy; satisfaction

阅读 A: 神奇的中医 The magical effect of traditional Chinese medicine

读前准备 Warm-up

一、简答题 Short-answer questions.

1　你听说过中医吗？你能说说中医跟西医有什么不同吗？

2　想象一下如果你去中国医院看中医，你会碰到什么情况？

3　请说说下面的词哪些用在中医，哪些用在中医、西医都可以：
　　把脉　喝药　诊断　看舌苔　复查　服药

课文 Reading

我先介绍一下我自己吧。我叫麦克，是两年前从美国来中国的，我在北京一个学校教英文。我身体很好，来中国以后没生过病，不过，我去过医院！

去年，我带一个朋友到浙江中医*大学附属第一医院看病。朋友得的是<u>肝炎</u>，<u>胃口</u>差，没有力气。他在美国也看了很多医生，都觉得很难治。

一位年近六十岁的老中医对朋友进行了<u>细致</u>检查后，告诉他："你这个病只要<u>按</u>要求坚持<u>服药</u>，可以治好。"朋友一听<u>喜出望外</u>。但是拿到大包小包的很多中药之后，他又不太<u>敢</u>相信，因为这些药<u>竟然</u>非常便宜，总共还不到一百元。谁知，朋友喝了一周的中药后，人有力气了，也能吃饭了。

我们去复诊的时候，那位中医又再次给朋友进行了检查。看着他<u>把脉</u>*、看<u>舌苔</u>，我<u>不禁</u>想：中医太神奇了，竟然能用如此简单的方法就<u>正确</u>地<u>诊断</u>疾病。朋友对这位老中医十分<u>佩服</u>，<u>一丝不苟</u>地按照他的话去做，什么时候服药，什么时候复查，都被他仔仔细细写在了每天的日程表上。

后来这位老中医又给朋友调整了几次处方，每次都只要几十块钱。半年后，朋友再去医院检查后欣喜地发现，他的肝炎<u>已经</u>基本<u>痊愈</u>了！我们都<u>惊叹</u>，中医诊断简单而正确，用药便宜但见效——中医真是<u>神奇</u>啊！

(472　字)

文：记者　薛京、吴尧、杨波　有删改
原载《健康时报》2011年10月19日
网络来源：
http://overseas.cn.yahoo.com/ypen/20111019/647174_5.html

生词注释 Vocabulary

1. 肝炎【gān yán】n. hepatitis

2. 胃口【wèi kǒu】n. appetite

3. 细致【xì zhì】細緻 adj. intricate, precise about details

4. 按【àn】prep.; v. according to, in accordance with; press (with the hand)

5. 服药【fú yào】服藥 vo. take medicine

6. 喜出望外【xǐ chū wàng wài】overjoyed, happy beyond expectations（成语）

7. 敢【gǎn】v. dare, have courage to (do sth)

8. 竟然【jìng rán】adv. unexpectedly, to one's surprise

9. 把脉【bǎ mài】把脈 vo. feel (take) somebody's pulse

10. 舌苔【shé tāi】n. coated tongue

11. 不禁【bù jīn】adv. cannot help (doing something)

12. 正确【zhèng què】正確 adj. correct, right, proper

13. 诊断【zhěn duàn】診斷 v.; n. diagnose; diagnosis

14. 佩服【pèi fú】v. admire, think highly of

15. 一丝不苟【yì sī bù gǒu】一絲不苟 conscientiousness and meticulousness about every detail（成语）

16. 复查【fù chá】復查 v.; n. reexamine; reexamining

17. 已经【yǐ jīng】已經 adv. already

18. 痊愈【quán yù】痊癒 v. completely cured or recovered (from an illness)

19. 惊叹【jīng tàn】驚嘆 v. exclaim with admiration, marvel at

20. 神奇【shén qí】adj. magical

文化/熟语注释 Culture/idiom notes

*中医【zhōngyī】中医是中国特有的医学，是中国传统文化的组成部分。中医是与西医相对而言的。中医是个庞大的体系，包括：中药、针灸、推拿、气功、食疗等。中医也用来指称中医的医生。

中医 refers to a broad range of traditional Chinese medicine practices sharing common theoretical concepts that have been developed over a long time in China. It is an important component in Chinese culture and a system independent and very different from that of Western medicine. Traditional Chinese medicine consists of Chinese pharmacy, acupuncture, traditional Chinese massage, tai-chi, diet therapy, etc. The word 中医 in this article also refers to the doctor who practices traditional Chinese medicine.

*把脉【bǎmài】又称为切脉，是中医师用手指按病人的动脉，根据脉象，以了解疾病内在变化的诊断方法。

把脉, also known as 切脉【qiēmài】, is a traditional Chinese method of diagnosis in which the doctor uses his fingers to feel (or take) the patient's pulse in order to discover whether there is a certain disease in the patient's body, a method that is based on the rhythm, strength, volume, and "quality" of the pulse.

语法/语言点注释 Grammar/language points

1 竟然 . . . . . . ; unexpectedly/surprisingly . . .

> 这些药竟然非常便宜，总共还不到一百元。
> These medicines are surprisingly cheap, no more than 100 yuan all together.

The word 竟然 is an adverb placed after the subject to express that something unexpected happened.

Example:

> 谁也没有想到，我们公司的经理竟然辞职了，留下一封信说她向往另一种生活。
> No one had had any idea that our company manager would suddenly quit her job, leaving a note saying that she wanted to pursue a different kind of life!

2 竟然 . . . . . . 就 . . . . . . ; unexpectedly . . . just . . .

> 中医太神奇了，竟然能用如此简单的方法就正确地诊断疾病。
> Chinese medicine is truly miraculous; it is almost beyond belief that a doctor can diagnose the disease so precisely just by using such simple methods.

In this sentence, the word 就 is an adverb used to emphasize the subsequent situation.

Example:

> 听说有一种特殊的花，竟然不需要水分和养料就能生长。
> It is said that there is a special flower, (and) it can grow without water or nutrients.

3 ......而......; ... and (yet) ...

> 我们都惊叹，中医诊断简单<u>而</u>正确，用药便宜但见效--中医真是神奇啊！
> We are all surprised that the diagnosis can be so simple yet precise, and the medicine is cheap but effective – how miraculous Chinese medicine is!

The word 而 is used as a conjunction to connect two words of either related or opposite meaning to indicate a slight tone of transition.

Example:

> 我的弟弟正在念中学，他活泼而好动，不仅参加了学校的表演社团，还参加了运动队。
> My younger brother is in middle school. He is vivacious and active; he not only participates in the acting club at school, but he is also in the sports team.

阅读理解 Comprehension

一、选择题 Multiple-choice questions.

1　关于麦克，下面哪个说法是错的？

　　a) 在北京教英文　　b) 来中国以后没生过病　　c) 没去过医院

2　关于麦克的朋友，下面哪些说法是对的？

　　a) 他得了胃病　　b) 没有胃口　　c) 没有力气

3　关于老中医第一次给麦克的朋友看病，下面哪个说法是错的？

　　a) 老中医觉得这个病很难治
　　b) 朋友既喜出望外，又不敢相信
　　c) 朋友觉得中药费很便宜

4　下面的说法，麦克和他的朋友不同意的会是哪一个？

　　a) 中医诊断方法简单，而诊断结果却非常正确
　　b) 中药虽然很便宜，但治病效果非常好
　　c) 只要花一星期时间，中医就能治愈肝炎

二、翻译题 Translate the following sentences into Chinese, using the words provided.

1　(My) friend admires the old Chinese medicine doctor very much, and he carefully follows the doctor's guidance.

　　（对......佩服　　一丝不苟）

2　He carefully marked on his daily schedule the times for taking the medicine and having a reexamination.

　　（服药　　复查　　仔仔细细　　日程）

根据提示完成课文结构图 Complete the text structure map according to the clues provided

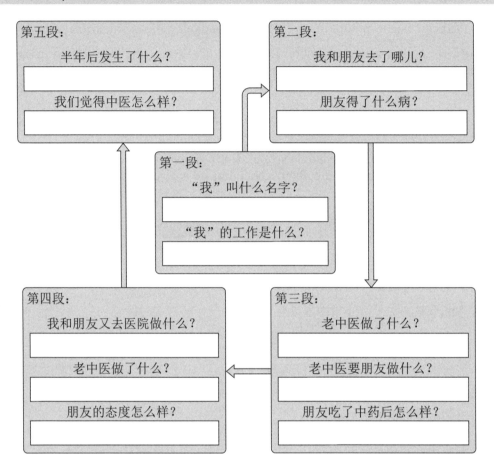

讨论 Discussion

1   读了这个故事后，你对中医有哪些了解？
2   如果在中国你生病了，你会去看中医吗？为什么？

阅读 B: 看病经历 The experience of visiting a Chinese hospital

课文 Reading	生词注释 Vocabulary

我是加拿大人，我叫唐纳德，我两个月前才刚到中国。我在杭州一家通信公司工作。上个月我的脚扭了，在一位中国同事的陪同下到一家医院看病。

到医院后先去了服务台，问那儿的工作人员我是否应该看骨科门诊？她很肯定地说，是的！骨科在二楼，因没有电梯，同事搀扶着我一步一步地走上楼梯，终于到了二楼，发现骨科门口很多人在等。没想到就要轮到我的时候，女护士说，你不能看门诊，得看急诊！可是刚刚楼下服务台的人明明是叫我看门诊的，没办法，只好去看急诊，而且不得不重新挂号。

没想到的是，新建好的急诊大楼看上去很气派，但结构复杂得不得了，我们得先从天桥过去，绕了半天还是找不到电梯。同事看我疼得要命，就自己跑到急诊大厅挂号，可是挂号处不让挂，让他先把我带到预检台，然后才能挂号。

真没想到在中国看病这么复杂，我的同事也很不耐烦了。从进医院大门开始已经30分钟了，居然还没看上病。终于办好了一系列手续坐到了医生眼前，医生却只用了3分钟的时间就开出处方让我们去拍片子。

交完费，我问护士小姐在哪里拍片？护士态度很好，耐心地说："先上3楼，过天桥，去急诊老楼，然后再下到1楼，左转！"我一听，差点没晕过去。又走了很长的路后，开始拍片，一大群看起来像学生的医生围着我指指点点。同事后来告诉我，那些是实习医生，当时我感到非常尴尬。

1. 扭【niǔ】v. turn round, twist, sprain

2. 骨科【gǔ kē】n. orthopedics

3. 搀扶【chān fú】攙扶 v. support gently by the hand or arm

4. 轮【lún】輪 v.; n. m. take turns; round

5. 挂号【guà hào】掛號 vo. register (at a hospital)

6. 气派【qì pài】氣派 n.; adj. imposing manner, dignified

7. 结构【jié gòu】結構 n. structure

8. 预检【yù jiǎn】預檢 v.; n. pre-examine; initial inspection

9. 处方【chǔ fāng】處方 n. prescription

10. 拍【pāi】v. take (an X-ray examination)

11. 片子【piàn zi】n. film, movie (here, film used for an X-ray examination)

12. 晕【yūn】暈 v.; adj. pass out; dizzy

13. 尴尬【gān gà】尷尬 adj. awkward, embarrassed

拍完片，又被告知得等两小时才能回来拿片子，同事开玩笑说："你可以利用这段时间四处转转。"我忍不住喊起来："饶命吧！我这脚还能再转吗？！"然后我俩不约而同地苦笑起来。

加拿大每个人都有家庭医生*，有病就找家庭医生看，我们和医生住得很近。没想到在中国看病却这么累人！

(671字)

文：记者　薛京、吴尧、杨波　有删改

原载《健康时报》2011年10月19日

网络来源：

http://overseas.cn.yahoo.com/ypen/20111019/647174_1.html

14. 饶命【ráo mìng】饒命 vo. spare one's life

15. 不约而同【bù yuē ér tóng】不約而同 take the same action or view without prior consultation（成语）

16. 苦笑【kǔ xiào】v.; n. make a wry smile; forced smile

文化/熟语注释 Culture/idiom notes

*家庭医生【jiātíng yīshēng】在中国，现在还没有家庭医生制度。许多人只是在有病的时候才去医院。每个人根据自己的病情直接找专科医生看病。比如脚扭了，就找骨科医生看病。

The family doctor system is not currently implemented in China. Most people would just visit the hospital if they felt sick. Patients would be directed to see a specialist. For example, if you had a foot or ankle sprain, you would need to visit an orthopedist.

语法/语言点注释 Grammar/language points

1 ......疼得要命;... "pain to death", in absolute agony

同事看我疼得要命，就自己跑到急诊大厅挂号，可是挂号处不让挂，让他先把我带到预检台，然后才能挂号。

Seeing that I was nearly dying of pain (i.e., in extreme agony), my colleague went to the emergency room to check in for me, but the check-in receptionist did not allow him to do so and asked him to take me to do a pre-check first before registering to see a doctor.

The word 要命 after 得 is used as a complement to indicate an extreme degree or to show emphasis on the part of the speaker.

Example:

最近我忙得要命，既要学习和打工，又要参加学校社团的活动。

I have been extremely busy lately as I need to study and work, and I also need to attend club activities at school.

阅读理解 Comprehension

一、填空题 Fill in the blanks, choosing from the words provided.

才　　上　　下　　出　　被

1　上个月，我在一位中国朋友的陪同＿＿到一家医院看病。
2　从进医院大门开始已经30分钟了，居然还没看＿＿病。
3　医生只用了3分钟的时间就开＿＿处方让我们去拍片子。
4　拍完片，又＿＿告知得等两小时才能回来拿片子。

二、对错题 True or false?

1　（　）我和同事坐电梯到了二楼的骨科门诊。
2　（　）我看病的地方在急诊新楼，而拍片的地方在急诊老楼。
3　（　）我走了很远的路，脚疼得要命，差一点晕过去。
4　（　）拍片的时候，一群实习医生围着我指指点点，我很尴尬。
5　（　）我一边等着拿片子，一边在医院四处转转。
6　（　）这是一次不愉快的看病经历。

第三课　年轻人喜欢的音乐

Chapter 3　Music young people like

课文导入 Introduction

　　摇滚乐这种音乐形式，以它动感的节奏、奔放的表演，受到全世界年轻人的喜爱，中国的大学校园里也有许多喜欢摇滚的学生。但在接受西方音乐的同时，随着传统文化的回归，也有不少年轻人越来越重视民乐这一传统音乐。

生词注释 Vocabulary

1. 摇滚乐【yáo gǔn yuè】摇滚樂 pn. rock and roll (music)

2. 节奏【jié zòu】節奏 n. rhythm

3. 奔放【bēn fàng】adj. bold and unrestrained

4. 回归【huí guī】回歸 v.; n. return to original place; regression

阅读 A: 一个大学生和他的摇滚乐队 A college student and his rock band

读前准备 Warm-up

一、简答题 Short-answer questions.

1　你喜欢摇滚乐吗？为什么？

2　你们学校有哪些乐队？你参加过乐队的活动吗？

二、选择题 Multiple-choice question.

你认为一支摇滚乐队通常需要有下面哪些乐器？

a) 吉他　　b) 贝司　　c) 鼓　　d) 钢琴

课文 Reading

夏亮是西安人，上中学时迷上了摇滚，对其他流行音乐一点也听不进去。那时，他买了许多摇滚乐队的海报，看各个摇滚乐队的演出，在纸上、衣服上画摇滚歌星的肖像。"这一切是我中学时期除学习之外的最大爱好。"夏亮说。

2007年，高考结束后，夏亮学吉他。2007年9月，夏亮背着一把吉他到了山东大学。室友没人会弹吉他，但在夏亮的影响和辅导下，大家后来都学会了。夏亮越来越想组建自己的乐队，实现摇滚梦想。

2008年9月，大二刚开学，夏亮终于成功组建了自己的第一支校园摇滚乐队。成员除了自己，还有两名室友和另外两名大学生。夏亮担任吉他手兼主唱。五个人凑钱买了音响、贝司、二手架子鼓。"没有钱，全是买便宜的，一共花了一千多元。"

乐队组起来了，却没有排练的地方，后来宿舍楼下的地下室成了他们吼唱的地方。但2009年3月，夏亮的乐队还是被人告发了，理由是"扰民"。夏亮和他的成员们只好把各种器材搬出了地下室，放回宿舍。这一年，乐队有两名成员毕业，又有两名成员退出，最后只剩下夏亮一个。但是夏亮仍然坚持着他的摇滚梦。

2009年9月，大三的夏亮找到三位热爱摇滚的同校学生，他们成立了一支新的摇滚乐队。夏亮还是担任主唱兼吉他手。在圣诞晚会上，乐队演唱了五首歌，其中三首是夏亮创作的摇滚歌曲。2010年3月，乐队又接收了外校一名热爱摇滚的女同学，担任乐队的主唱，夏亮只做吉他手。

大三结束前乐队的一次专场演出令他难忘。6月，夏亮要回老家西安，留在西安实习半年，乐队将再一次变得残缺。"所以暑假前搞一次专场演出，是每一个成员最大的愿望。"夏亮说。2010年6月10日，乐队在大学生活动中心进行了专场演出。从晚上6点到10点多，夏亮和

生词注释 Vocabulary

1. 迷上【mí shàng】v. fascinated by, crazy about

2. 海报【hǎi bào】海報 n. poster

3. 肖像【xiāo xiàng】n. portrait

4. 辅导【fǔ dǎo】輔導 v.; n. guide, coach; guidance, coaching

5. 兼【jiān】v.; adv. double; simultaneously, concurrently

6. 凑钱【còu qián】湊錢 vo. pool money

7. 架子鼓【jià zi gǔ】n. drum set

8. 吼【hǒu】v. roar, growl, shout

9. 告发【gào fā】告發 v. report (an offender), lodge an accusation against

10. 扰民【rǎo mín】擾民 vo. disturb residents

11. 仍然【réng rán】adv. still, yet

12. 创作【chuàng zuò】創作 v.; n. create, produce; work of literature or art

13. 残缺【cán quē】殘缺 v. incomplete (with parts missing)

他的乐队成员们演唱了二十多首摇滚歌曲。唱最后一首歌《古城》时，主唱哭了，五名成员都哭了。台下的观众也非常激动，感情很复杂。

14. 复杂【fù zá】複雜 adj. complicated, complex

大学四年里，夏亮带着他的前后两支摇滚乐队参加过大大小小二十几场演出。在即将告别大学时代的这个学期，为了找工作，夏亮剪掉了长发。问他是不是在毕业后还玩摇滚，他心里充满矛盾。"现实面前，也许会忍痛放弃吧。理性地去爱，正是摇滚的精神。"

15. 剪掉【jiǎn diào】v. cut off

16. 充满【chōng mǎn】充滿 v. filled with

17. 矛盾【máo dùn】n. contradiction

18. 忍痛【rěn tòng】vo. bear and suffer pain, reluctantly give up

19. 放弃【fàng qì】放棄 v. abandon, give up

(850字)

文：记者　李飞　实习生　任辉、徐青　有删改

原载《齐鲁晚报》2011年4月26日

网络来源：

http://sjb.qlwb.com.cn/html/2011-04/26/content_117801.htm?div=-1

文化/熟语注释 Culture/idiom notes

*摇滚乐【yáogǔnyuè】在中国: 中国摇滚始于1986年。最早的摇滚歌曲可以追溯到崔健的《一无所有》。中国摇滚被描述为一种反传统的工具，一种次文化、反抗主流意识形态的音乐。喜欢摇滚的人用歌声来倾诉自己追求的一种生活和理念。1990年代初，摇滚乐在中国大陆达到流行高潮，此后逐渐衰落但没有消亡。近几年，中国摇滚出现复苏迹象，2004年8月在贺兰山举行了大规模中国摇滚演唱会。

Rock music started to become popular in China in 1986. The earliest Chinese rock song is "Nothing to Lose," written by rock musician Cui Jian. In China, rock music is described as anti-conventional, as a subculture, and as the kind of music that goes against the mainstream. Rock musicians in China use their songs to describe the kind of life and ideas that they pursue. At the beginning of the 1990s rock music reached its peak in China, but after that, popularity plummeted. In recent years, however, it has started to make a comeback. In August 2004 the "Big China Rock Concert" was held on Helan Mountain, China.

语法/语言点注释 Grammar/language points

1 ......令......; ... make ...

大三结束前乐队的一次专场演出令他难忘。

The last special performance before the end of college junior year made him hard to forget.

The word 令 here is similar to 使 or 让 but conveys a slightly stronger tone. It is used to place somebody in some kind of emotional or physical situation.

Example:

> 我们的棒球队又赢了，这消息令所有的人激动万分。
> Our baseball team has won again; everyone is so excited about it.

2 将 (1) ......; will ...

> 乐队将再一次变得残缺。
> The band will once again become incomplete.

将 (1) is an adverb here used to indicate a future event, meaning something will happen at some point in the future.

Example:

> 明年这个时候我将大学毕业，回到自己家乡工作。
> By this time next year I will be graduating and shall return to my hometown to work.

阅读理解 Comprehension

一、选择题 Multiple-choice questions.

1 关于夏亮中学时期的爱好，下面哪个说法是错的？

   a) 买了许多摇滚乐队的海报
   b) 看各个摇滚乐队的演出
   c) 在纸上、衣服上画摇滚歌星的肖像
   d) 有时候也喜欢听其他流行歌曲

2 关于夏亮大学时期组建的乐队，下面哪个说法是对的？

   a) 大一的时候组建了一个乐队
   b) 大四的时候又组建了一个乐队
   c) 学校很支持夏亮的乐队
   d) 夏亮的第二支乐队里有一位外校女生

二、简答题 Short-answer questions.

1 夏亮组织乐队容易吗？为什么？

2 "理性地去爱，正是摇滚的精神。"这句话是什么意思？

三、海报设计 Design a poster.

   请给夏亮摇滚乐队2010年6月10日的专场演出设计一张海报（poster）。字数60-100字。

根据提示完成课文结构图 Complete the text structure map according to the clues provided

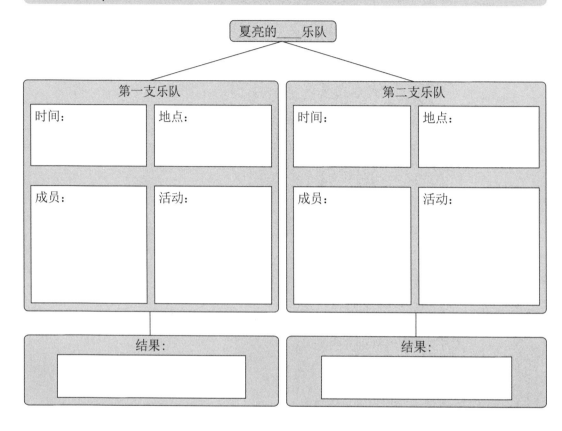

讨论 Discussion

1   年轻人为什么那么热爱摇滚？你所理解的"摇滚精神"是什么？
2   如果你是夏亮，你毕业后会再组织摇滚乐队吗？为什么？

阅读 B: 民乐热在校园升温 Revival of traditional Chinese music in schools

课文 Reading

臧选强是一名大学教师，学笛子已经3个月了，他的老师是杭州民乐*团的一位资深乐手。臧选强为什么学起民乐来了呢？他说，有一次他跟几个朋友吃饭，喝酒喝得很高兴，一个朋友吹起了葫芦丝，另一个朋友拉起了二胡。自己却什么也不会，只有在旁边干瞪眼*。

"当时只有一个感觉，自己太落伍了。"臧选强告诉记者，那次的尴尬经历，让他觉得民乐也是一种交际方式。虽然目前还只能吹简单曲子，但他已经尝到了甜头。不久前的大学教师联谊会上，他的笛声引来了不少女性朋友的侧目。

跟西洋乐器相比，学习民乐器的成本低多了。臧选强说，他的笛子118元，朋友的葫芦丝也就200元，而钢琴、小提琴这样的西洋乐器都要上万元。

不同年龄的学员，学民乐的目的也各不相同。高校学生和上班族大多是因为兴趣爱好，同时也把学习民乐当作娱乐活动。记者在琴行碰到一位姓许的年轻女子来换琵琶弦。小许告诉记者，她学琵琶已经有一年了，刚刚考出三级。小许说："像我这样去考级*没什么压力，空的时候就多练练，忙的时候就先不管它，反正是玩嘛。"

在采访中记者还了解到，有不少准备出国留学的学生，想在国外院校中展现具有民族特色的才艺，为留学生活增光，所以出国前突击学习民乐。

最近十年，民乐在中国迅速升温。全国学习民乐的青少年，据不完全统计，学古筝的有100多万人，学二胡的有60多万人，学扬琴的有50多万人，学笛子的也有40多万人。为什么现在掀起了民乐热呢？江南艺校的张老师告诉记者，如今民族性已经越来越受到重视。随着传统文化的回归，年轻人必然重视民乐这份艺术遗产。

(636 字)

文：通讯员 李莹 记者 陈宇浩 有删改
原载《今日早报》2010年7月3日
网络来源：
http://jrzb.zjol.com.cn/html/2010-07/03/content_436874.htm?div=1

生词注释 Vocabulary

1. 资深【zī shēn】adj. senior

2. 葫芦丝【hú lu sī】葫蘆絲 n. cucurbit flute (or hulusi)

3. 干瞪眼【gān dèng yǎn】ci. stand by anxiously (俗语)

4. 落伍【luò wǔ】vo.; adj. fall behind; out of date

5. 尝【cháng】嘗 v. taste, try

6. 侧目【cè mù】側目 vo. glance

7. 琴行【qín háng】n. musical instrument company

8. 碰到【pèng dào】v. run into, bump into

9. 弦【xián】n. string (of a musical instrument)

10. 增光【zēng guāng】v. dignify, add to the prestige of

11. 突击【tū jī】突擊 v. make a sudden attack, make a concentrated effort

12. 迅速【xùn sù】adj. rapid, prompt

13. 掀起【xiān qǐ】v. lift, surge

14. 必然【bì rán】n.; adv. inevitability; inevitably

文化/熟语注释 Culture/idiom notes

*民乐【mínyuè】中国民族音乐简称民乐，又称国乐，是指中国各个历史时期的本土音乐。中国地域辽阔，各地都拥有各具地方色彩的音乐，共同组成了中国民族音乐。著名的民乐乐器有：古筝、琵琶、二胡、笛子、葫芦丝等。

民乐 is a short form of 中国民族音乐 (traditional Chinese folk music). It is also called China's national music. It refers to a combination of local music in different periods throughout the history of China and the different regionalized music in that vast land. The most well-known traditional Chinese folk musical instruments include: 古筝【gǔzhēng】koto, 琵琶【pípa】 Chinese lute, 二胡【èrhú】two-stringed Chinese fiddle, 笛子【dízi】bamboo flute, and 葫芦丝【húlu sī】 cucurbit flute.

*干瞪眼【gāndèngyǎn】这是一个俗语，意思是非常着急却无可奈何，没有办法。

干瞪眼 is a colloquial idiom. It means to look anxiously on, while being unable to help, or to look on in despair. In this article, it means that the author admired other people playing musical instruments very much and felt anxious, being unable to join in because of not knowing how to play a musical instrument.

*音乐考级【yīnyuè kǎojí】音乐考级是指非音乐专业人士参加的考试，开始于1980年代。这种业余音乐考级在中国的青少年中非常盛行，考级是为音乐学习做一个鉴定。钢琴、小提琴、手风琴、大提琴、电子琴等种类的乐器及声乐都有考级。现在民族乐器也有了考级制度。

The "Level Test for Musicians" in China is for amateur musicians. It was first set in the 1980s. The Level Test is very popular among young people as a method of evaluating their music study. Piano, violin, accordion, cello, electronic piano, and other kinds of vocal musical instrument all have their own Level Test. Nowadays, Level Tests for performers of traditional Chinese folk music are also offered.

语法/语言点注释 Grammar/language points

1 ......引来了......; ... attract ...

他的笛声引来了不少女性朋友的侧目。
His flute has attracted the attention of lots of his female friends.

The word 引 is used with the complement 来 to indicate that something caused something else to happen, or that A is attractive to B.

Example:

她的歌声引来了一阵掌声。
Her singing drew a round of applause.

2 跟......相比......; compare with .../compare to ...

跟西洋乐器相比，民乐器的价格低多了。
Compared with that of a musical instrument in the West, the price for a traditional Chinese musical instrument is quite low.

This structure is used to make a comparison between two things.

Example:

我觉得跟汉语相比，学习西班牙文要容易多了。
I feel Spanish is much easier to learn compared to Chinese.

3 据......; according to ...

　　全国学习民乐的青少年，据不完全统计，学古筝的有100多万人，学二胡的有60多万人，学扬琴的有50多万人，学笛子的也有40多万人。
According to incomplete statistics, among young people who are learning a
traditional Chinese musical instrument, there are more than 1 million who are
studying the koto; more than 0.6 million are studying the two-stringed Chinese
fiddle; more than 0.5 million are studying the dulcimer; and more than
0.4 million are studying the bamboo flute.

The word 据 is used here as a preposition to introduce evidence or a resource.

Example:

据体检报告显示，麦克的肝炎已经痊愈了。
According to the medical report, Mark has fully recovered from hepatitis.

阅读理解 Comprehension

一、对错题 True or false?

1　(　)臧老师不会吹葫芦丝，也不会拉二胡。
2　(　)臧老师学笛子是为了引来女性朋友的侧目。
3　(　)民乐器没有西洋乐器那么贵。
4　(　)从学习人数来看，古筝是最受欢迎的民乐器。
5　(　)年轻人重视民乐是受了外国文化的影响。

二、填空题 Fill in the blanks, choosing from the words provided.

吹　　拉　　弹　　唱　　敲

1 ＿＿＿葫芦丝　　2 ＿＿＿二胡　　3 ＿＿＿琵琶
4 ＿＿＿小提琴　　5 ＿＿＿钢琴　　6 ＿＿＿大鼓

三、乐器知识 Knowledge of musical instruments.

　　你知道下面这些乐器吗？如果不知道，请上网查看图片，然后说说哪些是西洋乐器，哪些是中国民族乐器。Can you recognize the names of these musical instruments? (Check
the website!) Which are Western musical instruments and which are Chinese?

钢琴　　笛子　　小提琴　　葫芦丝　　吉他　　二胡　　萨克管
琵琶　　小号　　古筝　　长笛　　扬琴　　大鼓

第四课　运动与休闲

Chapter 4　Sports and leisure activities

课文导入 Introduction	生词注释 Vocabulary
怎样才能在<u>繁忙</u>的学习与工作中保持健康的身体呢？运动和休闲是最重要的<u>手段</u>。如果你知道中国人爱打太极拳、爱打麻将，你是不是也知道城市里的现代健身房越来越多？传统的休闲场所"茶馆"<u>依然</u>生意红火？	1. 繁忙【fán máng】adj. busy, bustling 2. 手段【shǒu duàn】n. means, method 3. 依然【yī rán】adv. still, as before

阅读 A: 瑜伽教练的体会 The experience of a yoga instructor

读前准备 Warm-up

一、简答题 Short-answer questions.

1　你常常锻炼身体吗？你喜欢哪种健身方式？

2　有的健身方式很激烈，有的很温和，你能说出一、两种温和的健身方式吗？

二、选择题 Multiple-choice questions.

你在选择一项健身运动的时候，会考虑下面的哪些因素？为什么？

a) 收费贵不贵　　b) 教练好不好　　c) 一起健身的学员是怎样的人

课文 Reading

2005年我体校*毕业后开始做瑜伽*教练。当时全城只有三、四家瑜伽馆，练的人很少，主要是三、四十岁的家中经济条件好的全职太太。那时练瑜伽好像是一种身份的象征。

如今可就不同了，瑜伽馆越开越多，来上课的人有办公室的白领、大学生，甚至有一些退休老人。上课的人比以前多了，纪律也比以前好了。以前常有人迟到，直接闯进教室，现在这种现象几乎不会发生。我并不要求学员的动作一定要做得多么标准，只要自己尽了力就够了，最重要的是坚持，让运动成为生活的一部分。

我曾经教过一个男学员，在海关工作，各方面条件都很好，就是因为太胖，一直没找到女朋友。小伙子刚来的时候很自卑，也不怎么和人交流，而且女学员们有点排斥他，毕竟一堆女人里面来了个男人，做动作会觉得不好意思。

不过小伙子很坚持，每天风雨无阻都来上课。为了帮他减肥，我每节课后，都会单独为他增加一些训练项目。渐渐地，他的坚持也感动了周围的人，女学员们都接纳了他。当时他每节课后都要做50个仰卧起坐，有时候人实在太累，躺下去就起不来了，这时候旁边的女学员都会一起帮他数数，为他加油。

我曾经开过一个自己的瑜伽馆，但是没开多久就陷入了困境，因为我懂的只是教学，对经营方面实在了解不多。现在的我也很满足，城里好几家健身中心和瑜伽馆请我做教练，我每天来往于各个健身房之间。

其实我的生活圈子很小，身边的朋友也大多是自己的学生。这么多年下来，我和他们的关系，与其说是师生，倒不如说是朋友。

(597字)

文/整理：记者　白蓓

原载《宁波晚报》2011年9月6日

网络来源：

http://daily.cnnb.com.cn/nbwb/html/2011-09/06/content_360827.htm

生词注释 Vocabulary

1. 瑜伽【yú jiā】n. yoga

2. 全职【quán zhí】全職 n.; adj. full time

3. 退休【tuì xiū】v. retire

4. 纪律【jì lù】紀律 n. rules, regulations

5. 闯进【chuǎng jìn】闖進 v. intrude into, suddenly get in

6. 标准【biāo zhǔn】標準 n. standard, norm, criterion

7. 坚持【jiān chí】堅持 v.; n. persist in; persistence

8. 自卑【zì bēi】adj. having low self-esteem

9. 排斥【pái chì】v. reject, exclude

10. 毕竟【bì jìng】畢竟 adv. after all, all in all

11. 风雨无阻【fēng yǔ wú zǔ】v. 風雨無阻 go as planned regardless of the weather（成语）

12. 接纳【jiē nà】接納 v. accept (into an organization), admit (as a member)

13. 仰卧起坐【yǎng wò qǐ zuò】仰臥起坐 phr. sit-ups

14. 陷入【xiàn rù】v. sink into, get caught up in

15. 经营【jīng yíng】經營 v. n. manage, run; operation

文化/熟语注释 Culture/idiom notes

　　*体校【tǐxiào】体校是从事体育教育和训练的学校，在校的学生都有运动专长。中国的运动员一般来说都是从省、市各级体校进入专业队的。但是对于绝大多数体校生来说，并不能成为专业运动员，他们从体校毕业后往往自己找工作。

体校 refers to sports schools that specialize in physical education and training. All the students in a sport school have their specialty in one or more sports. The professional athletes in the national teams are usually selected from the city or provincial sports schools. Most students in the sports schools who find they cannot become a professional athlete will seek other jobs after graduating.

　　*瑜伽【yújiā】瑜伽起源于印度，距今已发展、流传几千年，成为中国流行的一项健身、修心运动。瑜伽的印度梵语含义是一致、结合、和谐。

瑜伽 (yoga) originated in India and has been developing and spreading over thousands of years. It has become a popular form of fitness exercise and mind-cultivating activity in China. The word "yoga" in Sanskrit means consistency, integration, and harmony.

语法/语言点注释 Grammar/language points

1　可......了; surely...

　　　　如今<u>可</u>就不同<u>了</u>，瑜伽馆越开越多，来上课的人有办公室的白领、大学生，甚至有<u>一些</u>退休老人。
　　　But nowadays it is different. There are more and more yoga houses. And more and more white-collar office workers, college students, and even retired people are taking yoga classes.

可 in this sentence is used as an emphatic word meaning "surely," "certainly," or "finally." It is often used together with a particle such as 了, 呀, or 啦 at the end to further strengthen an emphatic tone.

Example:

　　我一直不知道你去了哪里，今天可找到你了！
　　I did not know where you were for a while, then finally, I found you today!

2　与其说是A不如说是B; A is less than B/B is more than A

　　这么多年下来，我和他们的关系，<u>与其说是</u>师生，倒<u>不如说是</u>朋友。
　　For many years, our relationship has been more like that of friends than of teacher and student.

This pattern is used to emphasize the elements after 不如, meaning A (or doing A) is not as good as B (or doing B). 倒 or 还 can be inserted before 不如。

Example:

今天太冷了，与其去公园看红叶，（倒）不如在家看电视吧。

It is very cold today. I'd rather stay at home watching TV than go to the park to appreciate the red leaves.

阅读理解 Comprehension

一、选择题 Multiple-choice questions.

1   关于以前的瑜伽馆，下面哪个说法是错的？

   a) 全城只有三、四家瑜伽馆
   b) 练瑜伽好像是一种身份的象征
   c) 练瑜伽的人，主要是家中经济条件好的全职太太
   d) 瑜伽课的纪律很好，没有人迟到

2   关于现在的瑜伽馆，下面哪些说法是对的？

   a) 瑜伽馆越开越多
   b) 练瑜伽的是各种各样的人
   c) 几乎没有迟到和直接闯进教室的现象
   d) 练瑜伽的人做的动作都非常标准

3   关于海关小伙子，下面哪个说法是错的？

   a) 长得太胖，一直没找到女朋友
   b) 刚来的时候很自卑，不爱和人说话
   c) 每天坚持来上课，每节课后做仰卧起坐
   d) 女学员们一开始就很喜欢他

4   关于这位瑜伽教练，下面哪些说法是对的？

   a) 曾经开过一个自己的瑜伽馆
   b) 只懂教瑜伽，不懂经营瑜伽馆
   c) 他在一家健身中心和一家瑜伽馆做教练
   d) 他和学生的关系很好，像朋友一样

二、翻译题 Translate the following sentences into English.

1   我一直都不知道，她每星期四晚上都不在宿舍是为了什么，今天可被我发现了。原来，她每星期四去练瑜伽。

2   我和老张的关系，与其说我们是师生，倒不如说我们是朋友。

根据提示完成课文结构图 Complete the text structure map according to the clues provided

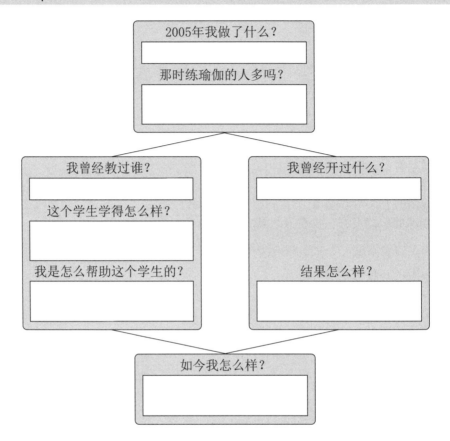

讨论 Discussion

1　在你的国家里，哪一个健身项目特别受欢迎？为什么？请你谈一谈自己最喜爱的运动或健身项目，你为什么喜欢这个项目？

2　读了课文以后，你认为这位教练为什么能够成为学员们的朋友？请举例说明。

3　如果有人想请你给他一些健身运动的建议，你会给他哪些建议呢？

阅读 B: 成都休闲生活 Leisure time in Chengdu

课文 Reading

成都人似乎从不说"玩",成都话"耍"把"玩"的意思都代替了。"耍"用普通话说就是"玩",用流行语说就是"休闲"。

成都人喜欢怎样的休闲生活呢? 众所周知, 文化休闲有影院、音乐厅、歌厅、KTV*等, 健身美容休闲有各类健身俱乐部、美容美发、洗浴按摩等。此外, 成都郊区的"农家乐"休闲方式, 非常吸引成都人。"农家乐"有丰富多彩的休闲项目, 如: 赏花、品果、垂钓、麻将*、棋牌、乒乓、桌球、篝火等。每到周末, 成都人喜欢到郊区的"农家乐"来耍。呼吸着清新的空气, 闻着花香果香, 吃着农家风味的饭菜, 耍着麻将和其他的娱乐活动, 是多么休闲愉快呀!

不过, 上面这些休闲方式在全国各地都很普遍, 并不能反映成都的特色。茶馆文化才是最具成都特色的休闲方式。成都到处是茶馆, 走到哪儿都能见到摆着竹桌竹椅的茶馆。与其说成都人爱喝茶, 不如说成都人爱泡茶馆。泡茶馆似乎已经成为许多成都人的一种生活方式了。许多成都人工作之余的时光, 大多在茶馆里度过。

市中心人民公园的少城茶庄, 大大的林荫场地上, 几百张茶桌椅常常座无虚席。备用的竹桌椅本来堆得有房子那么高, 生意红火的时候全都摆出来用。场地上摆得满满的, 让人惊叹。成都茶馆的竹椅比普通的椅子矮一点, 坐上去很舒服, 既可以坐, 也可以半躺。有的还有座垫、靠枕, 让你坐下去就不想再起来。众人在茶馆喝茶, 常常是一边喝, 一边聊天、打麻将, 累了就半躺着睡一觉, 饿了就叫一碗豆腐花, 来一碗成都馄饨。有的茶馆还有评书或川剧演出。掏耳朵、按摩也是茶馆的

生词注释 Vocabulary

1. 耍【shuǎ】v.; n. play, play with; play

2. 休闲 【xiū xián】休閑 v.; adj. have a leisure time activity; leisurely

3. 众所周知【zhòng suǒ zhōu zhī】眾所周知 known to all（成语）

4. 俱乐部【jù lè bù】俱樂部 n. club

5. 按摩【àn mó】v.; n. massage

6. 郊区【jiāo qū】郊區 n. suburb, outskirts

7. 垂钓【chuí diào】垂釣 v.; n. fish; fishing

8. 麻将【má jiàng】麻將 n. mahjong (see Culture/idiom notes)

9. 棋牌【qí pái】n. chess, board or card game

10. 篝火【gōu huǒ】n. campfire

11. 普遍【pǔ biàn】adj. universal, general

12. 反映【fǎn yìng】v. reflect

13. 摆【bǎi】擺 v. put, place

14. 泡【pào】v. soak, immerse

15. 林荫【lín yīn】林蔭 n. tree shade

16. 座无虚席【zuò wú xū xí】座無虛席 packed to capacity, "full house"（成语）

17. 座垫【zuò diàn】座墊 n. seat cushion

18. 靠枕【kào zhěn】n. supporting pillow

19. 馄饨【hún tun】餛飩 n. wonton

20. 掏【tāo】v. pull out, dig

一项特色服务。掏耳朵的人，背着工具包，最喜欢上茶馆<u>揽</u>生意。先掏耳朵，再做头、肩、颈部的按摩，能让你感觉<u>飘飘欲仙</u>，进入梦乡。难怪有不少外地人把下茶馆、掏耳朵列为到成都的必做之事。

成都以"坐茶馆"为特色的休闲生活<u>驰名</u>全国，很多外地人来成都就是为了享受这里的休闲生活。2011年，成都被评为中国"最佳休闲城市"。

(765字)

作者：五月采萧　有删改

网络来源：

http://wanghdingq.blog.163.com/blog/static/87928592007558142763/

21. 揽【lǎn】揽 v. seize, grasp, take (into one's arms)

22. 飘飘欲仙【piāo piāo yù xiān】飘飘欲仙 feeling as if in paradise, "in heaven"（成语）

23. 驰名【chí míng】驰名 adj. renowned, famous

文化/熟语注释 Culture/idiom notes

*KTV: 就是karaoke TV.卡拉OK是由日本传入港台及中国大陆的。KTV是指在包间唱歌的一种形式。

KTV is short for karaoke TV. Karaoke TV was introduced from Japan into Hong Kong, Taiwan, and mainland China. KTV in this article refers to a singing activity held inside a privately booked room.

*麻将【májiàng】麻将是一种源自中国的游戏，现在依然在世界华人中流行。在古代，麻将牌大多以骨面、竹背做成。游戏参与者一般为四人。赢家依靠的是技巧、计算、策略，但是运气也很重要。

Mahjong is a game that originated in China and remains popular among Chinese people all around the world. In ancient times each mahjong tile was made from two materials: the top side was made of bamboo and the bottom of animal bone. Mahjong is usually played by four people. In order to win the game, you have to rely on skill, calculation, and strategy. A bit of luck helps, too.

语法/语言点注释 Grammar/language points

1 每到......; every time/whenever . . .

<u>每到</u>周末，成都人喜欢到郊区的"农家乐"来耍。
Every weekend, the people from Chengdu like to come to tourist farms in the suburbs for fun.

The word 每 in Chinese is an adverb meaning an action or behavior that appears regularly.

Example:

> 每到总统大选年，电视上、报纸上就到处是有关竞选的报道。
> Whenever it's an election year, reports on the election will be all over the media.

2 才是......; really/very...

> 茶馆文化才是最具成都特色的休闲方式。
> Visiting the tea house is a really special leisure time activity in Chengdu.

The word 才 is an adverb, in this sentence meaning "really" or "very." 才是...... is often used to emphasize the topic introduced.

Example:

> 想要减肥的话，每天坚持运动才是最好的办法。
> If you wish to lose weight, the very best way is to keep on exercising every day.

3 ......之余的......; the time after...

> 许多成都人工作之余的时光，大多在茶馆里度过。
> Many Chengdu people spend most of their after-work hours in tea houses.

The word 之 in 之余 is a classic Chinese word. 之 here is used to connect the word 余 to make 工作之余 into a phrase meaning "the time after work."

Example:

> 小王工作之时不爱跟人说话，而工作之余却常常去KTV唱歌。
> Little Wang does not like to talk with other people while at work, but he often goes
>   to KTV to sing after work.

4 以......为......; take... as .../(is) considered ... as

> 成都以"坐茶馆"为特色的休闲生活驰名全国。
> "Sitting in a tea house" is considered a well-known leisure time activity in Chengdu.

This structure is used to name a representative.

Example:

> 我听说1980年代的中国人以自行车为主要交通工具。
> I heard that the Chinese considered bicycles a major form of transportation in
>   the 1980s.

阅读理解 Comprehension

一、对错题 True or false?

1   (   )许多成都人在工作之余就去泡茶馆。
2   (   )成都到处是摆着竹桌竹椅的茶馆。
3   (   )成都的茶馆除了喝茶，还吃得到豆腐花和馄饨。

4　(　)不少外地人到成都的必做之事是下茶馆、掏耳朵。

5　(　)掏耳朵的人也给客人提供头和脚的按摩服务。

6　(　)很多外地人来成都享受休闲生活。

二、简答题 Short-answer questions.

1　成都话"耍"是什么意思？

2　文化休闲是指哪些休闲方式？

3　健身美容休闲是指哪些休闲方式？

4　"农家乐"休闲方式到底有哪些活动项目？

三、自由回答 Open-ended questions.

1　　　文化休闲、健身美容休闲、"农家乐"休闲，以及具有地方特色的休闲方式（比方说成都的泡茶馆和掏耳朵），你最喜欢哪一种？为什么？

2　在你的国家，有哪些休闲方式？它们与成都的休闲方式有什么不同？

第五课　民以食为天

Chapter 5　Food is the most important staple of life

课文导入 Introduction	生词注释 Vocabulary
饮食与健康的关系是非常大的，不适当的饮食会让我们的身体出现很多问题。现代人<u>掌握</u>了科学知识、医学知识，<u>创造</u>了很多饮食新<u>概念</u>。中国人在饭桌上的一些传统习惯，也渐渐地有了改变。	1. 掌握【zhǎng wò】v.; n. grasp; mastery 2. 创造【chuàng zào】创造 v. create, produce 3. 概念【gài niàn】n. concept, notion

阅读 A: 轻食主义的饮食观 Light-meal philosophy

读前准备 Warm-up

一、简答题 Short-answer questions.

1　你喜欢吃肉类食物还是蔬菜类食物？

2　为了身体健康，你在饮食上常常注意哪些问题？

二、猜一猜下面这些词的意思 Guess the meaning.

轻食主义　　少食多餐　　素食主义　　节食

课文 Reading

轻食主义是一个来源于欧洲的概念，轻食主义意味着在饮食上吃清淡、热量低的食物。这和中国人传统的养生(中医养生*)饮食"少食多餐"、"少食多滋味"在概念上很相似，都属于健康的饮食理念。

轻食主义跟素食主义不同，轻食主义也不等于节食。轻食主义者虽然提倡少吃，但是不禁止吃肉，反而认为适当的肉类脂肪、蛋白质是人体需要的。轻食主义者也不禁止吃饱腹感强的食物。对于轻食主义者来说，日常挑选食物时，尽量让每天的食物种类符合"三低一高"原则，即低糖分、低脂肪、低盐分和高纤维。各种有色蔬菜、新鲜菌类、海鲜和鱼类等等都是轻食主义者喜欢的食物。烹饪的方式以蒸、炖、煮为主，避免煎炸过程中释放有害物质。

如何吃得少而又让人感到满足？轻食主义者有一些小技巧。先喝汤的办法不错，而放慢进食速度、养成细嚼慢咽的习惯，也是减少食物摄入的方法之一。另外，下午茶受到轻食主义者的欢迎，因为点心类的食物分量少、品种多、有营养，吃一份轻食点心，可以有效地增加饱腹感，在正餐的时候不会因为太饿而吃得过多。

轻食主义强调简单、适量、健康和均衡。当然，轻食态度也因人而异，总的来说，让自己觉得舒适的方式就是最适合的方式。

(481字)

文：苏文翰　有删改

原载《新快报》2012年2月6日

网络来源：

http://www.ycwb.com/ePaper/xkb/html/2012-02/06/content_1313900.htm

生词注释 Vocabulary

1. 来源【lái yuán】來源 v.; n. originate; origin, source

2. 意味【yì wèi】v.; n. mean; meaning

3. 养生【yǎng shēng】養生 v. keep in good health, care for life (see Culture/idiom notes)

4. 理念【lǐ niàn】n. idea

5. 节食【jié shí】節食 v.; n. diet

6. 提倡【tí chàng】v. advocate, promote

7. 禁止【jìn zhǐ】v. prohibit

8. 脂肪【zhī fáng】n. fat

9. 蛋白质【dàn bái zhì】蛋白質 n. protein

10. 饱腹感【bǎo fù gǎn】飽腹感 n. sense of satiety

11. 菌类【jūn lèi】菌類 n. fungus

12. 烹饪【pēng rèn】烹飪 v.; n. cook, cooking; culinary art

13. 煎炸【jiān zhá】v. fry and deep fry (cooking method)

14. 细嚼慢咽【xì jiáo màn yàn】細嚼慢咽 chew well and swallow slowly （成语）

15. 摄入【shè rù】攝入 v. absorb, ingest

16. 均衡【jūn héng】v.; n.; adj. balance; balanced

17. 因人而异【yīn rén ér yì】因人而異 vary with each individual, different from person to person （成语）

文化/熟语注释 Culture/idiom notes

*中医养生【zhōngyī yǎngshēng】中医养生是指以传统中医理论为指导，对人体进行科学调养，保持身体健康。中医养生有食养、药养、针灸、按摩、气功等丰富多样的养生技术。"少食多餐"、"吃饭七分饱"等都是中医养生的饮食原则。

The traditional Chinese medical method of staying healthy is guided by traditional Chinese medicine theories. It aims to nourish and recuperate the body and keep it in a good, healthy condition. It includes diet therapy, methods using herbs, acupuncture, Chinese massage, qigong breathing exercises, and other techniques. "Eat little and often," and "Don't eat yourself full" are traditional Chinese sayings about keeping fit.

语法/语言点注释 Grammar/language points

1 来源于......; originated in .../comes from ...

轻食主义是一个<u>来源于</u>欧洲的概念，轻食主义意味着在饮食上吃清淡、热量低的食物。

The light-meal philosophy originated in Europe; it means to eat a light, low-calorie diet.

Example:

心理学家说，女孩子对粉色的喜欢不是来源于她的内心，而是来源于商业广告。

Psychologists say that girls' passion for pink comes not from their heart, but from commercials.

2 反而......; on the contrary ...; instead ...

轻食主义者虽然提倡少吃，但是不禁止吃肉，<u>反而</u>认为适当的肉类脂肪、蛋白质是人体需要的。

The light-meal philosophy advocates that we embrace the eating of light meals, but it does not restrict meat eating. On the contrary, it is considered vital that the body takes in a moderate amount of fat and protein from meat.

The word 反而 is an adverb expressing a tone of transition – something contrary to the previous comments or something unexpected or out of the ordinary.

Example:

那些吃素的人并不觉得每天吃豆腐很没有意思，反而觉得豆腐可以被做成各种美味的菜肴，每天吃着各种风味不同的豆腐是一种享受。

Vegetarians do not feel bored if they eat only tofu every day; on the contrary, they think that tofu can be made into a wide variety of delicious dishes, and eating those various tofu dishes is a joy.

3 以......为主......; take ... as ...

以蒸、炖、煮为主，避免煎炸过程中释放有害物质。
Steaming, stewing, and boiling are alternative cooking methods to the unhealthy method of deep frying.

以......为主 is used to introduce something as principal or foremost.

Example:

这家中国饭店以经营各种北方面食为主，因此很多学生都去那儿吃面条。
This Chinese restaurant mainly serves all kinds of wheat-based food from Northern China; therefore, many students go there for noodles.

阅读理解 Comprehension

一、选择题 Multiple-choice questions.

1 关于轻食主义，下面哪个说法是错的？

a) 吃清淡、热量低的食物
b) 可以吃肉，认为肉对人体有用
c) 提倡吃得少，禁止吃得饱
d) 以"三低一高"原则挑选食物

2 轻食主义者喜欢下面哪些食物？

a) 有色蔬菜
b) 新鲜菌类
c) 海鲜和鱼类
d) 煎炸过的食物

3 下面哪一种不是轻食主义者的饮食习惯？

a) 先喝汤，再吃主食
b) 放慢进食速度，细嚼慢咽
c) 下午茶的时候，吃一份点心
d) 正餐的时候尽力多吃

二、填空题 Fill in the blanks.

1 "三低一高"的意思是低_____、低_____、低_____和高_____。
2 轻食主义者喜欢的烹饪方式是____、____、____，避免____和____。

三、简答题 Short-answer questions.

I　轻食主义者为什么不禁止吃肉？

2　下午茶为什么受到轻食主义者的欢迎？

根据提示完成课文结构图 Complete the text structure map according to the clues provided

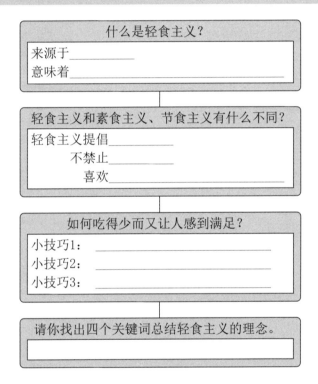

什么是轻食主义？
来源于_____
意味着_____

轻食主义和素食主义、节食主义有什么不同？
轻食主义提倡_____
　　不禁止_____
　　　喜欢_____

如何吃得少而又让人感到满足？
小技巧1：_____
小技巧2：_____
小技巧3：_____

请你找出四个关键词总结轻食主义的理念。

讨论 Discussion

I　在你的家人、同学、朋友中，你观察到哪些不健康的饮食习惯？请给他们好的建议。

2　在你看来，东方人和西方人的饮食习惯有什么相同之处和不同之处？

3　你接受轻食主义的观点吗？为什么？

阅读 B: 可怕的 "腻爱" "Greasy love" is bad for your health

课文 Reading

　　我和所有的母亲一样，爱自己的家，爱孩子。作为家庭主妇的我，每天用自己的厨艺，用美食来满足家人的胃。我认为再没有比这更合适的方式来表达我对他们的爱了。

　　可是真没想到，最近我丈夫体检，年纪轻轻的他居然有了三高：高血压、高血脂、高血糖，医生说是因为不健康的饮食习惯引起的。接着，女儿的幼儿园老师也说，女儿在幼儿园不喜欢运动，吃饭的时候挑食，喜欢吃荤菜，不喜欢吃素菜。让我这个当妈妈的要适当引导，小孩子吃饭要养成好习惯，荤素搭配，营养均衡才能更健康。

　　医生和老师的话让我有点懵，我想，让家人吃得好点儿难道有错吗？就在这时，我无意中看见一本《家庭医生》，里面有篇文章写道："把最好吃的留给最爱的，这是中国人表达爱的一种方式。但是如果这种爱带给家人的却是高热量、高脂肪的肥腻食物，那这种爱就是'腻爱'，是可怕的'杀手'。""适量是营养，过量是毒物，当我们用食物表达爱的时候，请别用'腻爱'害了自己的亲人。"这样的句子吓坏了我。

　　我开始关注有关科学饮食方面的信息，不看不知道，一看吓一跳，原来食物不是越贵越好，也不是荤菜比素菜好，这么长时间里，我一直在用食物表达错误的爱，后果严重到有可能成为可怕的杀手！这实在是个极大的误会。我开始改变全家人的饮食习惯。我花更多的时间去做菜，想办法保持食物的原汁原味，把荤菜做得不油腻。

生词注释 Vocabulary

1. 厨艺【chú yì】廚藝 n. culinary skill

2. 居然【jū rán】adv. unexpectedly, to one's surprise

3. 营养【yíng yǎng】營養 n. nutrition

4. 懵【měng】adj. muddled

5. 肥腻【féi nì】肥膩 adj. rich, greasy

6. 杀手【shā shǒu】殺手 n. professional killer, hitman

7. 吓坏【xià huài】嚇壞 v. scare, frighten

8. 误会【wù huì】誤會 v.; n. misunderstand; misunderstanding

我虽然还是喜欢用食物来表达爱，不过不再是腻
爱，而是健康的爱。"民以食为天*"，注重身边家人
"吃"的质和量，就是保住大家健康的最大的"天"。

（619字）

文：林墨瞳　有删改

原载《扬子晚报》2008年10月21日

网络来源：

http://epaper.yangtse.com/yzwb/2008-10-21/content_11819549.htm

文化/熟语注释 Culture/idiom notes

*民以食为天【mín yǐ shí wéi tiān】"民以食为天"这句话出自汉代，已有两千多年历史，意思是人活着吃饭是最重要的事情。这句话反映了中国的饮食文化精神。自古以来中国人就特别重视饮食以及饮食的礼节文化。

The expression 民以食为天 originated in the Han dynasty some 2,000 years ago and literally means "food is of primary importance in people's lives." This expression is a reflection of Chinese eating culture and how Chinese people have emphasized different eating and drinking styles and manners since ancient times.

语法/语言点注释 Grammar/language points

1 用……来……; use . . . to . . .

作为家庭主妇的我，每天<u>用</u>自己的厨艺，<u>用</u>美食<u>来</u>满足家人的胃。我认为再没有比这更合适的方式来表达我对他们的爱了。

As a housewife, I use my culinary skills and delicious food to satisfy my family members' stomachs. I think there is no better way to express my love for them than this.

This structure is used to express using certain means to reach certain goals.

Example:

我父亲用他的全部工资来养活我们一家四口人。

My father uses all his salary to support his family of four.

2 不再是A而是B; is no longer A but B

我虽然还是喜欢用食物来表达爱，不过<u>不再是</u>腻爱，<u>而是</u>健康的爱。

Although I still like to use food to express my love, it is no longer "greasy love" but a healthy kind of love.

This structure is used to indicate the negation of a former action or event and the confirmation or emphasis of the latter one. 不再 placed before 是 is used to emphasize the negation.

Example:

> 有人说，现在世界首富已经不再是美国微软公司的比尔·盖茨，而是瑞典家具制造商宜家公司的创始人英格瓦·坎普拉德。
>
> It is said that the world's wealthiest person is no longer Bill Gates of Microsoft in the USA, but Ingvar Kamprad, the Swedish founder of the retail company IKEA.

阅读理解 Comprehension

一、对错题 True or false?

1 （ ）"我"每天做很多好吃的来表达对家人的爱。
2 （ ）医生说丈夫得了"三高"是因为他不喜欢运动。
3 （ ）幼儿园老师发现女儿的饮食习惯是不健康的。
4 （ ）看了《家庭医生》上的文章我才知道自己错了。
5 （ ）我以前觉得食物越贵越好，荤菜比素菜好。
6 （ ）现在我知道做菜应该保持食物的原汁原味。

二、填空题 Fill in the blanks, choosing from the words provided.

> 荤　　素　　适　　过　　营养　　血压　　血脂　　血糖

1 年轻的丈夫居然有了"三高"：高_____、高_____、高_____。
2 女儿吃饭的时候挑食，喜欢吃___菜，不喜欢吃___菜。
3 _____量是营养，_____量是毒物。请别用"腻爱"害了自己的亲人。
4 吃饭要养成好习惯，_____搭配，_____均衡才能更健康。

三、自由回答题 Open-ended questions.

1 你平时喜欢吃哪些食品？你觉得那些食品健康吗？

2 如果你是餐馆的老板，你会建议餐馆给顾客提供哪些菜？为什么？

3 你的父母也用厨艺和美食来表达对家人的爱吗？你觉得是腻爱还是健康的爱？

第六课　留学与海归

Chapter 6　Study abroad and overseas returners

课文导入 Introduction	生词注释 Vocabulary
每年中国有许多年轻人告别家人、朋友，到<u>异国他乡</u>去留学。他们学成归国以后，又把在国外学到的各方面知识与经验用于中国的创业。年轻人的留学<u>潮</u>与海归潮，改变着他们的人生也改变着中国与世界的<u>距离</u>。	1. 异国他乡【yì guó tā xiāng】異國他鄉 n. foreign country（成语） 2. 潮【cháo】n. tide, current, trend 3. 距离【jù lí】距離 v.; n. be apart from; distance, interval

阅读 A: 出国留学改变年轻人的生活 Studying abroad changes young people's lives

读前准备 Warm-up

一、简答题 Short-answer questions.

1　你去过外国吗？你是去旅游、留学还是去工作？

2　你的出国经历对你有什么影响？

二、选择题 Multiple-choice questions.

1　他们<u>学成</u>后会带着和以前有很大不同的价值观回国。
The underlined word 学成 means:

a) fully grown　　b) accomplish　　c) turn into

2   在过去的两年中，就有62万中国学生出国留学。
     Which one of the following numbers is 62万？

     a) 6,200   b) 62,000   c) 620,000

3   这所学校去年的600名毕业班学生中，有10%已经出国留学。
     10% is read as:

     a) 十之一百   b) 一百之十   c) 百分之十

课文 Reading	生词注释 Vocabulary

英国《金融时报》国际版4月4日刊登一篇文章说，现在出国留学*的中国年轻人越来越多，而国外留学期间正是他们转变价值观的重要阶段，他们学成后会带着和以前有很大不同的价值观回国。

在过去的两年中，就有62万中国学生出国留学，这是自1978年中国开始恢复留学以来的留学生总数的四分之一。中国实行了30多年的独生子女政策*，使绝大多数家庭只有一个孩子。在中国家长看来，孩子现在的最好前途就是出国留学，许多中国家庭现在也负担得起送孩子留学的学费。

文章作者采访了石家庄第42中学。校方说，这所学校去年的600名毕业班学生中，有10%已经出国留学。现在学校专门为希望毕业后出国留学的学生成立了一个特殊的班，有30名学生。一名16岁女生的父亲说，以前都认为女孩子不能出远门，但现在观念变了，所以准备送她上沃顿商学院读精算。

一项由英国诺丁汉大学和中国清华大学共同进行的对中国在英留学生的调查结果显示，中国留学生刚开始时不习惯西方的生活和教育方式，很少与西方同学交朋友。但是几年之后，他们中的大多数都承认，出国的这几年时间，永远改变了他们的人生。

一位接受调查的学生说，由于中国人生活在单一文化背景中，出国留学帮助他们了解生活在其他文化背景下的人，然后发现彼此的共性。文章最后引用一位在爱

1. 金融时报【jīn róng shí bào】
金融時報 pn. *Financial Times*

2. 阶段【jiē duàn】階段 n. stage,
phase, period

3. 价值观【jià zhí guān】價值觀
n. values

4. 恢复【huī fù】恢復 v. recover,
restore

5. 负担【fù dān】負擔 v.; n. bear
or shoulder (responsibility);
burden

6. 特殊【tè shū】adj. special,
particular, exceptional

7. 沃顿商学院【Wò dùn shāng
xué yuàn】沃頓商學院 pn.
Wharton School of the University
of Pennsylvania

8. 精算【jīng suàn】n. actuarial
science

9. 诺丁汉大学【Nuò dīng hàn dà
xué】諾丁漢大學 pn. University
of Nottingham

10. 彼此【bǐ cǐ】pr. each other,
one another

丁堡读书的中国留学生的话说，越多中国人出国，并重

新审视自己，中国与外部世界的关系就会越正常。

II. 审视【shěn shì】审视 v. look at carefully, examine

(565字)

文：易彪　有删改

原载《羊城晚报-家园周刊》2012年4月13日

网络来源：

http://www.ycwb.com/ePaper/jyzk/html/2012-04/13/content_1368200.htm

文化/熟语注释 Culture/idiom notes

　　*出国留学【chūguó liúxué】中国结束十年文革以后，1978年中国在邓小平领导下走上了改革开放的道路，从此以后，中国社会各方面发生了巨大的变化。在教育领域，恢复了高考制度和出国留学制度。同时无数青年把好奇的目光投向了外面的世界, 社会上渐渐掀起了一股出国留学热潮。

　　After ten years of Cultural Revolution, China entered a new era and started on the path to reform and opening up, led by Deng Xiaoping in 1978. Since then China has undergone changes in every aspect of society. In the field of education, the college entrance exam system and studying abroad system were restored. Meanwhile, many young people were driven by their curiosity about the outside world; thus studying abroad became popular among college students.

　　*独生子女政策【dúshēng zǐnǚ zhèngcè】1980年9月，为了控制中国增长过快、过多的人口，中国政府实施了"一对夫妇只生一个孩子"的政策，因此，1980年代出生的孩子大部分都是独生子女。

　　In September 1980 the Chinese government started to advocate the "one family, one child" policy nationwide, aiming to control the fast growing population. Thus, the generation born in 1980s China became known as 独生子女, the "only children."

语法/语言点注释 Grammar/language points

1 自......以来; since . . .

　　在过去的两年中，就有62万中国学生出国留学，这是自1978年中国开始恢复留学以来的留学生总数的四分之一。

　　In the past two years 0.62 million Chinese students went abroad to study. This number is about a quarter of the total number of students studying abroad since 1978 when the studying abroad system was restored.

This structure indicates that the time of an action or the continuation of something is from a certain point in the past up to now.

Example:

中国人自古以来一直崇拜龙，认为龙是天上的神物。

Chinese people have admired dragons since ancient times, believing that they are supernatural beings from heaven.

2 由 . . . . . . 对 . . . . . . ; by . . . toward . . .

> 一项由英国诺丁汉大学和中国清华大学共同进行的对中国在英留学生的调查结果显示，中国留学生刚开始时不习惯西方的生活和教育方式，很少与西方同学交朋友。
>
> A study of Chinese students studying in the UK co-conducted by the University of Nottingham in England and Tsinghua University in China showed that many Chinese students were not used to Western ways of living and education at the beginning and seldom made friends with Western students.

The proposition 由 is used to introduce the subject–verb phrase "英国诺丁汉大学和中国清华大学共同进行的." This phrase serves as the first attribute in the sentence. 对 is also a preposition used to specify a target group. The phrase 对中国在英留学生的调查 serves as the second attribute in the sentence. The two phrases introduced by 由 and 对 both serve as attributes for the subject 结果 in this compound sentence.

Example:

> 由中国红十字会发起的对失学儿童的支助活动已经在上个星期开始了。
>
> The activities organized by the Red Cross in China to support school-dropout students has already started – they've been going on since last week.

阅读理解 Comprehension

一、填空题 Fill in the blanks, choosing from the words provided.

> 得　　成　　由　　对　　并

1　他们学＿＿＿后会带着和以前有很大不同的价值观回国。
2　这项调查是＿＿＿中国和英国两所大学共同进行的。
3　越多中国人出国，＿＿＿重新审视自己，中国与外部世界的关系就会越正常。

二、选择题 Multiple-choice questions.

1　关于中国人出国留学，下面哪个说法是错的？

　　a) 中国1978年恢复了留学政策
　　b) 从恢复留学到两年以前，中国有62万人出国留学
　　c) 现在的中国家长认为出国留学能给孩子好的前途
　　d) 现在的中国家庭有经济能力送孩子出国留学

2　关于中国在英留学生调查，下面哪些说法是对的？

　　a) 这项调查是中英两所大学共同进行的
　　b) 留学初期在生活上和学习上都不习惯
　　c) 出国留学改变了他们单一的文化背景
　　d) 留学生发现中国人与英国人没有共性

三、简答题 Short-answer questions.

1   读课文第三段，说说关于出国留学，孩子们家长的想法有什么变化？

2   读课文第四段，说说中国留学生出国后与出国前相比有什么变化？

根据提示完成课文结构图 Complete the text structure map according to the clues provided

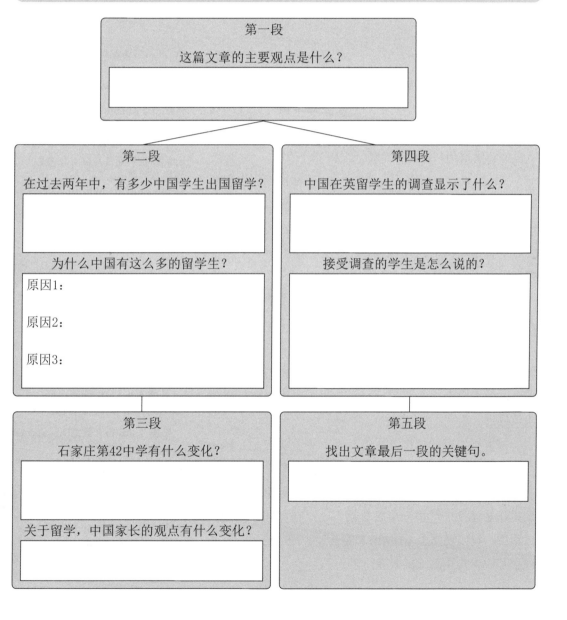

第一段

这篇文章的主要观点是什么？

第二段

在过去两年中，有多少中国学生出国留学？

为什么中国有这么多的留学生？

原因1：

原因2：

原因3：

第四段

中国在英留学生的调查显示了什么？

接受调查的学生是怎么说的？

第三段

石家庄第42中学有什么变化？

关于留学，中国家长的观点有什么变化？

第五段

找出文章最后一段的关键句。

讨论 Discussion

1　　　很多中国家长认为孩子现在的最好前途就是出国留学，你认为中国家长为什么会有这样的想法？

2　　你的父母鼓励你去外国留学吗？你的父母和你自己对留学有什么看法？

阅读 B: 做一本不同的DM杂志 Running a different direct mail magazine

课文 Reading

　　甘雷是一位还不到三十岁的年轻人。他二十多岁的时候在法国留学了五年，然后回家乡郑州在一家日产汽车公司工作，后来又去阿尔及利亚做翻译，最后于2009年春节回到郑州，办起了DM（直投广告）杂志。

　　"出国以前不知道什么是DM，去了法国以后发现那里有很多DM杂志，我经常看，慢慢开始感兴趣。找工作、购物需要的信息，百分之八、九十都是从DM里得到的。"甘雷回国后发现国内DM的发展相比国外差了很多，于是决定自己创办一份不同的DM杂志。

　　"一开始很多人都不看好，觉得我一个学计算机的人怎么办起杂志来了？"甘雷在法国克莱蒙费朗大学学习的专业是计算机，后来的两份工作也是计算机方面的，但最近他却选择了办DM杂志。"其实，我的专业并没有丢下，因为办杂志需要用计算机技术来处理数据，提供决策依据。"

　　甘雷不但有计算机方面的技术，更重要的是，他还有与DM杂志相关的工作经验。2005年的寒假，甘雷获得了法国一个叫《信息》的DM杂志社实习的机会。他的主要工作是建立一个用户信息数据库。"在与同事接触的过程中，我慢慢熟悉了DM杂志经营、管理的模式，这是我在那次实习中最大的收获。"

生词注释 Vocabulary

1. 郑州【Zhèng zhōu】鄭州 pn. Zhengzhou (capital of Henan Province, China)

2. 阿尔及利亚【Ā ěr jí lì yà】阿爾及利亞 pn. People's Democratic Republic of Algeria

3. 克莱蒙费朗【Kè lái méng fèi lǎng】克萊蒙費朗 pn. Clermont-Ferrand

4. 处理【chǔ lǐ】處理 v.; n. handle, deal with; disposal

5. 数据【shù jù】數據 n. data

6. 决策【jué cè】決策 v.; n. make policy; policy decision

7. 依据【yī jù】依據 v.; n. judging by; basis

8. 相关【xiāng guān】相關 adj. related, interrelated

9. 数据库【shù jù kù】數據庫 n. database

甘雷说："国内的DM杂志只面向高收入人群，<u>忽略了</u>大多数中等或中等以下收入水平的人群，而我的杂志恰恰是定位在这个群体，他们数量<u>庞大</u>，对各种实用信息有强烈的需求。这也正是目前国内DM杂志市场所缺少的。"

像甘雷这样<u>敢于</u>打破常规、挑战<u>风险</u>的<u>海归</u>*，在<u>各行各业</u>还有很多。这些海归充分运用在国外所学的专业知识和理念，结合国内实际情况来创业，往往能很好地<u>弥补</u>国内某些行业的不足。

（636字）
文：记者 林琳 有删改
原载《人民日报海外版》2009年3月21日
网络来源：
http://paper.people.com.cn/rmrbhwb/html/2009-03/21/content_215711.htm

10. 忽略【hū lüè】 v. ignore, neglect

11. 庞大【páng dà】龐大 adj. big, huge, enormous

12. 敢于【gǎn yú】敢於 adv. dare to

13. 风险【fēng xiǎn】風險 n. risk, danger

14. 各行各业【gè háng gè yè】各行各業 all professions（成语）

15. 海归【hǎi guī】海歸 v.; n. return from oversea; returnees

16. 弥补【mí bǔ】彌補 v. compensate, make up for

文化/熟语注释 Culture/idiom notes

*海归【hǎi guī】中国人称从海外回到中国的人为"海归"，这是一种幽默的说法，因为它的发音与"海龟"相同。"海归"常常用来指那些获得相当的国外学习和工作经验后，回到中国生活和工作的高素质人才。

This refers to highly competent and talented people who have had the experience of studying and working abroad. Chinese people refer to such people who return home as 海归, which is a humorous way of referring to them, because the pronunciation of 海归 is the same as 海龟 (which means sea turtle!).

语法/语言点注释 Grammar/language points

1 并 . . . . . .; actually . . ., really . . .

其实，我的专业<u>并</u>没有丢下，因为办杂志需要用计算机技术来处理数据，提供决策依据。
In fact, I did not actually drop my specialization. Running a magazine means you need to use computer skills to handle statistics, in order to provide a basis for decision making.

The word 并 is placed before the negation word such as 没有 or 不 to emphasize the negation.

Example:

我只希望我的男朋友一心一意爱我，并不在乎他是不是有钱。
I only want my boyfriend to love me wholeheartedly. I really don't mind if he is rich or not.

2 与 . . . . . . 相关; (is) related to . . .

> 甘雷不但有计算机方面的技术，更重要的是，他还有与DM杂志<u>相关</u>的工作经验。
> Lei Gan not only has computer skills; more importantly, he has related experience in running a direct mail magazine.

This structure is used to state that a certain thing is related to or connected to another.

Example:

> 自从学习中文以后，我对一切与中国相关的事情都很好奇。
> Since I started to learn Chinese, I have become very interested in all things related to China.

3 所 . . . . . . 的; what . . .

> 这也正是目前国内DM杂志市场<u>所</u>缺少<u>的</u>。
> This is what the current domestic direct mail magazine market is lacking.

The word 所 is used together with 的 to form a "的 construction" to make the phrase a noun phrase.

Example:

> 在赛场上获得金牌是每一个运动员所渴望的。
> To win the gold medal is what every athlete yearns for in the sporting world.

阅读理解 Comprehension

一、对错题 True or false?

1　(　)甘雷第一次看到DM杂志是在法国留学期间。
2　(　)甘雷回国后发现中国的DM杂志发展得也很好。
3　(　)甘雷创办杂志很多人并不看好，因为他太年轻了。
4　(　)甘雷在法国DM杂志社的实习工作跟自己的专业没有关系。
5　(　)甘雷创办的DM杂志面向中等或中等以下收入水平的人群。

二、连线题 Using a line, connect the word in the left column with the corresponding one in the right.

打破　　　　　实际情况
挑战　　　　　专业知识和理念
运用　　　　　不足
结合　　　　　风险
弥补　　　　　常规

三、写简历 Write a résumé.

青年报社一位记者要采访甘雷，你是甘雷的秘书，请你为给甘雷写一份简历交给记者。
（字数：250-300字）

第七课　就业与失业

Chapter 7　Employment and unemployment

课文导入 Introduction

　　找工作是每个毕业生最关心的大事。如何才能通过面试得到工作机会呢？一旦找到工作，就步入了职业生涯，而任何人的职业生涯都不可能总是顺利的，有一天失业了，又该怎么办？下面两篇文章从不同方面反映了应聘者与失业者对这两个问题的看法。

生词注释 Vocabulary

1. 生涯【shēng yá】n. career, profession, livelihood

2. 应聘者【yīng pìn zhě】應聘者 n. job applicant

3. 失业者【shī yè zhě】失業者 n. unemployed person

阅读 A: 我的工作面试经历 My job-interviewing experience

读前准备 Warm-up

一、选择题 Multiple-choice questions

1　工作面试的时候，你认为下面哪一项是最重要的？

　　a) 自信　　b) 微笑　　c) 诚实　　d) 良好的外貌

2　要是面试迟到了，你会怎么做？

　　a) 告诉面试官一个听起来很可信但不是真实的理由
　　b) 告诉面试官真实的原因，虽然这个原因有可能会影响到是否被录用
　　c) 别的办法

　　如果选c，请说明你的办法：＿＿＿＿＿＿＿＿＿＿＿＿＿＿＿。

课文 Reading

大四那年，为了找工作*，我四处<u>奔波</u>。一个<u>偶然</u>的机会，我从报上看到某保险公司<u>招聘咨询师</u>的信息，于是决心试试。寄出去简历没多久，我就收到了面试通知。

下午1点，我准时到达面试场所。我应聘的是咨询师<u>岗位</u>，这个岗位的<u>职责</u>就是解答客户的来电问题，处理客户的<u>投诉</u>，类似于客户服务的工作内容。

第一轮<u>测试</u>很简单，我轻松过关。第二轮考试的时候，我戴上耳机听问题，用话筒回答。尽管有些<u>紧张</u>，但我也顺利通过了。晚上6点，<u>最终</u>面试的名单贴了出来，我再次看见自己的名字。进入最后面试的有15个人，就在晚上7点20分开始。

我是外地人，看来晚上回不去家了。我顾不上吃晚饭，赶紧去公司附近找住宿的旅馆。这一忙时间就给<u>耽误</u>了，眼看就要迟到了，我飞奔回面试地点，结果还是迟到了10分钟。不过，晚上7点20分是所有参加面试的人集合的时间，而每个人的面试时间都各不相同，我被安排在后面，所以严格意义上说，我没有迟到。

但老实的我，还是很为那10分钟过意不去。见到<u>面试官</u>的第一<u>反应</u>就是<u>鞠躬道歉</u>："不好意思，我迟到了，因为出去找旅馆了，所以没能及时赶回来。"考官却<u>严肃</u>地说："迟到是没有任何理由的，你说呢？"我只好老实回答，"我知道迟到是没有借口的，迟到就是迟到，就是不对，所以我很<u>抱歉</u>。但是，我不是给自己的迟到找借口，只是想解释一下。"

考官笑着认可了我的解释，他似乎看出了我真诚的歉意。接着问了我对整个面试过程的感想和看法。我个人认为整个过程很<u>严谨</u>，考试方式很科学。考试的环节一步接一步，效率很高。

一个小时后，面试结果出来了——我得到了这份工作！

(642字)

文：邢燕　有删改
原载《新民晚报》2006年11月25日
网络来源：http://www.gdchrc.com/art/ArticleShow.aspx?ArticleID=7733

生词注释 Vocabulary

1. 奔波【bēn bō】v. be busy running about, rush about

2. 偶然【ǒu rán】adj.; adv. accidental, unusual; accidentally

3. 招聘【zhāo pìn】v. invite applications, give public notice of vacancies to be filled

4. 咨询师【zī xún shī】諮詢師 n. consultant, counselor

5. 岗位【gǎng wèi】崗位 n. post, position

6. 职责【zhí zé】職責 n. duty, obligation, responsibility

7. 投诉【tóu sù】投訴 v.; n. complain; complaint

8. 测试【cè shì】測試 v.; n. test; testing

9. 紧张【jǐn zhāng】緊張 adj. nervous, intense

10. 最终【zuì zhōng】最終 n. ultimate, final

11. 耽误【dān wù】耽誤 v. delay, hold up

12. 面试官【miàn shì guān】面試官 n. interviewer

13. 反应【fǎn yìng】反應 v.; n. react, respond; reaction

14. 鞠躬【jū gōng】vo. bow (to show respect)

15. 道歉【dào qiàn】vo.; n. apologize; apology

16. 严肃【yán sù】嚴肅 v.; adj. strictly enforce; serious (attitude), solemn

17. 抱歉【bào qiàn】v. sorry, regret

18. 严谨【yán jǐn】嚴謹 adj. rigorous, strict, precise

文化/熟语注释 Culture/idiom notes

*找工作【zhǎo gōngzuò】中国以前的政策是，大学毕业生的工作由国家分配，所以大学生毕业后不用自己找工作。但是到20世纪80年代以后，毕业生不再由国家分配工作，而是自己找工作。因为经济和社会方面存在的问题，在当代中国，大学生就业难已成为一个社会现象。

In the past, a job after graduation was guaranteed for college students as it was assigned by the government. Since the 1980s graduates are no longer assigned jobs by the government, but have to seek jobs for themselves. Nowadays, due to the economy and other social problems, it has become a common phenomenon that it is more and more difficult for college graduates to find a job.

语法/语言点注释 Grammar/language points

1 某......; one (a certain) . . .

一个偶然的机会，我从报上看到某保险公司招聘咨询师的信息，于是决心试试。
Coincidentally, I saw in the newspaper that an insurance company was recruiting consultants. I decided to give it a try.

The word 某 is used before a noun as an indefinite reference meaning "one" or "a certain."

Example:

他从某网站上看到了这个招聘广告，决定应聘这个工作。
He saw the job advertisement on a website and decided to apply for the job.

2 类似于......; (is) similar to . . .

我应聘的是咨询师岗位，这个岗位的职责就是解答客户的来电问题，处理客户的投诉，<u>类似于客户服务的工作内容</u>。
The position I applied for is that of consultant. It mainly involves being in charge of answering questions from clients and handling customer complaints over the phone, which is similar to customer service.

类似于 is used to compare the similarity of two things.

Example:

我过敏的时候，常常会出现打喷嚏、流眼泪等类似于感冒的症状。
When I get allergic, I usually have flu-like symptoms such as sneezing and watery eyes.

3 尽管......但......; despite . . .

<u>尽管有些紧张</u>，<u>但</u>我也顺利通过了。
Despite my being a little nervous, I still passed (the test) smoothly.

This pattern is used to express a tone of transition similar to "虽然......但是......" but lighter in tone.

Example:

这个电影我尽管已经看过三遍了，但还想再看一遍。

Despite the fact that I have watched this movie three times, I still want to see it one more time.

4 严格意义上说......; strictly speaking . . .

晚上7点20分是所有参加面试的人集合的时间，而每个人的面试时间都各不相同，我被安排在后面，所以严格意义上说，我没有迟到。

The assembly time for the evening interview is 7:20, yet everyone had different interview times. I was arranged to be one of the later ones, so, strictly speaking, I was not late (for the interview).

严格意义上说 is an adverbial phrase that is usually placed before the sentence that the phrase is referring to.

Example:

我丈夫忙着自己的工作，很少回家，更不用说做家务，带孩子，严格意义上说，他没有尽一个父亲和丈夫的职责。

My husband is busy with his job; he is seldom at home, not to mention being around to do housework or take care of the children; strictly speaking, he is not fulfilling his "duty" as a father and a husband.

5 不是......只是......; it is not A . . . but . . . B

我不是给自己的迟到找借口，只是想解释一下。

I'm not trying to find an excuse for being late (to the interview), but just want to explain a bit.

This structure is used to convey a reason for the statement or situation presented in the previous sentence.

Example:

虽然我的生活情况不太好，但是每次给我父母打电话我都对他们说我很好，这不是故意要骗他们，只是不想让他们担心。

Although my living situation is not so good, I always tell my parents that I'm doing fine when I call them; I'm not intentionally lying to them, it is just that I don't want them to worry about me.

阅读理解 Comprehension

一、对错题 True or false?

1　(　)同学告诉我有一家保险公司在招聘咨询师。
2　(　)我应聘的岗位先得通过两轮笔试，然后进入面试。
3　(　)因为我出去吃晚饭，结果面试迟到了10分钟。
4　(　)我的面试时间不是7点20分，也不是7点半。
5　(　)面试的时候考官请我解释为什么迟到10分钟。

二、填空题 Fill in the blanks, choosing from the words provided.

还是 　 但 　 只是 　 对 　 于是 　 总是

1 我从某网站上看到一则招聘启事，跟我的专业很符合，_____我想去应聘。

2 这是我第一次参加工作面试，尽管有些紧张，_____我回答得还可以。

3 虽然我自己觉得面试的时候表现不错，结果却_____没有通过。

4 我给面试官写了一封信去，我不是想请他重新考虑我，_____想咨询一下。

5 我在信上问了面试官_____我整个面试过程的看法和建议，我想在以后的面试中改正缺点。

三、简答题 Short-answer questions.

1 "我"为什么要向考官道歉？你认为这位面试者迟到了吗？

2 "我"对这家公司的面试有什么感想和看法？

根据提示完成课文结构图 Complete the text structure map according to the clues provided

我应聘的是什么工作？

下午有几轮考试？

什么事让我没吃晚饭？

我迟到了吗？

找出说明我通过考试的关键词。

见到面试官我为什么要道歉？

用一句话总结这次面试的过程与结果。

讨论 Discussion

1   如果你是课文中的面试官，你会录用一个迟到的面试者吗？请说明。
2   有人说找工作主要靠"运气"，也有人说找工作得靠"实力"，请说说你的看法。

阅读 B: 走出被裁员的阴影 Walking out of the shadow of unemployment

课文 Reading

苏小姐刚刚从外地出差回来，手头的项目还在进行中，然而没想到的事情还是发生了。就在那天一早，<u>人力资源部</u>经理把她叫到办公室，告诉她一个坏消息：她被<u>裁员</u>了。

苏小姐从<u>跨国公司</u>白领变成了一个失业者。此后几天里，她一直想不通，自己工作那么努力，为什么偏偏是她被裁员？接下来该怎么办？还能找到工作吗？要是被朋友们知道自己被裁了，多丢人！"24小时内走人，一个月工资补偿"——这样的事情真的就发生在自己身上，苏小姐一天比一天<u>苦闷</u>。接下来的两个多月里，她虽然也寄出了不少找工作的简历，可是都<u>石沉大海</u>，没什么收获。

巨大的压力下，苏小姐敲响了职业生涯咨询*的大门。职业规划专家耐心地开导她，给了她很多有效的建议。"当你刚被裁员的时候，心情不好，这些<u>消极情绪</u>很可能影响求职中的表现，找工作就不顺利。假如你还没做好重新工作的准备，那还不如先静下心来想一想。"

"所以，关键是要调整心情，要让自己的精神面貌变得积极、向上。你要花点时间去休闲、娱乐，保持健康的生活方式，这样才能走出<u>阴影</u>，迎接新的<u>挑战</u>。"

"还有，你也可以试着理性分析被裁的原因。是自己能力不够，还是公司状况不佳？是单个<u>企业</u>不景气，还是整个行业不景气？假如是自己能力不够，那就通过各种方法增强竞争力；假如是你的公司单个企业不景气，

生词注释 Vocabulary

1. 人力资源部【rén lì zī yuán bù】人力資源部 n. human resources department

2. 裁员【cái yuán】裁員 vo. lay off employees

3. 跨国公司【kuà guó gōng sī】跨國公司 n. international corporation

4. 苦闷【kǔ mèn】苦悶 adj. depressed, downhearted

5. 石沉大海【shí chén dà hǎi】never seen or heard again (like a stone dropped into the sea)（成语）

6. 消极【xiāo jí】消極 adj. negative, passive, dispirited

7. 情绪【qíng xù】情緒 n. emotion, feeling, mood

8. 阴影【yīn yǐng】陰影 n. shadow

9. 挑战【tiǎo zhàn】挑戰 vo.; n. challenge; contest

10. 企业【qǐ yè】企業 n. enterprise, company

那么可以看看同行的公司有没有机会；假如是整个行业
不景气，也许就要做转行的准备了。"

这一<u>番</u>话说得苏小姐<u>茅塞顿开</u>，她慢慢地终于走出
了裁员阴影。她在空闲时间积极地给自己"充电"，考
出了一个市场<u>营销</u>方面的证书。如今，她已经成功找到
了一份市场方面的工作，重新找回了自信。

(657字)

文：向阳生涯职业规划中心　有删改
原载《新民晚报》2005年7月25日
网络来源：

http://www.fesco.com.cn/210/2009_10_10/1_210_25690_0_1255167121968.html

11. 番【fān】 m. kind, sort, for counting occurrences

12. 茅塞顿开【máo sè dùn kāi】茅塞頓開 suddenly enlightened （成语）

13. 营销【yíng xiāo】營銷 n. marketing

文化/熟语注释 Culture/idiom notes

　　*职业生涯咨询【zhíyè shēngyá zīxún】职业生涯是指一个人一生中从事和负担的职业、职务、职位的过程。职业生涯咨询是当某个人在求职或工作中有困难时，向别人求助解决问题的方法。咨询师的工作一般是帮助客户分析自身的兴趣爱好、性格特征、能力特长从而能在职业选择上做出恰当的决策；也帮助客户学习在准备简历、面试方面的技巧和提高应对职场上挫折和困境的能力。在中国，这种咨询服务是近年来受西方文化影响后逐步发展起来的。

职业生涯 refers to the profession, responsibility, and position that you have taken in your life. Career consultation is a service providing for people who have encountered difficulties in their career and are looking for a solution. A career consultant is someone who helps clients determine their personal traits, characteristics, skills, and specialties so as to make a decision on career choices. He will help clients to develop their skills in writing a resumé and dealing with interviews, as well as improving their ability to handle difficult situations. In China, this kind of consulting service is gradually increasing due to the influence of West.

语法/语言点注释 Grammar/language points

1 假如......，还不如......; If ..., it is better ...

<u>假如</u>你还没做好重新工作的准备，那<u>还不如</u>先静下心来想一想。
If you are not ready to start a new job, you'd better calm down and think about it
　a bit.

The first part of the compound sentence led by 假如 raises an assumption and the second part of the sentence with 还不如 usually gives suggestions under that assumed condition.

Example:

假如你现在又累又困，那还不如先去睡觉，等休息好了再学习。
If you feel so tired and sleepy right now, you'd better go to bed and study (again) after you've rested.

阅读理解 Comprehension

一、选择题 Multiple-choice questions.

1   关于苏小姐被裁员，下面哪个说法是错的？

    a) 苏小姐没想到自己被裁员了
    b) 苏小姐的工作项目刚做完
    c) 公司让她24小时内离开
    d) 公司多付她一个月的工资

2   关于职业规划专家的建议，下面哪些说法是对的？

    a) 花点时间去休闲、娱乐，调整心情
    b) 理性分析被裁的原因，找到解决的办法
    c) 应该立即找新的工作，这样才能走出阴影
    d) 保持健康的生活方式和积极的精神面貌

二、填空题 Fill in the blanks, choosing from the words provided.

自信　　证书　　裁员　　充电　　阴影　　丢人　　收获

    苏小姐一开始想不通为什么自己努力工作却被_____，她不知道以后怎么办，是不是能找到工作，她还觉得被裁员很_____，怕朋友笑话自己。在职业规划专家的开导下，苏小姐在空闲时间积极地给自己_____，考出了一个_____，找到了新的工作。苏小姐重新找回了_____，走出了裁员的_____。

三、连线题 Using a line, connect the phrase in the left column with the corresponding one in the right.

假如是自己能力不够　　　　　　　　那么可以看看同行的公司有没有机会
假如是你的公司单个企业不景气　　　也许就要做转行的准备了
假如是整个行业不景气　　　　　　　应该去请教职业规划专家
　　　　　　　　　　　　　　　　　那就通过各种方法增强竞争力

四、翻译题 Translate the following sentences into English.

1   假如是自己能力不够，那就通过各种方法增强竞争力。

2   当你刚被裁员的时候，心情不好，这些消极情绪很可能影响求职中的表现，找工作就不顺利。

第八课　现代网络生活

Chapter 8　The role of the internet in modern life

课文导入 Introduction

　　网络的发明给人类社会带来了深刻的变化，世界因为网络而成为一体。互联网进入千家万户以后，给全球公众的日常生活带来了方便、乐趣和不断的惊喜。下面两篇课文将跟你分享中国网友的网络故事。

生词注释 Vocabulary

1. 网络【wǎng luò】網絡 n. network
2. 千家万户【qiān jiā wàn hù】千家萬戶 thousands of families and households（成语）
3. 分享【fēn xiǎng】v. share

阅读 A: 虚拟年夜饭 Virtual New Year's Eve dinner

读前准备 Warm-up

一、简答题 Short-answer questions.

1　你觉得在网上可以做哪些有意思的事？

2　你觉得有什么办法请客吃饭既不麻烦又不用担心吃胖？

二、选择题 Multiple-choice questions. Circle an appropriate English translation for the underlined words.

1　小王的朋友郑小姐刚打开人人网，就收到了这条留言。

　　a) language　　b) missed call　　c) message

2　与郑小姐有类似经历的网友不在少数。

　　a) common　　b) similar　　c) all kinds of

3   王欣已<u>成功</u>做出了一个叫"兔年烧卖"的点心。

    a) easily   b) successfully   c) finally

4   这一活动，吸引了很多白领网友的<u>加入</u>。

    a) editing   b) deleting   c) participating

课文 Reading

    没有<u>舟车劳顿</u>，也不用担心吃胖，时下一些都市<u>白领</u>流行在自家的<u>虚拟</u>餐厅请客。随着春节的日益临近，有不少白领正在网上<u>筹备</u>年夜饭*，准备在大年三十和朋友们"网络团圆"。在某外企工作的白领王欣日前就加入了"人人"年夜饭一<u>族</u>。

    "我正在准备兔年*<u>烧卖</u>，能送我一根<u>腊肠</u>吗？"昨日，小王的朋友郑小姐刚打开人人网，就收到了这条<u>留言</u>。郑小姐想了半天都没反应过来，经旁人提醒才知道：原来小王是在"人人餐厅"里筹备除夕年夜饭*。与郑小姐有类似经历的网友并不在少数，王欣给她的许多好友都发送了邀请，有人被她<u>雇佣</u>洗碗上菜，有人帮她找做饭的食材，就连王欣的上司也被她雇来做大厨。"虽然是在虚拟的环境里和朋友们一起做年夜饭，但同样会让人觉得很开心、很有过年的<u>气氛</u>"，小王高兴地说。目前，王欣已成功做出了一个"兔年烧卖"，她打算在大年三十之前多做几个，与更多的朋友一起享用。

    王小姐在"人人餐厅"里筹备着年夜饭，她的男友程先生则在"人人派对"里<u>装扮</u>年夜饭的场地。"红彤彤的兔年<u>墙纸</u>和圆形年夜饭桌<u>象征</u>着圆圆满满、合家团圆；福字地灯很有中国风情，看上去很喜庆，特别有年味儿。"小程<u>自豪</u>地介绍着自己的"装扮"成果。

    在兔年春节<u>前夕</u>，一些<u>社交</u>网络推出了主题年夜饭、春节装扮、新春大拜年*等活动，吸引了很多白领网友的加入。

(536字)
文：记者 李少峰 通讯员 陶铭东 有删改
原载《长江日报》2011年1月31日
网络来源：
http://cjmp.cnhan.com/cjrb/html/2011-01-31/content_4753071.htm

生词注释 Vocabulary

1. 舟车劳顿【zhōu chē láo dùn】fatigued by a long journey（成语）

2. 白领【bái lǐng】n. white collar worker

3. 虚拟【xū nǐ】adj. virtual, fictitious

4. 筹备【chóu bèi】v. prepare, arrange, plan

5. 族【zú】n. nationality, class or group of things or people with common features

6. 烧卖【shāo mài】n. Cantonese steamed dumpling (a type of dim sum)

7. 腊肠【là cháng】n. Chinese sausage

8. 留言【liú yán】vo.; n. leave comments, leave a message; message

9. 雇佣【gù yōng】雇傭 v. employ, hire

10. 气氛【qì fēn】n. surrounding feeling, atmosphere

11. 装扮【zhuāng bàn】v. dress up, attire, decorate

12. 墙纸【qiáng zhǐ】n. wallpaper

13. 象征【xiàng zhēng】v.; n. symbolize, signify, stand for; symbol

14. 自豪【zì háo】v. take pride in oneself

15. 前夕【qián xī】n. eve, on the eve of

16. 社交【shè jiāo】n. social contact, social life

文化/熟语注释 Culture/idiom notes

*兔年【tù nián】中国文化里有12生肖，分别是鼠、牛、虎、兔、龙、蛇、马、羊、猴、鸡、狗、猪。每十二年为一个轮回，2011年是兔年。

The Chinese zodiac is a system that relates each year to an animal in a 12-year cycle. The 12 zodiac animals are the rat, the ox, the tiger, the rabbit, the dragon, the snake, the horse, the sheep, the monkey, the rooster, the dog and the pig. 2011 was the Chinese Year of the Rabbit.

*年夜饭【niányè fàn】中国农历一年最后一天晚上叫"除夕"。除夕夜晚全家人在一起吃"团圆饭"，也就是"年夜饭"。中国农历一年最后一天通常叫作"大年三十"。

除夕 (Chinese New Year's Eve) is the last evening of the year according to the lunar calendar. It is the time when Chinese families gather for their annual reunion dinner, also known as "年夜饭" (New Year's Eve dinner). The last day of the year in the lunar calendar is often called "大年三十."

*新春大拜年【xīnchūn dà bàinián】中国农历正月初一叫"春节"。春节期间向别人祝贺新年叫"拜年"。拜年一般从家里开始，再走亲访友。初一、初二、初三、初四、初五这几天，都可以是拜年的日子。新春大拜年是指大的有许多人加入的拜年活动。

春节 is the first day of the first month in the lunar calendar. 拜年 means to pay a New Year call to send New Year's wishes to others during the festival, normally to close family members first and then to friends and other relatives. It starts on the first day of the New Year and lasts through to the fifth day. 大拜年 means the 拜年 activity is joined by many people.

语法/语言点注释 Grammar/language points

1 随着......临近; as ... close by ...

随着春节的日益临近，有不少白领正在网上筹备年夜饭。
As the Spring Festival approaches, many office workers are preparing a virtual New Year's Eve dinner online.

This pattern is used to indicate that a certain thing approaching will bring about a change in another thing.

Example:

随着毕业考试的临近，为了让大家有更多的时间复习，图书馆每天开放的时间也延长了。
As the graduation exam is close, the library has extended its opening hours to let everyone have longer hours in which to study.

2 连......也......; even ... also ...

连王欣的上司也被她雇来做大厨。
Even Xin Wang's boss was hired by her (Xin Wang) to be the chef.

This structure is used to express emphasis. The element placed after 连 is the element to be emphasized.

Example:

> 我的朋友最近因为失业，心情很不好，不想跟别人交流，连他女朋友的电话也不接。
> My friend has been in a bad mood lately because he lost his job. He does not want to communicate with others and doesn't even answer his girlfriend's calls.

3 A......, B则......; A..., and (or while) B...

> 王小姐在"人人餐厅"里筹备着年夜饭，她的男友程先生则在"人人派对"里装扮年夜饭的场地。
> Ms. Wang is preparing her virtual New Year's Eve dinner in the "Renren Restaurant," while her boyfriend, Mr. Cheng, is decorating the virtual "Renren Party Room" for the New Year's Eve dinner.

The word 则 placed after the subject of the second sentence indicates a parallel relation between this sentence and the previous sentence.

Example:

> 我妈妈每个星期六都要做家务，上午去超市买菜，下午则在家整理房间和洗衣服。
> My mom always does the housework on Saturdays. She goes to the market to do grocery shopping in the morning, and cleans the rooms and does the laundry in the afternoon.

阅读理解 Comprehension

一、选择题 Multiple-choice questions.

1   关于虚拟餐厅，下面哪个说法是错的？

   a) 去虚拟餐厅，路上没有交通问题，不辛苦
   b) 在虚拟餐厅吃饭，不用担心吃胖
   c) 到虚拟餐厅吃饭，得白领才行

2   为什么郑小姐收到留言没反应过来？

   a) 因为她不认识王欣
   b) 因为她不知道腊肠是什么
   c) 因为王欣没告诉她正在筹备虚拟年夜饭

3   关于王欣筹备的虚拟年夜饭，下面哪个说法是对的？

   a) 王欣的上司是年夜饭的大厨
   b) 王欣做了三十个"兔年烧卖"
   c) 洗碗、上菜的人还没有找到

4　关于小程装扮的年夜饭场地，下面哪个说法是对的？

　　a) 金黄的兔年墙纸
　　b) 红色的灯笼
　　c) 圆形的年夜饭桌子

5　根据文章内容，哪些人对社交网络感兴趣？

　　a) 大学生网友
　　b) 饭店服务员网友
　　c) 白领网友

根据提示完成课文结构图 Complete the text structure map according to the clues provided

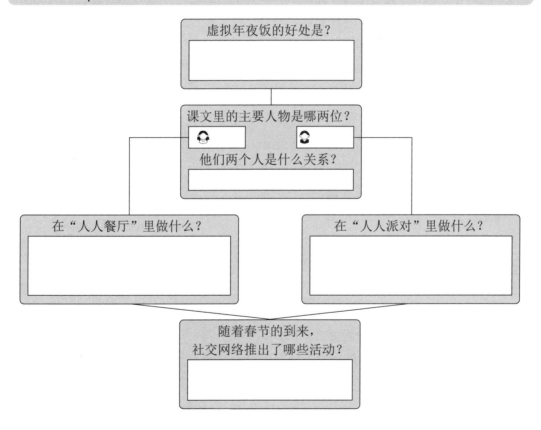

虚拟年夜饭的好处是？

课文里的主要人物是哪两位？

他们两个人是什么关系？

在"人人餐厅"里做什么？

在"人人派对"里做什么？

随着春节的到来，
社交网络推出了哪些活动？

讨论 Discussion

1　你喜欢网上虚拟餐厅吗？为什么？
2　网络给你的生活带来了什么样的变化？说说你会用网络做什么事？

阅读 B: 网络广播剧 Internet radio play

课文 Reading

　　网络广播剧是由策划人提交一份策划书，在网上发帖征招合作伙伴，包括编剧、配音、导演、美工等不同工种而制作完成的，然后通过微博*和论坛进行宣传，供网友免费下载。网络广播剧兴起于2002年，目前，正在火热创作中的网络广播剧社团就有上百个，不少社团还成了圈内"明星"，拥有不少"粉丝"。在网上已颇有名气的马晓天，从事网络广播剧制作已有5、6年，他的不少作品成了网友们争相下载的"名作"。在马晓天看来，一部成功的网络广播剧，最重要的是选择一个好的剧本。"策划人选中本子后，经过作者授权、改编、制作后，我们会放在微博上宣传，网友可随意下载。"

　　马晓天说："听网络广播剧，就像看电影，注重听众的画面感。而传统广播剧更像有声小说，有太多的旁白和独白，缺少吸引人的场景对话。"在网友看来，网络广播剧最大的特点，便是听起来画面感更强。在剧中加入了喷火、滴水、或是一些动物发出的声音等现场音效，让听众能够听音成像，在脑海里面形成边"看"边听的效果。

　　马晓天告诉记者，广播剧的制作过程都是"远程遥控"，再加上我们都是业余爱好者，所以制作花费的时间比较长。一部网络广播剧的制作周期在三个月到半年。

（480字）

文：吴璟　有删改

原载《四川日报》2011年10月19日

网络来源：http://news.163.com/11/1019/07/7GN9AM6E00014AED.html

生词注释 Vocabulary

1. 广播剧【guǎng bō jù】n. radio play
2. 策划【cè huà】v. plot, plan
3. 发帖【fā tiě】vo. post (a thread, message, advertisement)
4. 编剧【biān jù】vo.; n. write a play; playwright, screenwriter
5. 配音【pèi yīn】vo.; n. to dub (a film, etc.); dubbing
6. 通过【tōng guò】通過 prep. v. by means of; pass through
7. 微博【wēi bó】n. microblog
8. 论坛【lùn tán】n. forum, tribune, place to express oneself in public
9. 宣传【xuān chuán】v.; n. propagate, disseminate; propaganda
10. 粉丝【fěn sī】n. fans
11. 选择【xuǎn zé】v.; n. choose, select; selection, option
12. 授权【shòu quán】v. empower, authorize, license
13. 旁白【páng bái】v.; n. say as an aside; aside (in a play)
14. 独白【dú bái】v.; n. utter a monolog; monolog
15. 遥控【yáo kòng】v.; n. control remotely; remote control

文化/熟语注释 Culture/idiom notes

*微博【wēibó】"微博"可以理解为"微型博客"或者"一句话博客"。用户可以写一句话，或发一张图片，通过电脑或者手机随时随地分享给朋友，也还可以即时看到朋友们发布的信息。全球使用者最多的微博提供商为美国的Twitter和中国的新浪微博。

The microblog is a kind of miniblog or "one-sentence posting blog"; users can post a simple sentence or a picture to share it with anyone at anytime and at any place through their iPhone or computer. They can also see postings instantly from their friends as well. The two microblog providers that have the largest number of users in the world are Twitter in the USA and Sina weibo (www.weibo.com) in China.

语法/语言点注释 Grammar/language points

1 通过......; by means of/through . . .

网络广播剧是由策划人提交一份策划书，在网上发帖征招合作伙伴，包括编剧、配音、导演、美工等不同工种而制作完成的，然后通过微博和论坛进行宣传，供网友免费下载。

The online radio play starts with a proposal by the planner. The planner posts the proposal online to recruit partners to work on the playwriting, dubbing, directing, editing, and other kinds of work. The finalized play is published through microblogs and forums for the audience to download for free.

The word 通过 here is a proposition to indicate reaching a goal or conclusion by means of certain methods or ways.

Example:

我听说中医师只要通过"切脉"就能知道病人得的是什么病。
I heard that a doctor of traditional Chinese medicine could tell the patient's disease by (means of) just checking his pulse.

2 再加上......; in addition . . .

马晓天告诉记者，广播剧的制作过程都是"远程遥控"，再加上我们都是业余爱好者，所以制作花费的时间比较长。
Xiaotian Ma told the reporter that the production of radio plays is all done remotely. In addition, because they are all amateur fans of the play, it takes longer to produce.

This pattern is used to state an additional reason, condition or further information.

Example:

最近我的室友太忙了，每天要去一家公司实习，睡得很少，再加上有时候顾不上吃饭，结果他就病倒了。
My roommate has been very busy lately what with going to the company as an intern every day, having had very little sleep, and sometimes not even having enough time for meals. As a result, he gets sick.

阅读理解 Comprehension

一、对错题 True or false?

1　(　)网络广播剧完成以后，会在电视或报纸上做广告。
2　(　)下载网络广播剧是不用付费的。
3　(　)一个网络广播剧社团一般来说有上百个人。
4　(　)网络广播剧的剧本是策划人选定的。
5　(　)网络广播剧比传统广播剧更像有声小说。
6　(　)网络广播剧加入了各种各样的真实声音。

二、填空题 Fill in the blanks, choosing from the words provided.

　　征召　　周期　　现场　　业余　　从事

1　马晓天_____网络广播剧制作已经好几年了。
2　网络广播剧听起来画面感很强，因为剧中加入了不少_____音效。
3　网络广播剧社团的成员并不是专业制作者，而是_____爱好者。
4　一部网络广播剧的制作_____在三个月到半年。

三、自由回答 Open-ended questions.

1　你觉得这篇文章的标题如果改为"网络社团"或"马晓天与网友"合适吗？为什么？

2　网络给人们带来了很多好处，但是它同时是否也带来了负面作用？请谈谈你的看法。

第九课 传统节日新过法

Chapter 9 New ways of celebrating traditional festivals

课文导入 Introduction

　　中国有许多传统节日*。随着时代的<u>变迁</u>，过节日的风俗习惯也在悄悄地改变，人们将传统习俗与现代生活结合，<u>涌现</u>出丰富多样的传统节日的新过法。

生词注释 Vocabulary

﹨1. 变迁【biàn qiān】變遷 v.; n. change of situation; development

﹨2. 涌现【yǒng xiàn】涌現 v. emerge in a large number, spring up

阅读 A: 不一样的过年 New ways of celebrating New Year

读前准备 Warm-up

一、简答题 Short-answer questions.

1　中国的春节是在哪一天？中国人过春节有哪些传统习俗？

2　中国的清明节是在哪一天？中国人过清明节有哪些传统习俗？

3　除了春节、清明节，你还知道哪些中国的传统节日？

课文 Reading

　　"什么最重要，身体健康最重要！"这是今年春节餐桌上的一个新话题。餐桌上喝白酒的人数在减少，喝酒的数量也在减少。纯牛奶、果汁等受到大家的欢迎。农历大年初三晚上，36岁的市民宋先生在酒店宴请远方归来的同学。"酒喝多了伤身，白酒带一瓶就够了，多带几瓶果汁。"宋先生出发去酒店时，他的母亲叮嘱他。宋先生说，在酒桌上，几名同学纷纷拒绝喝白酒，这个说有脂肪肝，那个说胃不好。还有一位同学说自己是开车来的，不能喝酒。

　　以前是长辈给晚辈发红包，如今晚辈也开始给长辈发红包了。市民小涛的爷爷今年八十岁了，住在农村。今年春节，小涛和父母一起回农村老家过年。农历大年初一早上，小涛拿出两个红包，给了爷爷奶奶。小涛的爷爷奶奶拿着孙子给的红包，高兴极了。

　　小涛告诉记者："爷爷年龄大了，习惯了农村的生活，不愿到城市生活。我们不能在身边照顾他，只能让他们物质上过得好一点。"记者在采访中发现，给长辈发红包的现象很普遍。很多不和子女一起住的老人，在辞旧迎新之际，都收到了子女给的红包。

　　小荣在深圳一家企业工作，因为工作忙，没有时间回家和父母过团圆年。农历大年三十晚上，小荣的父母做好饭菜后，打开了QQ视频*，他们边吃饭，边看春晚，边和在深圳的小荣聊天。小荣的父亲说QQ视频不收费，图像很清晰，一家人就像团圆了一样。

　　多喝饮料少喝酒、晚辈给长辈发红包、QQ视频里拜年，这些新习俗承载了传统春节文化的内涵，同样寄托了人们对新年的美好祝福。不少市民说，换种过法也喜气！

(608字)

文：记者　朱晔　有删改

原载《天中晚报》2011年2月9日

网络来源：

http://www.zmdnews.cn/Info.aspx?ModelId=1&Id=323270

生词注释 Vocabulary

1. 纯【chún】純 adj.; adv. pure; purely

2. 宴请【yàn qǐng】宴請 v. invite (someone to a banquet)

3. 叮嘱【dīng zhǔ】叮囑 v.; n. exhort; exhortation

4. 拒绝【jù jué】拒絕 v.; n. refuse; rejection

5. 辞旧迎新【cí jiù yíng xīn】辭舊迎新 farewell to the old year and welcome to the new（成语）

6. 视频【shì pín】視頻 n. video

7. 清晰【qīng xī】adj. clear, explicit

8. 承载【chéng zài】承載 v. bear the weight of, carry a load

9. 内涵【nèi hán】內涵 n. connotation, implied meaning

10. 寄托【jì tuō】寄託 v. place (one's hopes, feeling, etc.) on

文化/熟语注释 Culture/idiom notes

*中国传统节日【Zhōngguó chuántǒng jiérì】中国有很多传统节日，一到过节，举国同庆。这些节日大多跟农耕节气相关。节日风俗代代相传，成为中国文化的一部分。目前，国家法定休假的传统节日有春节、清明、端午、中秋。

There are many traditional festivals in China. Whenever there is a traditional festival, the whole nation celebrates. Most of the festivals are related to the traditional Chinese agricultural seasons. The traditions of each festival have been passed from generation to generation and have been a part of Chinese culture for ever, it seems. The nationally recognized traditional holidays in mainland China include the Spring Festival, Tomb-Sweeping Day, the Dragon Boat Festival, and Mid-Autumn Festival.

*QQ视频【shìpín】QQ腾讯公司成立于1998年，是中国最大的互联网综合服务提供商之一，构建了QQ、腾讯网、QQ游戏以及拍拍网这四大网络平台，形成中国规模最大的网络社区。QQ软件为中国目前使用人数最多的即时通讯软件。

The QQ Tencent Inc. was established in 1998. It is one of the major comprehensive online service providers in China. It provides the four major online platforms: Tencent QQ, Tencent website, QQ game, and Paipai Internet. QQ Tencent has formed the largest online community in China.

语法/语言点注释 Grammar/language points

1 这个......，那个......; this ... that ...

> 宋先生说，在酒桌上，几名同学纷纷拒绝喝白酒，<u>这个</u>说有脂肪肝，<u>那个</u>说胃不好。
> Mr. Song said that many of his classmates refused to drink white wine at the dinner table. One said that he had liver disease, and another said that he had stomach problems.

"这" and "那" are both pronouns. They are used here as an indefinite reference indicating "this (person) and that (person)."

Example:

> 大学快毕业的时候，每天都听到同学们的好消息，这个找到了高薪工作，那个考上了医学院研究生。
> There was lots of good news from our classmates before graduation. I heard that this person had found a job with a high salary, and that person had been admitted into the graduate program of a medical school.

2 在......之际; at the time of ...

> 很多不和子女一起住的老人，<u>在辞旧迎新之际</u>，都收到了子女给的红包。
> Many older people who do not live with their children receive red envelopes from them around the time of the New Year Festival.

This structure is used to indicate a certain time for an event or a situation.

Example:

> 在告别校园之际，这支摇滚乐队进行了最后一场难忘的演出。
> At the time of graduating and saying goodbye to the campus, the rock band gave a last memorable performance.

阅读理解 Comprehension

一、对错题 True or false?

1　（　）农历大年初三晚上，宋先生在家宴请同学。
2　（　）宋先生的同学都不喜欢喝果汁，而喜欢喝酒。
3　（　）小涛给爷爷奶奶发红包，因为这是春节的传统。
4　（　）只有住在农村的长辈，才能收到子女给的红包。
5　（　）农历大年三十晚上，小荣工作很忙。
6　（　）QQ视频让小荣一家人像团圆了一样。

二、简答题 Short-answer questions.

1　课文介绍了哪三种过年的新习俗？

2　跟以前比，宋先生、小涛、小荣今年春节过得有什么不同？

根据提示完成课文结构图 Complete the text structure map according to the clues provided

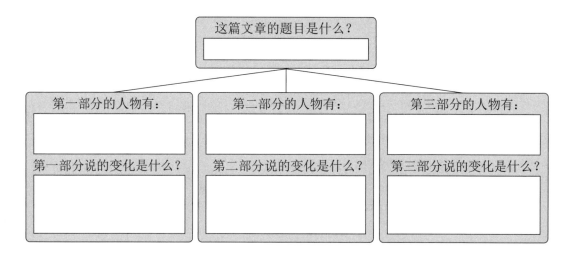

讨论 Discussion

1　在你的国家，哪一个节日最重要？你们怎么庆祝这个节日？
2　现代社会改变着人们的生活，在你的国家里，哪些传统习俗也在渐渐改变？

阅读 B: 过清明节 On Tomb-Sweeping Day

课文 Reading

　　春节过后不久，人们将迎来中华民族传统节日——清明节*。记者采访了北京几位著名的民俗专家，听取他们对于清明节传统的评说，以及关于清明节活动的新建议。以下是记者根据采访写出的报道。

　　清明其实既是悲伤的日子，又是欢乐的日子，还是社交的日子。清明是一个综合节日。祭奠先人是清明节的主题之一，不过，清明节扫墓并不应该在清明当天进行。扫墓的时间，最好是在节前10天或节后10天进行。清明当天，则是僧人扫墓的时间，僧人在这一天表达自己不能为祖先传宗接代的歉意。

　　很多人在清明节扫墓时习惯烧纸，专家们都认为这种做法既不安全也不文明，而且也并非传统的祭奠形式。在中国历史上，大家采用的最原始的祭扫办法是把纸钱向空中扬去，或者在先人墓前用砖头压住一张纸钱，表示这家后继有人。不过，现在较好的办法是买一束鲜花，祭拜过后将花瓣撒在墓前。

　　清明节期间，除了各家各户开展祭奠活动外，专家们建议还可以开展公众纪念活动。档案馆可以在节日当天向公众开放，方便人们查阅家族档案或历史档案。图书馆、档案馆也可以举办展览，让市民了解我们的先辈都有哪些光荣业绩。

生词注释 Vocabulary

1. 民族【mín zú】n. ethnic group, nation

2. 采访 【cǎi fǎng】採訪 v.; n. have an interview with; interview

3. 民俗【mín sú】n. folk custom

4. 建议【jiàn yì】建議 v.; n. propose, suggest; suggestion

5. 悲伤【bēi shāng】悲傷 n.; adj. sorrow; sad, sorrowful

6. 祭奠【jì diàn】v.; n. hold a memorial ceremony for; memorial ceremony

7. 扫墓【sǎo mù】掃墓 vo. sweep a grave, pay respect to the dead

8. 僧人【sēng rén】n. shaman, monk

9. 花瓣【huā bàn】n. pedal

10. 档案馆 【dàng àn guǎn】檔案館 n. archives

11. 查阅【chá yuè】查閱 v. read, look up

12. 展览【zhǎn lǎn】展覽 v.; n. display, show; exhibition

13. 光荣【guāng róng】光榮 n.; adj. honor, glory; honorable, glorious

亲近大自然也是清明节的主题。过去清明节有个习俗就是折柳枝，编成花环戴在头上。但这种做法破坏环境，如今大家可以结伴郊游，还可以进行植树活动。专家们还提到，古时的人们过清明节还开展各种户外体育、娱乐活动，例如踢<u>蹴球</u>、抖空竹、放<u>风筝</u>、荡<u>秋千</u>、<u>拔河</u>、踢毽子、跳房子等。文人则聚在一起作诗、画画、写书法。现代人的生活太忙了，没有了这样的<u>雅兴</u>。专家们建议结合传统，在清明节举办放风筝、诗歌朗诵等活动。

14. 蹴球【cù qiú】蹴球 n. ancient type of Chinese football

15. 风筝【fēng zheng】風筝 n. kite

16. 秋千【qiū qiān】鞦韆 n. swing

17. 拔河【bá hé】v.; n. play tug-of-war; game of tug-of-war (a Chinese sports game)

18. 雅兴【yǎ xìng】雅興 n. aesthetic mood, refined interest

（647字）

文：记者　李洋　有删改

原载《西安晚报》2008年3月5日

网络来源：http://www.cefla.org/news_view.jsp?nid=217

文化/熟语注释 Culture/idiom notes

*清明节【qīngmíng jié】清明节是中国传统的祭祀节日，中国人在清明节扫墓。祭扫活动既能体现对死者的怀念，又能表达对祖先的感恩。清明节在冬至后的第108天，即每年的阳历四月五日。

Tomb-Sweeping Day is a traditional memorial day in China. Chinese people usually visit the tombs of the deceased to mourn and express gratitude to their ancestors. Tomb-Sweeping Day is on April 5 of the lunar calendar, which is the 108th day after the winter solstice.

语法/语言点注释 Grammar/language points

1 将(2) ......; have/get ...

不过，现在较好的办法是买一束鲜花，祭拜过后<u>将</u>花瓣撒在墓前。

But a better way is to buy a bunch of flowers and have the petals sprinkled over the tomb after the memorial ceremony.

将 in this sentence is a preposition. Its meaning is similar to 把.

Example:

《泰坦尼克号》电影里，杰克将生存的机会给了爱人罗斯。

In the movie *Titanic*, Jack gave his lover, Rose the opportunity to live.

2 既......又......还......; both ... and ..., besides ...

清明其实既是悲伤的日子，又是欢乐的日子，还是社交的日子。
Tomb-Sweeping Day is both a sad and a joyful day, and also a day of social
   interaction.

既......又......还...... in this compound sentence are used to list parallel things
or to describe two or more properties or situations of one thing.

Example:

应聘这个职位，既要有学历，又要有工作经验，还要精通英语和计算机。
To apply for this position, you need to have not only a degree, but also work
   experience; moreover, you should also be proficient in English and the use of
   a computer.

阅读理解 Comprehension

一、选择题 Multiple-choice questions.

1   关于清明节扫墓，下面哪个说法不是民俗专家说的？

   a) 普通人扫墓最好节前10天或节后10天进行
   b) 僧人扫墓应该在清明节当天
   c) 扫墓时烧纸不是传统的做法
   d) 扫墓的传统做法是买一束花，把花瓣撒在墓前

2   关于清明节开展别的活动，下面哪个活动不是民俗专家建议的？

   a) 开放档案馆，并且在图书馆和档案馆举办展览
   b) 结伴郊游，亲近大自然
   c) 折柳枝，编成花环戴在头上
   d) 进行植树活动

二、填空题 Fill in the blanks with the phrases provided.

1   将花瓣撒在墓前   买一束鲜花   压住一张纸钱   把纸钱向空中扬去

      很多人在清明节扫墓时习惯烧纸，而在中国历史上，大家采用的最原始的祭扫
办法是_____，或者在先人墓前用砖头_____。不过，现在较好的
办法是_____，祭拜过后_____。

2   植树   结伴郊游   折柳枝，编成花环戴在头上   放风筝、诗歌朗诵

      过去清明节有个习俗就是_____。但这种做法破坏环境，如今
大家可以_____，还可以进行_____活动。古时的人们过清明节还开展各种户外
活动，文人则聚在一起作诗、画画、写书法。现代人的生活太忙了，清明节可以举办
_____等活动。

第十课 爱情和婚姻

Chapter 10 Love and marriage

课文导入 Introduction

　　人的一生会有许许多多的感情。爱情、亲情、友谊，像阳光一样温暖着我们。在中国越来越自由的社会里，年轻人还努力维持婚姻吗？他们怎么看待传统的与现代的婚恋方式？他们又怎么理解婚姻的幸福之源？你也许能在下面的文章中找到答案。

生词注释 Vocabulary

1. 感情【gǎn qíng】n. feeling, emotion, affection
2. 维持【wéi chí】维持 v. maintain, keep, support
3. 幸福之源【xìng fú zhī yuán】phr. source of happiness

阅读 A: 爱：怎样走得更稳 Love: How to keep it

读前准备 Warm-up

一、简答题 Short-answer questions.

1　你觉得现代男女什么年龄结婚比较合适？

2　要是你已经有了男/女朋友，你还会再爱上别人吗？

3　要是你已经有了男/女朋友，却又爱上了别人，你会怎么办？

课文 Reading

　　我和小媛决定结婚时，她家强烈地反对，说我学历不高，工作也不大稳定。多亏了小媛坚定的态度，她父母才勉强答应了我们的婚事。我们结婚时才23岁。

　　早婚*，会让一个男人迅速成熟起来，我暗下决心要赚钱，给小媛一个真正的家，让她的父母改变对我的看法。我那时最多兼过三份工作，有时忙得站着都能睡着。小媛也很辛苦，她在一家百货商场的专柜卖衣服，业绩不大好。我的工作有了起色后，就不让她工作了。凭着我的努力，我们过得越来越好。

　　但是就在去年，我在工作中遇到了一个女孩，年轻、漂亮，我得承认，我喜欢她身上那种积极上进的态度，而小媛只会拿着我的信用卡拼命消费，不关心我的事业，完全就是一个家庭主妇。我情不自禁地喜欢上了那女孩。或许，她才是未来更适合和我生活的人。这个念头产生时，我心里有一种罪恶感，我说过这辈子都不会放弃小媛，不管她变成什么样，然而一旦有了比较，我竟动摇了。

　　我当然可以像别的男人一样，选择离婚，给对方一笔赡养费。但想到小媛已经很久没出去工作了，又缺乏独立生活的经验，离婚对她的打击可想而知。我这些年一直忙于事业，很少去想夫妻间需要不断培养默契，才不会渐行渐远。后来，我有意识地带她出席一些工作场合，又把一些不太难的事情交给她做。她很快在公司里得心应手。只要给她机会，她也一样可以闪亮动人。我用行动证明了，我真的很爱她。

(553字)
作者：榛果　有删节
原载《扬子晚报》2012年1月19日
网络来源：
http://edu.gmw.cn/2012-01/19/content_3415846.htm

生词注释 Vocabulary

1. 强烈【qiáng liè】强烈 adj. strong, powerful, intense

2. 勉强【miǎn qiǎng】勉强 v.; adj.; adv. force sb to do sth; reluctant; reluctantly

3. 下决心【xià jué xīn】下决心 vo. make up one's mind

4. 兼【jiān】v.; adv. do concurrently

5. 起色【qǐ sè】n. improvement, sign of recovery

6. 凭【píng】憑 v. rely on, depend on

7. 情不自禁【qíng bù zì jīn】cannot help doing（成语）

8. 念头【niàn tou】念頭 n. thought, idea, intention

9. 罪恶感【zuì è gǎn】罪惡感 n. guilty feeling

10. 这辈子【zhè bèi zi】這輩子 n. this life

11. 动摇【dòng yáo】動搖 v. vacillate, wave, shake

12. 赡养费【shàn yǎng fèi】贍養費 n. alimony

13. 可想而知【kě xiǎng ér zhī】one can well imagine（成语）

14. 默契【mò qì】n. tacit understanding

15. 渐行渐远【jiàn xíng jiàn yuǎn】漸行漸遠 go far gradually, get apart gradually（成语）

16. 得心应手【dé xīn yìng shǒu】得心應手 do with high proficiency, handy（成语）

17. 闪亮【shǎn liàng】閃亮 adj. twinkle, brilliant, shiny

18. 动人【dòng rén】動人 adj. moving, charming

文化/熟语注释 Culture/idiom notes

*早婚【zǎohūn】根据《婚姻法》第六条，结婚年龄男不得早于二十二周岁，女不得早于二十周岁。中国政府提倡晚婚晚育。晚婚是男性满25周岁，女性满23周岁。因为作者是23岁结婚的，所以他认为自己是早婚。

According to Article 6 of the Marriage Law in China, males under the age of 22 and females under 20 are not allowed to get married. The government encourages "late marriage" and having children afterwards. Late marriage is defined as being between males aged 25 or above, and females aged 23 or above. Because the author (male) got married at the age of 23, he considered himself as having got married early.

语法/语言点注释 Grammar/language points

1 都......不管......; all ... regardless of ...

> 这个念头产生时，我心里有一种罪恶感，我说过这辈子<u>都</u>不会放弃小媛，<u>不管</u>她变成什么样，然而一旦有了比较，我竟动摇了。
>
> When this idea came into my mind, I felt guilty, as I promised that I would never give up on Xiaoyuan regardless of how she was, but once I had made a comparison, I unexpectedly changed my mind (not to keep my word).

Usually, the sentence introduced by 不管 precedes the sentence with 都. For the sample sentence above, the position of the two simple sentences is reversed for rhetorical purposes. This pattern is used to indicate that the action introduced in the sentence (containing 都) takes place unconditionally.

Example:

> 不管在世界哪个国家，葡萄酒都受到人们的喜爱。
>
> Regardless of differences among countries, wine is always well-loved by people.

阅读理解 Comprehension

一、选择题 Multiple-choice questions.

1 下面哪些词和短语可以用来介绍课文中的丈夫？

a) 学历不高　　b) 工作努力　　c) 业绩不好　　d) 忙于事业

2 下面哪些词和短语可以用来介绍课文中的妻子小媛？

a) 工作态度坚定　　b) 喜欢消费　　c) 能独立生活　　d) 闪亮动人

3 下面哪些词和短语可以用来介绍课文中的丈夫在工作中遇到的那位女孩？

a) 年轻漂亮　　b) 积极上进　　c) 兼三份工作　　d) 关心"我"的生活

二、简答题 Short-answer questions.

1　课文中的"我"和小媛结婚的时候，小媛家为什么强烈反对？

2　他们结婚后，为什么丈夫不让小媛出去工作了？

3　这个丈夫用怎样的行动证明了他真的很爱她？

根据提示完成课文结构图 Complete the text structure map according to the clues provided

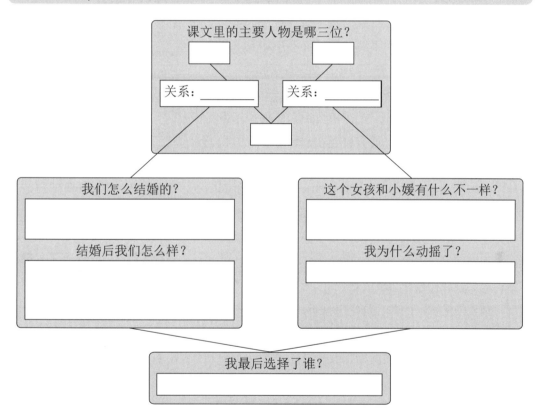

课文里的主要人物是哪三位？

关系：_____　　关系：_____

我们怎么结婚的？

结婚后我们怎么样？

这个女孩和小媛有什么不一样？

我为什么动摇了？

我最后选择了谁？

讨论题 Discussion

1　要是课文中的"我"跟小媛离婚，你是支持还是反对？为什么？

2　在你看来，女人是不是应该有自己的工作，有经济独立的能力？你对女人做全职家庭主妇有什么看法？

阅读 B: 关于爱情、婚姻的对话 A conversation about love and marriage

课文 Reading

小林：你知道什么是"闪婚"吗？

小陈：当然知道了。就是闪电式结婚，从认识到结婚时间相当短。我的朋友小芸跟同一幢写字楼里的一个美国人认识以后，<u>情投意合</u>，一个月内就结婚了。婚后，他们一直<u>恩爱如初</u>，生活幸福。

小林：闪婚很<u>浪漫</u>，但有时候闪婚也会导致"闪离。"由于婚前双方了解不够，婚后又不能相互<u>宽容</u>，结果进入婚姻生活时间不长就<u>草草</u>离婚。

小陈：可不是嘛！现在盛行网恋，<u>足不出户</u>就可以通过网络谈恋爱，时间上是比较自由，然而由于双方没有面对面接触，很有可能在结婚之前双方缺乏了解，刚结了婚就又"闪离"了。

小林：今天的报纸上说，我们E时代的年轻人要找的是一个像EXCEL一样的朋友——想隐藏就隐藏，想<u>筛选</u>就筛选，想<u>删除</u>就删除，一不高兴，嘿，那就不保存了。

小陈：是的，我们被社会看成是一群思想和行为都不同于前人的怪物，什么"闪婚"、"闪离"、"网恋"、"裸婚*"……这些词都是用来<u>形容</u>我们的。

小林：然而事实上，据我所知，我们并没有完全<u>摒弃</u>传统。比方说相亲*，我的一些朋友甚至不反对父母跟着去相亲，她们觉得父母都是过来人，挺有眼光的。

小陈：当然，我们常说婚姻是人生的头等大事，在这样一个重要的问题上，多听取父母的意见是非常有必要的。再说，新时代的相亲是一种很时尚的社交活动，即使不能成为男女朋友也还可以做普通朋友嘛。

生词注释 Vocabulary

1. 情投意合【qíng tóu yì hé】find one another congenial, hit it off perfectly（成语）

2. 恩爱如初 【ēn ài rú chū】恩爱如初 love and respect like before（成语）

3. 浪漫【làng màn】adj. romantic

4. 宽容【kuān róng】寬容 v.; adj. show forebearing; tolerant

5. 草草【cǎo cǎo】adv. careless, hasty

6. 足不出户【zú bù chū hù】keep to the house, stay home （成语）

7. 隐藏【yǐn cáng】隱藏 v. hide, conceal, keep out of sight

8. 筛选【shāi xuǎn】篩選 v. filter

9. 删除【shān chú】刪除 v. delete

10. 形容【xíng róng】v. describe

11. 摒弃【bìng qì】摒棄 v. discard, abandon

小林：现代人的确拥有了更多的自由去追寻爱情，这是时代进步的表现。我爷爷、奶奶所处的是一个<u>婚姻包办</u>的年代，他们的婚事是由双方父母决定的。婚后，他们一心一意<u>善待</u>对方，恩恩爱爱过了一辈子。

小陈：<u>白头偕老</u>的爱情是人生最理想和完美的境界！只要两人恩爱，就算物质条件艰苦，生活也一定是幸福的。我爸爸妈妈<u>相遇</u>的那个年代，自由恋爱已经开始走向主流。那时候我妈妈是文化馆的独唱演员，有一次演出的时候，爸爸就坐在台下。那时候妈妈常常收到别人送的花，而我爸爸献给她的是自己写的诗。我妈妈被这些诗打动了，就嫁给了他。他们真可以说是"<u>一见钟情</u>、永结同心"。

小林：你父母的爱情同样令人<u>羡慕</u>！看来，时代再怎么变，幸福婚姻的基本<u>秘诀</u>却始终没变。

（848字）

作者：虞农　冰清

12. 婚姻包办【hūn yīn bāo bàn】婚姻包辦 phr. marriage is arranged

13. 善待【shàn dài】v. be kind to

14. 白头偕老【bái tóu xié lǎo】白頭偕老 remain married until old age（成语）

15. 相遇【xiāng yù】v. meet

16. 一见钟情【yī jiàn zhōng qíng】一見鐘情 fall in love at first sight（成语）

17. 羡慕【xiàn mù】v.; n. admire; admiration

18. 秘诀【mì jué】秘訣 n. secret (of success)

文化/熟语注释 Culture/idiom notes

*裸婚【luǒhūn】"裸婚"是2008年出现的网络新词，是指不买房、不买车、不办婚礼甚至没有婚戒而直接领证结婚的一种简朴的结婚方式。赞成"裸婚"的年轻人认为爱情应该抛开金钱的世俗，真心相爱才是最重要的。

裸婚 (naked wedding) is a new internet word that appeared in 2008. It refers to the kind of marriage that occurs when the bride and groom just want a marriage certificate for the sake of the marriage itself, sometimes not even having a wedding ring. They hold no wedding ceremony either. The young people who support this kind of marriage hold that true love is beyond materialism.

*相亲【xiāngqīn】相亲是中国传统婚配礼仪之一。媒人说媒以后，在议婚阶段，由媒人联系安排，双方父母或长亲见面议亲。旧时相亲，男女双方当事人并不相见，而由父母或长亲包办。相亲以后，则由媒人传话，互通意愿。现代意义的相亲，则泛指男女双方经人介绍而见面，可由家长或介绍人陪同。

An arranged blind date is a traditional Chinese marriage ritual. In the past, after the matchmaker made the match, she would then arrange for the heads of the two families to meet to discuss the marriage and wedding ceremony. The husband- and wife-to-be, however, would not meet each other, but simply obey their parents' instructions. After the arrangement had been settled, the two families would pass what they wanted to say through the matchmaker. Nowadays a blind date refers to a meeting during the course of which a single man and a single woman will be introduced to one another by an introducer. They may be accompanied by their parents or just the introducer when going to such a meeting.

语法/语言点注释 Grammar/language points

1　由于......，又......，结果......; because (of) ..., and ..., as a result ...

> 由于婚前双方了解不够，婚后又不能相互宽容，结果进入婚姻生活时间不长就草草离婚。
>
> Because the couple did not get to know each other well before getting married, and furthermore, (they) could not tolerate each other afterwards, the marriage quickly broke up and (they) got divorced.

This is a compound sentence. The word 由于 is used to introduce a clause. The word 又 is used to list an additional clause, while 结果 is used to introduce a result.

Example:

> 由于他酒后驾驶，又不系安全带，结果警察毫不客气地把他带走了。
>
> Because he drove under the influence of alcohol (DUI) and without his seatbelt on (as a result), the police took him into custody.

2　可不是嘛; this is exactly right

> 小陈：可不是嘛！
> Chen: Exactly!

This phrase is normally used to express agreement with what the other person said. Here, 可不是 means 就是; 可 is used to place an emphasis so the tone is stronger than 就是. 嘛 is a modal particle, used to convey a strong tone.

Example:

> 学生甲：昨天那场关于中国历史的讲座来了好多人啊！
> 学生乙：可不是嘛！座无虚席，连走道上都站满了人。
> Student A: There were so many people at the Chinese history lecture yesterday.
> Student B: (You are) exactly right! Every seat was taken and the hallway was packed, too.

3　即使......也......; even if ... still ...

> 再说，新时代的相亲是一种很时尚的社交活动，即使不能成为男女朋友也还可以做普通朋友嘛。
>
> In addition, nowadays an arranged blind date is regarded as a fashionable type of social activity. Even if the two people did not become boyfriend and girlfriend, they could certainly become friends.

即使 in the first simple sentence is used to introduce an extreme supposition; the second simple sentence, introduced by 也, states the result or consequence under the supposition.

Example:

我的室友可真能睡啊，即使在房间里开音乐会，他也能睡得很香。

My roommate is such a heavy sleeper: even if a concert were performed in the room, he would still be sound asleep.

4 只要......，就算......，......也......; as long as ... , even ... , still ...

只要两人恩爱，就算物质条件艰苦，生活也一定是幸福的。

As long as the two people are in love, even if they are not well-off, their life would still be happy.

In this compound sentence, the structure 就算......也 is similar to 即使......也, only more colloquial. 只要 is used to introduce a condition.

Example:

只要你住在公共交通发达的大城市，就算你没有车，去哪儿也都是方便的。

As long as you live in a big city with a well-developed public transport system, you can go anywhere conveniently even if you do not have a car.

阅读理解 Comprehension

一、名词解释 Explain the meaning of the following words in Chinese.

网恋　　闪婚　　闪离　　裸婚　　婚姻包办

二、对错题 True or false?

1　（　）有的恋人认识不久就"闪婚"了，婚后一样非常幸福。
2　（　）"网恋"的双方往往缺乏面对面的接触与了解。
3　（　）相亲这种方式是从E时代开始流行的。
4　（　）小陈的爸爸妈妈是自由恋爱以后结婚的。

三、填空题 Fill in the blanks, choosing from the words provided.

老　　令　　初　　知　　心　　头　　永

1　婚后，他们一直恩爱如＿＿＿，生活幸福。
2　然而事实上，据我所＿＿＿，我们并没有完全摒弃传统。
3　我们常说婚姻是人生的＿＿＿等大事。
4　白头偕＿＿＿的爱情是人生最理想和完美的境界。
5　你父母的爱情同样＿＿＿人羡慕！

四、简答题 Short-answer questions.

1   你跟你的男/女朋友是怎么认识的？

2   你的家庭中三代人婚恋方式有什么不同？

3   课文最后一句说："时代再怎么变，幸福婚姻的基本秘诀却始终没变。"你同意吗？

第十一课　中华民族的图腾 — 龙

Chapter 11　The Chinese national totem – the dragon

课文导入 Introduction	生词注释 Vocabulary
在中国文化中，"龙"有着重要的地位和影响。你对中国龙的<u>形象</u>与文化了解多少呢？下面两篇课文会告诉你，无论是日常的用词用语，还是节日的庆祝活动，中国人的生活时时处处都体现出中华民族丰富的龙文化。	形象【xíng xiàng】n. image

阅读 A: 龙的传人 Descendants of the dragon

读前准备 Warm-up

一、简答题 Short-answer questions.

你听说过龙吗？它应该是什么样的？

二、选择题 Multiple-choice questions.

请选择"a) 龙 b) 狮子 c) 鹰 d) 公鸡"这四种动物中的一种，写到国家名字的后面：

美国　（　　）
英国　（　　）
中国　（　　）
法国　（　　）

课文 Reading

　　每个民族都有图腾*。古代人们崇拜某种动物的能力，渐渐地这种动物就用来代表这个民族的精神，成为这个民族的图腾。比方说英国是狮子，美国是鹰，法国是公鸡。中国人崇拜龙，所以龙就成了中国人的图腾。中国人称自己是"龙的传人"，即龙的子子孙孙。

　　狮子、鹰、公鸡都是人类见过的动物，而"龙"却是想象中的一种动物。龙是什么样的呢？这个问题可真是不好回答。因为从古至今，谁也没有见过真正的龙，人们有多丰富的想象，龙就有多丰富的形象。据说龙的身体能粗能细，能长能短。龙能上天，也能入水。根据传说，龙是九种动物的综合体，所以它看起九不像。

　　可以说在中国人的生活中，龙是无处不在的。以语言为例，我们一开口就会用到很多带"龙"字的成语。比方说，父母希望自己的子女在学业和事业上获得成功，那么用四个字就能说明这种情况，即"望子成龙"。这里的"龙"代表的是成功人士。另外一个常常用到的成语"画龙点睛"，说的是中国古代一位画家画龙而不画眼睛，说画了眼睛龙就会飞走，众人都不信，让他给龙画上眼睛。结果，等眼睛画好，龙真的就飞走了。这个成语后来表示画画或者讲话、写文章的时候，画上关键的一两笔或者说出关键的一两句话，就使内容生动起来。像这样关于"龙"的成语*，中文里有两三百个。

　　传说中的龙，也有人说它长得像一座起伏的大山，所以中国人常常把山比作"龙"，把山梁比作龙身上的血管，即"脉"。"来龙去脉"这个成语最早的时候指山峦的地理走向，后来人们用这个词表示一件事情的前后关系、来历和发展。

　　据说，把"龙"译作 Dragon 的是一位传教士，他热爱中国文化，但在明代，这位意大利人无法在英文单词中找到能表达中国"龙"的词，他只好用 Dragon 这个词。希望你读了这篇课文，对中国龙的"来龙去脉"有了一些了解。

(719字)

编写：虞农

生词注释 Vocabulary

1. 图腾【tú téng】圖騰 n. totem
2. 崇拜【chóng bài】v.; n. worship
3. 某【mǒu】pr. certain (referring to a certain person or thing)
4. 鹰【yīng】鷹 n. eagle
5. 传说【chuán shuō】傳說 v.; n. pass from mouth to mouth; legend
6. 综合【zōng hé】綜合 v.; n. synthesize; synthesis
7. 获得【huò dé】獲得 v. obtain, acquire
8. 关键【guān jiàn】關鍵 n. key point, crucial importance
9. 起伏【qǐ fú】v.; adj. rise and fall; rising and falling
10. 山梁【shān liáng】n. ridge (of a mountain or hill)
11. 血管【xuè guǎn】n. blood vessel
12. 脉【mài】脈 n. pulse
13. 山峦【shān luán】山巒 n. chain of mountains
14. 地理【dì lǐ】n. geography
15. 传教士【chuán jiào shì】傳教士 n. missionary

文化/熟语注释 Culture/idiom notes

*图腾【túténg】图腾为印第安语 totem 的音译，被视为图腾的一般是与某个氏族有特殊关系的某种动物或植物。图腾被看成是整个部族的标记，也是一种原始的宗教标志，大约出现在旧石器时代晚期。

图腾 is a literal translation of the Native American word "totem." It is a certain animal or plant that is specially related to a tribe and is regarded as the sign of the tribe. It is also a kind of primitive religious symbol. It appeared, as far as we can tell, in the late Paleolithic Age.

*成语【chéngyǔ】成语是汉语特有的语言形式，每个成语都是一个固定短语，大多数由四个汉字组成，许多成语都有其历史故事，在文言文中被广泛使用，在现今的白话文书写或日常会话中，仍有不少古代成语被保留下来。在现代汉语中，有许多成语是人们长期以来的习惯用语，用简洁的词语表达一种现象或观点，不一定有历史故事。如果想了解更多的成语，可以查看各种《成语词典》。

成语 (Chinese idiom) is a type of traditional Chinese idiomatic expression, most of which consist of four characters and which originated from Chinese historical accounts. Those traditional 成语 were widely used in classical Chinese and are still commonly used in vernacular Chinese, in both written and spoken forms. In modern Chinese, many 成语 are condensed expressions of a certain phenomenon or an idea, and they may not necessarily have a historical basis. (For more information about 成语, refer to a dictionary of Chinese idiomatic expressions.)

语法/语言点注释 Grammar/language points

1 用来......; is used to . . .

　　古代人们崇拜某种动物的能力，渐渐地这种动物就用来代表这个民族的精神，成为这个民族的图腾。

Ancient people worshipped the ability of a certain animal, and gradually used this animal to represent the spirit of the nation. Hence, the animal became the totem of the nation.

This pattern is used to express the use of something to serve a certain purpose or reach a certain goal.

Example:

"画蛇添足"这个成语可以用来形容做了一件多余的事。

The idiom "gilding the lily" is used to describe doing something superfluous and unnecessary.

2 却......; but . . .

狮子、鹰、公鸡都是人类见过的动物，而"龙"却是想象中的一种动物。

The lion, hawk, and rooster are all animals that people have actually seen and that exist, but the dragon is an imaginary animal.

The adverb 却 in the second simple sentence of this compound sentence indicates a tone of transition for introducing an action, behavior, or situation that is inconsistent with the one in the first simple sentence.

Example:

> 男人们爱看足球赛，女人们却喜欢逛街。
> Men love to watch football, while women enjoy window shopping.

3 比作 . . . . . .; is likened to . . ./compared to . . .

> 中国人常常把山比作"龙"，把山梁比作龙身上的血管，即"脉"。
> Chinese people often compare a mountain to a dragon and the ridge to the dragon's scaly spine.

This pattern is used to point out partial similarity between two things.

Example:

> 在中国，人们习惯把男人比作太阳，把女人比作月亮，把孩子比作花朵。
> In China, people like to use the sun to describe men, the moon for women, and a flower for children.

阅读理解 Comprehension

一、对错题 True or false?

1 (　)龙是想象中的一种动物。
2 (　)传说龙是九种动物的综合体。
3 (　)龙的传人意思是龙变成了人。
4 (　)根据课文内容，龙是很有力量的动物。

二、选择题 Multiple-choice questions.

1 画龙点睛的"点"跟下面哪个句子中的"点"意思相近？

   a) 现在几点？
   b) 老王，你来点菜吧。
   c) 我一点儿咖啡都不能喝。
   d) 电脑上的这个广告，你只要点击一下就能打开。

2 "龙看起来九不像"这句话的意思是：

   a) 龙看起来不像汉字"九"
   b) 看不出龙跟九种动物有像的地方
   c) 看得出龙像九种动物中的一种
   d) 龙看起来跟九种动物像，但又有不像的地方

三、简答题 Short-answer questions.

1 "望子成龙"的"龙"是指什么意思？

2 "画龙点睛"故事中的画家为什么不画龙的眼睛？

3 "来龙去脉"这个成语现在用来表示什么意思？

根据提示完成课文结构图 Complete the text structure map according to the clues provided

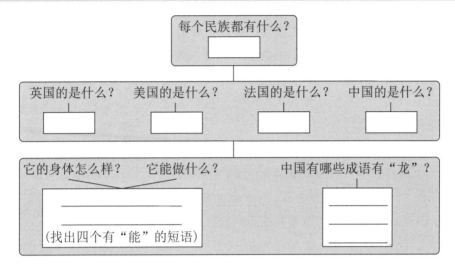

每个民族都有什么？

英国的是什么？　美国的是什么？　法国的是什么？　中国的是什么？

它的身体怎么样？　它能做什么？　中国有哪些成语有"龙"？

(找出四个有"能"的短语)

讨论 Discussion

1 在你的国家，哪一种动物得到人们特别的崇拜？为什么？

2 你认为每一个民族或国家都应该有图腾吗？为什么？

阅读 B: 节日里体验龙文化 Experiencing dragon culture in Chinese festivals

课文 Reading

五月初五赛龙舟，对中国人来说是一项重要的活动。赛龙舟最早是中国南方部落的祭神活动。他们祭的神就是龙，因为他们认为龙会带给人们雨水、丰收和生命。虽然现代人再也不需要祭神求雨，但是赛龙舟这项活动在中国人生活中长期保留下来了。

生词注释 Vocabulary

1. 赛【sài】賽 v.; n. compete; contest

2. 部落【bù luò】n. tribe

3. 祭神【jì shén】vo.; n. offer sacrifice to gods; worship, sacrifice

4. 丰收【fēng shōu】豐收 n. harvest

龙舟，是一条长十四、五米，形状像龙的木船。船头做成龙头的样子。举行赛龙舟活动的时候，五、六十只龙舟同时参赛。每条船的颜色都不一样，龙头的样子也不同。有金龙、黄龙、白龙、乌龙等。这些龙舟看起来就像一条条帅气的龙。比赛的时候，龙舟上鼓声阵阵，喊声阵阵，而河的两岸欢声震天。

在中国人最重要的节日春节，一定能看到龙的身影。欢乐的人们，身穿彩衣，敲锣打鼓，舞起了鲜艳的大龙。这条舞动的大龙，是人们手工制作的，用了草、竹、木纸、布等材料。龙身上的节数有九节、十一节、十三节，最多可达二十九节。舞起来的时候，龙身游走飞动，非常好看。

在中国少数民族*中，同样有很多与龙有关的节日和民俗。鄂西土家族农历六月初六是晒龙袍节，同时有祭神活动。相传六月六日是土家族的土王战败遇难的日子，为纪念他，土家人在这一天家家都要把新衣物放在太阳下晒，来表示晒土王的战袍，称为晒龙袍。

云南普米族也有一个自己的节日，叫"龙潭祭节"，时间是农历一月、二月，或者农历三月、七月。每家都在山林里有自家的"龙潭"，到祭潭的节日，要在龙潭边住三日，还要建一个"龙塔"，让龙神居住，然后把祭品放在塔前，求龙神保佑。传说很久很久以前普米人为躲避战争，逃到外乡去。他们回来的时候，所有东西都被毁掉了，只有放在井里的饭碗还是好好的。普米人认为是水中的龙神保佑了自己，祭龙潭的节日就这样开始了。

由此看来，不仅是汉族，许多少数民族也都有龙崇拜和祭龙节庆活动。各族龙文化不断融合，最终形成了中华民族丰富的龙文化。

（735字）

编写：虞农

5. 欢声【huān shēng】歡聲 n. cheerful sound

6. 震天【zhèn tiān】vo. shake (the air), shock

7. 敲锣打鼓【qiāo luó dǎ gǔ】敲鑼打鼓 beat drums and gongs（成语）

8. 鲜艳【xiān yàn】鮮艷 adj. brightly colored

9. 晒【shài】曬 v. be exposed to the sun

10. 龙袍【lóng páo】龍袍 n. dragon robe, imperial robe

11. 战败【zhàn bài】戰敗 v. lose a battle or war, be defeated

12. 遇难【yù nàn】遇難 vo. killed, die in an accident

13. 普米族【Pǔ mǐ zú】pn. Pumi minority

14. 潭【lóng tán】潭 n. deep pool, pond

15. 保佑【bǎo yòu】v.; n. bless and protect; blessings

16. 躲避【duǒ bì】v. hide, avoid

17. 战争【zhàn zhēng】戰爭 n. war

18. 逃【táo】v. escape, flee, run away

19. 毁掉【huǐ diào】v. damage, ruin

20. 井【jǐng】n. well

21. 融合【róng hé】v.; n. mix together, fuse, merge; mixture

文化/熟语注释 Culture/idiom notes

*少数民族【shǎoshù mínzú】中国辽阔的土地上，生活着56个不同的民族。汉族人口占总人口的90%以上，所以，另外的55个民族被称为少数民族。人口较多的少数民族有：藏族、回族、壮族、蒙古族、满族等。

In the vast land of China, there are altogether 56 different nationalities. Over 90% of China's population are Han. Therefore, the other 55 nationalities are referred to as minorities. The minorities with larger populations include: Tibetans, Hui, Chuang, Mongols, and the Manchu.

语法/语言点注释 Grammar/language points

1 再也不 . . . . . .; will never appear or do it again . . .

虽然现代人<u>再也不</u>需要祭神求雨，但是赛龙舟这项活动在中国人生活中长期保留下来了。

Although modern people no longer need to pray for rain, the dragon-boat race has remained a tradition in Chinese people's lives.

再也不 is an emphatic form of 不再 (not again). It means an action or a situation that will never occur again.

Example:

我看父亲咳得厉害，我真为他担心，劝他再也不能抽烟了。

Seeing how hard my father coughs, I'm really worried about him and am trying to persuade him never to smoke again.

2 所有 . . . . . . 都 . . . . . .; all . . .

他们回来的时候，<u>所有</u>东西<u>都</u>被毁掉了，只有放在井里的饭碗还是好好的。

When they returned, all the goods and property had been destroyed; only the bowls in the well remained in good condition.

This pattern is used to indicate that all things are included, or everybody is included.

Example:

由于今天大雾，北京机场所有的航班都被取消了。

Because of the dense fog today, all flights from Beijing airport are cancelled.

阅读理解 Comprehension

一、选择题 Multiple-choice questions.

1　关于五月五赛龙舟，下面哪个说法是错的？

　　a) 赛龙舟最早出现于中国南方　　b) 在古代，赛龙舟是为了祭龙
　　c) 龙舟是一条形状像龙的木船　　d) 比赛的时候，龙舟上的鼓声、喊声停了

2   关于春节舞龙，下面哪个说法是错的？

   a) 春节舞龙用的龙，是手工做的
   b) 做龙用了草、竹、木纸、布等材料
   c) 龙身上的节数最常见的是八节
   d) 这条舞动的大龙很鲜艳，非常好看

3   关于土家族的晒龙袍节，下面哪些说法是对的？

   a) 晒龙袍节是农历六月初六
   b) 传说这天是土王战败遇难的日子
   c) 晒龙袍节是为了纪念土王
   d) 家家都要把很多年前的衣物拿出来晒

4   关于普米族的龙潭祭节，下面哪些说法是对的？

   a) 一年有四个龙潭祭节
   b) 每家都有自己家的"龙潭"
   c) 祭潭的时候，人在龙潭边住三日
   d) 还要建一个"龙塔"，让龙神居住

二、填空题 Fill in the blanks, choosing from the words provided.

1   节日   民俗   祭神   纪念   保佑

      土家族的晒龙袍节是为了＿＿＿土王，而普米族的祭龙潭节是为了感谢龙神＿＿＿
   了普米人。在少数民族中，还有很多与龙有关的＿＿＿和＿＿＿。

2   逃   遇难   战争   毁掉   躲避

      在我看来，晒龙袍节和祭龙潭节都跟＿＿＿有关系。土家族的土王战败时，身上
   穿着战袍。普米族人则为了＿＿＿战争而＿＿＿到外乡去，回来的时候发现井里的碗还
   是好的，没有被＿＿＿。

三、简答题 Short-answer questions.

1   赛龙舟活动中的"龙舟"是怎样的？

2   春节舞龙活动中的"龙"是怎样的？

3   土家族人为什么把土王的战袍叫做"龙"袍？

第十二课　中国家庭

Chapter 12　A typical Chinese family

课文导入 Introduction　　　　　　　　**生词注释 Vocabulary**

　　"父母在，不远游"是一句中国老话，意思是父母健在，子女就不能去外地，而应该留在家陪伴父母。在新时代，这种观念是不是还被人接受呢？另外，中国人的家庭关系正在变得简单，这是不是意味着年轻人可以放弃那些复杂的亲戚称谓了呢？下面的文章表达了对这些问题的看法。

1. 称谓【chēng wèi】稱謂 n. appellation, title

阅读 A: 父母在, 不远游 Don't stray too far from home if your parents are waiting for you there

读前准备 Warm-up

一、选择题 Multiple-choice questions.

在你以后的人生中，你比较接受下面哪一种家庭生活方式？

a) 跟父母住在一起，给他们最好的关心与照顾
b) 跟父母住在一起，让他们帮你照顾你的孩子
c) 不跟父母住在一起，而愿意去外地独立生活、工作
d) 不跟父母住在一起，但生活在同一个城市，并经常去看他们

二、简答题 Short-answer questions.

1　你的父母希望你留在身边，还是告诉你可以自由选择？

2　你的父母如果只有你一个孩子，你是不是会花更多时间照顾他们？

课文 Reading

中国家庭的传统观念是"养儿防老"，"父母在，不远游"。在新时代这种观念是不是<u>一如既往</u>呢？

<u>即将</u>毕业正在找工作的大四学生小琳说："我想所有父母都是这样的，他们表面上<u>装作</u>不<u>在意</u>，希望你不要因为他们影响自己的决定，但心里肯定希望孩子留在自己身边。"小琳是家里的独生女，她告诉记者："虽然父母有工作，并不需要经济上的<u>援助</u>，但他们确实更需要有人陪在身边，哪怕只是说说话也好。"

去年国家公务员招考*时，小琳报考了离家较近的城市的公务员职位，并且进入了复试。"我现在希望能在离家较近的城市工作，虽然不如一线城市*发达，但重要的是离家近，可以照顾父母。"

一位姓钮的母亲在接受采访时告诉记者："有一次，我和同事们一起吃饭。饭桌上有人讲起了这样一个故事：老师让小明在黑板上写下十个对他最重要的人，小明写下了父母、<u>伴侣</u>和八个要好的朋友。然后，老师对他说，如果让你在这十个人中只能选择九个，你会选谁？小明<u>擦掉</u>了一个朋友的名字，然后是八个、七个……一直到黑板上只剩下了父母和伴侣。老师说，在这两个中你只能选一个，你会选谁？小明想了很久，<u>含泪</u>擦掉了父母的名字。老师问他为什么，他说，父母只能陪伴你走过人生的一<u>段</u>路，而只有你的爱人才是那个要陪伴你走过一生的人。"

这个故事，是钮女士在饭桌上听到的，用她自己的话来说，这是<u>醍醐灌顶</u>，突然发现自己的想法已经太<u>陈旧</u>了。"父母虽然是孩子人生中最重要的人之一，但父母<u>终归</u>会离去，不能陪伴孩子一生。我忽然认识到，父母也要学会独立生活，与其把希望寄托在孩子身上，希望他们照顾你、陪伴你，还不如让自己<u>充实</u>起来，发现人生的乐趣。"

生词注释 Vocabulary

1. 一如既往【yí rú jì wǎng】just as before, in the past or as always（成语）

2. 即将【jí jiāng】即将 adv. soon, upcoming

3. 装作【zhuāng zuò】装作 v. act, pretend to

4. 在意【zài yì】v. care about, mind

5. 援助【yuán zhù】v.; n. help, support; assistance

6. 伴侣【bàn lǚ】伴侣 n. companion, partner, husband, wife

7. 擦掉【cā diào】v. wipe out, scrub off

8. 含泪【hán lèi】vo. with tears, in tears

9. 段【duàn】m. n. section, part

10. 醍醐灌顶【tí hú guàn dǐng】醍醐灌頂 realize suddenly, be enlightened（成语）

11. 陈旧【chén jiù】陳舊 adj. old, outdated, old fashioned

12. 终归【zhōng guī】終歸 adv. eventually, in the end, after all

13. 充实【chōng shí】充實 v.; adj. enrich; rich, abundant

自从孩子去外地上学后，钮女士开始"重新发现自己"。她对记者说："以前天天围着孩子转，也没有时间想想自己要干些什么，现在时间多了，<u>正好</u>可以培养一些兴趣爱好。"除了这些兴趣爱好，她还结交了一些跟她一样儿女在外的朋友，有机会就聚在一起聊天<u>打牌</u>。"人老了，最大的问题在于寂寞，有了朋友，生活也就不寂寞了，就让儿女们自己选择他们希望过的生活吧。"钮女士说。

14. 正好【zhèng hǎo】adv. just right, just enough, happen to

15. 打牌【dǎ pái】vo. play mahjong or cards

(836字)
文：记者　吴敏　实习生　江艳博　有删改
原载《南方日报》2012年2月24日
网络来源：
http://epaper.nfdaily.cn/html/2012-02/24/content_7060348.htm

文化/熟语注释 Culture/idiom notes

　　*国家公务员考试【guójiā gōngwùyuán kǎoshì】国家公务员考试是中国各级政府部门招聘工作人员的专门考试，一般安排在10-11月间。公务员职位在中国被认为是"金饭碗"，每年参加公务员考试的人数相当巨大。

The Chinese civil service examination is a specialized exam for Chinese government agencies at all levels to recruit new employees. The exam normally takes place between October and November every year. A job in a government agency is considered to be a "golden rice bowl" (a stable and well-paid job) in China; therefore, the number of people taking the exam every year is quite large.

　　*一线城市【yíxiàn chéngshì】根据城市的大小及政治或经济地位的重要性，中国人把城市划分为一线、二线、三线不同的等级。目前被公认的一线城市是北京、上海、广州、深圳，简称北上广深。

In China, cities are divided into first-tier, second-tier, and third-tier according to their population and political or economic importance in the country. The nationally recognized first-tier cities include Beijing, Shanghai, Guangzhou, and Shenzhen. 北上广深【běi shàng guǎng shēn】is the abbreviation of the four cities as a collective.

语法/语言点注释 Grammar/language points

1 哪怕......（也好）; even if...

　　"虽然父母有工作，并不需要经济上的援助，但他们确实更需要有人陪在身边，<u>哪怕</u>只是说说话<u>也好</u>。"
"Even if parents have jobs and don't need financial support; they still need company, someone to talk to."

The word 哪怕 is a conjunction and introduces a hypothetical condition that is similar to 即使, but in a more colloquial form.

Example:

在我看来，想要身体健康就得坚持跑步，哪怕每天只跑十分钟也好。

It seems to me that you have to keep running if you want to be fit, even if just for ten minutes every day.

2 围着......转; follow . . . around

她对记者说：“以前天天围着孩子转，也没有时间想想自己要干些什么，现在时间多了，正好可以培养一些兴趣爱好。”

She told the reporter: "In the past the kids were the center of my attention. I had no time to think about myself; now I have more free time so this time is just about cultivating my own interests and hobbies."

The original meaning of 围着......转 is "to revolve around a center point." Its extended meaning is to do everything for just one purpose or for one person.

Example:

月亮围着地球转，地球围着太阳转，可我不愿意我的父母围着我转。

The moon circles around the earth and the earth circles around the sun, but I don't want my parents to follow me around all the time.

3 在于......; is about . . .

“人老了，最大的问题在于寂寞，有了朋友，生活也就不寂寞了，就让儿女们自己选择他们希望过的生活吧。”钮女士说。

"When you get old, the biggest problem is feeling lonely. Once you have friends, you will no longer feel lonely in your life, so you can let your children go free and choose the life they wish to live," said Ms. Niu.

The word 于 is a preposition that is used together with 在 to introduce the object of the sentence.

Example:

上次我的工作面试不太顺利，主要原因在于我太紧张了，没能好好表现自己。

The last job interview did not go so smoothly, mainly because I got so nervous and could not give it all I had.

阅读理解 Comprehension

一、选择题 Multiple-choice questions.

1   关于小琳，下面哪个说法是错的？

   a) 小琳是大四学生，正在找工作
   b) 小琳没有兄弟姐妹，她是父母的独生女
   c) 小琳报考了一线城市的公务员职位
   d) 小琳希望在离家较近的城市工作

2   关于钮女士，下面哪个说法是对的？

　　a) 钮女士的儿子叫小明

　　b) 钮女士的孩子在外地上学

　　c) 钮女士越来越希望孩子毕业后照顾她、陪伴她

　　d) 钮女士觉得现在的生活太寂寞了

二、填空题 Fill in the blanks, choosing from the words provided.

　　会　　到　　掉　　下

1   小明擦＿＿＿了一个朋友的名字。黑板上只剩＿＿＿了父母和伴侣。

2   我忽然认识＿＿＿，父母也要学＿＿＿独立生活。

三、完成对话 Finish the conversation.

1   A: 听说你放弃了一线城市的工作，决定回家乡小城？

　　B: 是的。我家乡虽然＿＿＿＿＿＿＿，但重要的是＿＿＿＿＿＿＿。

2   A: 孩子们都去外地工作了，生活真寂寞啊！我真希望孩子们就在身边。

　　B: 与其＿＿＿＿＿＿＿，还不如＿＿＿＿＿＿＿。

根据提示完成课文结构图 Complete the text structure map according to the clues provided

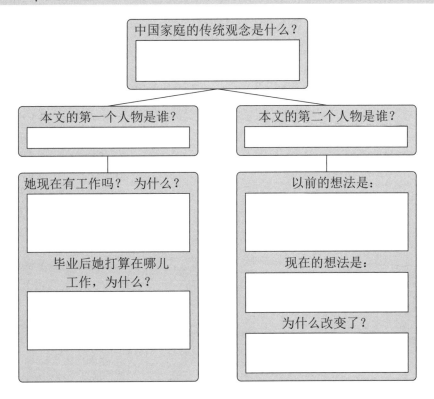

讨论 Discussion

I   如果你是课文中的小明，你会把黑板上谁的名字留在最后？为什么？

2   你认为"父母在，不远游"是不是子女对父母表达爱的最佳方式？在你看来，子女应该用哪些方式来表达对父母的爱呢？

阅读 B: 亲戚称谓 Addressing relatives

课文 Reading

每到春节，许许多多年轻人都要回家过年，和亲人团聚。平常不怎么走动的亲戚们也要多联络联络。然而，复杂的亲戚关系让很多年轻人头疼，姑姑舅舅，表兄堂兄，究竟如何区别？为此，一位网友自制了一张亲属关系图发布在网上。图上面有祖父母、外祖父母、孙子、孙女、外孙、外孙女、叔叔、伯伯、姑姑、婶婶、舅舅、舅妈、嫂子、堂哥、表弟等等，把所有亲属关系都清清楚楚画了出来，年轻人高兴地称它为"过年必备"。

中国原本是一个极重视家庭的国家。一个家庭，有很多直系、旁系的亲属，这是中国文化的特色。在古代每个小孩子都要学习如何辨别这些亲属关系。各种亲戚关系的称谓应该是常识，为什么今天的年轻人却不懂呢？著名的礼学*学者、清华大学教授彭林说："现代年轻人家庭观念不强，逐渐失去了中国文化的特质。他们崇尚西方文化。中西方是不同的，中国是一种家庭文化，西方则是一种宗教文化。许多西方人认为是神造了人，所有人都是神的子女，父母在家庭的地位远远没有像在中国这么重要。中国人认为血浓于水，血缘关系不可割裂。西方人则不然，他们成熟的标志之一是脱离父母，可以晚上不回家了。"彭教授特别强调："中国人见到没有血缘关系的人，也叫叔叔伯伯，这正是把家庭推而广之的结果。"

生词注释 Vocabulary

1. 走动【zǒu dòng】走動 v. walk about, (of relatives and friends) visit each other

2. 联络【lián luò】聯絡 v.; n. contact, communicate; liaison

3. 究竟【jiū jìng】n.; adv. outcome; actually, after all

4. 直系【zhí xì】adj. immediate (family members)

5. 旁系【páng xì】adj. collateral

6. 亲属【qīn shǔ】親屬 n. relatives, kinship

7. 辨别【biàn bié】辨別 v. differentiate, distinguish

9. 崇尚【chóng shàng】v. uphold, advocate

10. 宗教【zōng jiào】n. religion

11. 血浓于水【xuè nóng yú shuǐ】血濃於水 blood is thicker than water（成语）

12. 割裂【gē liè】v. cut, sever

13. 不然【bù rán】conj.; v. otherwise; (it) is not so

14. 脱离【tuō lí】脫離 v. separate oneself from, away from, out of

15. 推而广之【tuī ér guǎng zhī】推而廣之 apply broadly（成语）

　　虽然在今天，中国人的家庭关系正在变得简单，但是这是不是意味着我们就可以放弃那些复杂的称谓了呢？如果那样，恐怕孩子们看中国传统的典籍时，可能很多地方由于不了解这些家庭关系而看不懂。

16. 典籍【diǎn jí】n. classical books or records

（598字）

文：记者　周怀宗

原载《北京晨报》2012年1月27日

网络来源：

http://www.morningpost.com.cn/fukan/rwgc/2012-01-26/279312.shtml

文化/熟语注释 Culture/idiom notes

　　*礼学【lǐxué】礼学是以"礼"为研究对象的专门学术。"礼"是中国传统儒学的核心部分，是中国古代社会人们行为规则的总称。

礼学 is the study of Chinese ritual. It is a core component in traditional Chinese Confucianism; it is also a general term for behavioral norms in ancient Chinese society.

语法/语言点注释 Grammar/language points

1　由于......而......; due to/because of...

　　　　如果那样，恐怕孩子们看中国传统的典籍时，可能很多地方由于不了解这些家庭关系而看不懂。

　　If so, I'm afraid that when reading the traditional Chinese classics, children will not be able to understand the text due to lack of knowledge of kinship relations.

The word 由于 in this sentence is used to introduce a cause and 而 is used to introduce a result.

Example:

　　老人往往由于子女不在身边而感到寂寞。

　　Old people often felt lonely because their children did not live nearby.

阅读理解 Comprehension

一、对错题 True or false?

1　（　）年轻人把亲属关系图称为"过年必备"。

2　（　）在古代，亲戚称谓对中国人来说是常识。

3　（　）到了现代，亲戚称谓对年轻人来说不是一件容易的事。

4　（　）中国以前一个家庭有很多直系、旁系的亲属，家庭里父母的地位非常重要。

5　（　）现在中国人的家庭关系正在变得简单，有的亲戚平常不怎么走动。

二、填空题 Fill in the blanks, choosing from the words provided.

家庭   脱离   割裂   崇尚   观念   宗教   辨别

1   现代年轻人家庭_____不强，逐渐失去了中国文化的特质。
2   中西方是不同的，中国是一种家庭文化，西方则是一种_____文化。
3   中国人认为血浓于水，血缘关系不可_____。
4   对于西方人来说，成熟的标志之一是_____父母，可以晚上不回家了。
5   如果不能_____这些亲属关系，那么就会看不懂中国的传统古籍。

三、请你用中文称呼制作一张你家的亲属关系图。Draw a family tree using Chinese kinship names for your own family.

第十三课　明星的生活

Chapter 13　Celebrity life stories

课文导入 Introduction

　　生活在众人视线下的明星，他们每天都受到粉丝们的<u>追捧</u>。可是他们在获得成功或拥有<u>知名度</u>的同时，失去了什么？他们的个人生活和内心世界又是怎样的？你也许可以在下面的文章中找到答案。

生词注释 Vocabulary

1. 追捧【zhuī pěng】v. follow, pursue, admire
2. 知名度【zhī míng dù】n. popularity, fame

阅读 A: 我好想家 I really miss home

读前准备 Warm-up

一、资料查找 Search for information.

1　"巩俐"是谁？你能介绍一下吗？

2　要是你不了解她，请上网查找巩俐(Li Gong)，阅读维基百科(Wikipedia)关于她的介绍。

二、选择题 Multiple-choice questions.

你认为生活中的巩俐很可能符合下面哪些选项？

a) 她作为公众人物，常常被人误解和贬损
b) 她得到了家人的理解和支持
c) 她和家人去饭馆吃饭会把剩菜带回家
d) 她的衣服都很漂亮，很贵，是名牌

课文 Reading

我在演艺<u>圈</u><u>闯荡</u>了几年以后，发现我最钟情的地方是家。有时想起家中餐桌上的<u>咸菜</u>，有时想起妈妈身上那件旧毛衣。我问自己，为什么会想起这些？慢慢地我懂了，心会随家一起走。无论我走到哪里，家已深深<u>扎根</u>在我的心里。作为公众人物，被人误解、被人<u>贬损</u>是常有的事，这时，我一定会想起家。家一直作为一种力量<u>支撑</u>我、伴随我。

我结婚前回老家接母亲<u>赴</u>香港参加婚礼，才得知母亲患了重病住在医院。当时，我的心情很复杂，深深地陷入了两难境地。作为母亲唯一的女儿，我没有理由在她有生命危险的时候不在她的身边，但婚礼<u>请柬</u>已经发出，如果被<u>媒体</u>知道婚礼<u>延期</u>，一定会有很多猜测，这对我产生什么后果，<u>不言而喻</u>。母亲以婚礼延期对我不利为由，坚持要我先回香港。三个哥哥也让我以公众<u>信誉</u>为重。他们都是我至爱的亲人，他们的理解让我觉得我在社会上不是孤单的，我不仅仅是为自己而工作，我代表着巩家，我的心里升起一种力量。

母亲有一件<u>套头</u>毛衣，是我几年前为她买的，被虫子咬过，已经很旧了。母亲患病以后，右臂<u>抬</u>上抬下有困难，穿套头衫很不方便。我想给她买件开衫，母亲不允许。她把毛衣中间剪开，找颜色接近的毛线<u>织</u>了一条边，把套头衫变成了开衫。我看着母亲这样做，真是很感动。他们那代人都是伴着苦和汗生活的，现在儿女有条件让他们享福了，他们为什么还这样？这就是一种观念、一种精神。这些东西<u>潜移默化</u>地<u>渗透</u>在我的生命里，影响着我，我做任何事，<u>别无选择</u>地带着家的印迹。

有一次，我们在饭店吃完饭<u>打包</u>回家，有位记者写了《巩俐*吃不了"<u>兜</u>"着走*》一文。其实，我妈每次都这样。那次，我和妈妈一起在外边吃饭，一碗鱼汤没有喝完。我觉得汤不好拿，就说算了。妈妈说不行。她让服务员把汤水倒出去，把汤里的鲫鱼和豆腐打包带回家。

可能很多人都不相信，我经常到北京的"秀水街"<u>地摊</u>买衣服，只要不是演戏和<u>应酬</u>，我平时几乎不戴任何首饰。我不喜欢珠光宝气，因为母亲就是这样……

（786字）

文：巩俐　有删改　原载《生活时报》1999年6月26日
网络来源：

http://www.gmw.cn/01shsb/1999-06/26/GB/1021%5ESHI-2636.HTM

生词注释 Vocabulary

1. 圈【quān】v.; n. circle

2. 闯荡【chuǎng dàng】闖蕩 v. leave home to make a living

3. 咸菜【xián cài】鹹菜 n. pickled vegetables

4. 扎根【zhā gēn】vo. rooted in

5. 贬损【biǎn sǔn】貶損 v. disparage, derogate

6. 支撑【zhī chēng】支撐 v. hold up, sustain, support

7. 赴【fù】v. go to, attend

8. 请柬【qǐng jiǎn】請柬 n. invitation card, written invitation

9. 媒体【méi tǐ】媒體 n. news media

10. 延期【yán qī】v. postpone, put off, delay, extend

11. 不言而喻【bù yán ér yù】it goes without saying, it is self-evident（成语）

12. 信誉【xìn yù】信譽 n. prestige, credit, reputation

13. 套头【tào tóu】套頭 adj. turtleneck, pullover

14. 抬【tái】v. lift, raise

15. 织【zhī】織 v. knit, weave

16. 潜移默化【qián yí mò huà】潛移默化 imperceptibly influence, influence unconsciously（成语）

17. 渗透【shèn tòu】滲透 v.; n. permeate, infiltrate; infiltration

18. 别无选择【bié wú xuǎn zé】別無選擇 no other choice（成语）

19. 打包【dǎ bāo】v. pack

20. 兜【dōu】v.; n. wrap up; bag, sack

21. 地摊【dì tān】地攤 n. street stall

22. 应酬【yìng chou】應酬 v.; n. socialize with; social engagement

文化/熟语注释 Culture/idiom notes

*巩俐【Gǒng Lì】中国大陆著名电影女演员，生于山东济南。她被认为是中国在世界影坛成就、地位最高和影响力最大的女演员。

Gong Li is a famous movie actress in mainland China. She was born in Jinan, Shandong Province. She is regarded as an actress who has achieved great things and exercised considerable influence in the film world.

*吃不了兜着走【chībùliǎo dōuzhezǒu】课文中的意思是说上馆子吃饭有吃剩的，不浪费，打包带走。但是通常我们用这一俗语来比喻某一事件的后果很严重，当事人很可能会陷入某种困境。

吃不了兜着走 is a colloquial idiom. In this article, it means if you are dining out and cannot eat the whole meal, the leftovers can be packed into a box (a doggy bag) so as not to waste the food. On most other occasions, this idiom is used to describe a serious consequence of an event or bearing all the consequences for an incident.

语法/语言点注释 Grammar/language points

1 作为......; as ...

作为公众人物，被人误解、被人贬损是常有的事，这时，我一定会想起家。
As a public figure, it is quite common to be misunderstood and disparaged by
    others; whenever it happens, I certainly miss home.

The word 作为 is used as a preposition to introduce a certain identity or property of the subject in the sentence.

Example:

玫瑰花和巧克力作为情人节的礼物，送给心爱的人是最合适的。
Roses and chocolates are the best presents to send to the one you love on
    St Valentine's Day.

阅读理解 Comprehension

一、对错题 True or false?

1 （　）想到家人巩俐的心里就有了力量。
2 （　）巩俐的家人不支持她将婚礼延期。
3 （　）因为套头衫被虫子咬了，所以巩俐母亲把它改成了开衫。
4 （　）记者写《巩俐吃不了"兜"着走》这是贬损巩俐。
5 （　）生活中的巩俐并不讲究衣饰。

二、填空题 Fill in the blanks, choosing from the words provided.

以　　被　　对　　猜测　　公众信誉　　支撑

　　婚礼请柬已经发出，如果＿＿＿媒体知道婚礼延期，一定会有很多＿＿＿，这＿＿＿我产生什么后果，不言而喻。母亲＿＿＿婚礼延期对我不利为由，坚持要我先回香港。三个哥哥也让我以＿＿＿为重。

三、简答题 Short-answer questions.

1　　如果媒体知道巩俐的婚礼延期，会有什么猜测？

2　　根据课文描述，你认为巩俐作为一个电影演员有哪些难处？

根据提示完成课文结构图 Complete the text structure map according to the clues provided

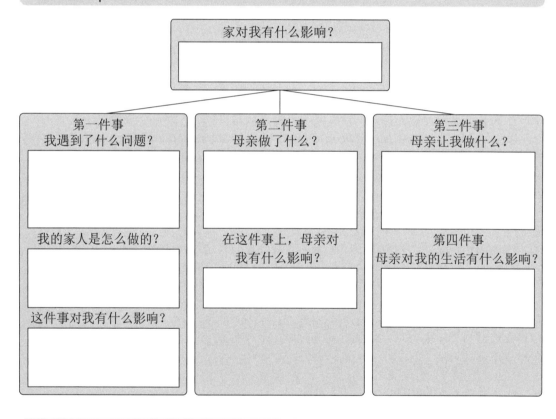

讨论 Discussion

1　　如果巩俐是你的家人，你更希望她生活幸福（比如说有美满的婚姻、可爱的孩子）还是更希望她事业成功？为什么？

2　　明星的生活往往跟人们想象中的并不一样。除了巩俐，你能举出另外一些明星的例子来说明吗？

阅读 B: 我和我的儿子 My son and I

课文 Reading

我跟我儿子是一个悲剧。他小时候我不能跟他在一起。

我跟我的爱人约会时就有一个日本女孩跳火车自杀了，我很怕这样的悲剧重演，所以我和我爱人讲好不公开我们的私生活。因为一些女孩子真的太痴情，她们会做很多傻事出来，为此我把我整个家庭藏起来。我儿子在医院出世，我看见他出生后我就上飞机走了。我的工作不是朝九晚五，我的工作是飞来飞去。

我没有跟儿子一起度过他的童年生活。我看他一次觉得他长高很多，看一次长高很多。从来没有牵着他的手或抱着他在街上走，也从来没有带他到迪士尼去玩，永远是半夜三更的时候我收工了，马路上也没什么人了，我回家去，把他叫起来，他还在睡梦中，我把他带出去开车兜风，也没有风景可看。我一直开，然后回家把他放到床上睡觉我又走了。就是这样子。

一次我跟叶倩文表演的时候，她跟我说，你知道吗你儿子最大的梦想就是有一天爸爸接他放学。我说好的，谢谢你提醒我，我会记住。有一天从美国回香港，早上七点飞机，不能睡，一睡晚上睡不着，就会有时差，所以通常我不睡。我想不如去接儿子放学，给他一个惊喜。12点半到了学校门口，我就打开车，整个马路都是车，都是接儿子的，我就停在那儿，戴着墨镜等儿子。校门一开，一大堆人走出来。我一直等，一直等。等到一个人都没有了。车接一个走一个，接一个走一个，最后车都走了。电话响了，我的司机问我在哪里，我说我在学校门口。他问清楚以后说，对不起，陈先生*，那是小学，你儿子现在读中学。我赶紧问司机到中学去怎么走。开到那里以后，一个小孩子站在斜坡上，他认识我

生词注释 Vocabulary

1. 悲剧【bēi jù】悲劇 n. tragedy

2. 痴情【chī qíng】n.; adj. unreasoning passion; be infatuated

3. 傻事【shǎ shì】n. silly things

4. 藏【cáng】v. hide, conceal, store away

5. 朝九晚五【zhāo jiǔ wǎn wǔ】work from nine to five every day（成语）

6. 牵【qiān】牽 v. lead along

7. 迪士尼【dí shì ní】pn. Disney, Disneyland

8. 半夜三更【bàn yè sān gēng】late at night（成语）

9. 收工【shōu gōng】vo. stop work for the day

10. 兜风【dōu fēng】兜風 v.; n. ride, going out for a drive

11. 墨镜【mò jìng】墨鏡 n. sunglasses

12. 堆【duī】v.; m. n. pile up; pile

13. 斜坡【xié pō】n. slope

的车，他一开门，上车，一年半没有见，一句话都没有。
他一开门就瞪我，然后脸就看着窗口，我看着他，我也
说不出话，他转过脸说"我已经读中学了"，那一刹那
我的眼泪一直在眼眶里打转。他又说"我的同学都
走了"，我就觉得非常对不起他。把他送到家，他下了
车，头也不回就走了。我也很不开心地回公司，但是
一到公司我的精神就又全在工作上了，把刚才的事情
忘了。

　　有时候我问我自己，我这样做对还是不对呢？是否
应该放弃我的事业，每天接他放学？我真的不懂。

14. 瞪【dèng】v. stare at, glare with displeasure

15. 一刹那【yí chà nà】一刹那 phr. in a flash, a very short time, in the twinkling of an eye

16. 眼眶【yǎn kuàng】n. eye socket, rim of the eye

17. 打转【dǎ zhuàn】打轉 v. spin, rotate

18. 是否【shì fǒu】adv. whether or not, is it so or not

(843字)
作者：成龙*
注：本文节选自成龙2005年10月18日在北京大学的公开
演讲，有删改。

文化/熟语注释 Culture/idiom notes

　　*成龙【Chéng Lóng】成龙生于香港，祖籍山东。香港著名电影演员，国际功夫电影
巨星。原名陈港生，所以课文中司机称他陈先生。

Jackie Chan was born in Hong Kong, China, but his ancestral home is in Shandong Province. He is a famous Hong Kong movie star and an international kung-fu action star. His original name was Gangsheng Chen; therefore, in this article, his driver called him Mr. Chen.

语法/语言点注释 Grammar/language points

1 从来没......; never ...

从来没有牵着他的手或抱着他在街上走，也从来没有带他到迪士尼去玩。
I never held his hand, or carried him in my arms strolling in the street, and I also
　　never took him to Disneyland to play.

The word 从来 indicates a time period from past to present; 从来没 is used in this sentence to indicate an unchanged state from past to present.

Example:

我父亲虽然喜欢喝酒，却从来没喝醉过。
My father is very fond of drinking but has never been drunk.

阅读理解 Comprehension

一、选择题 Multiple-choice questions.

1　关于成龙的个人生活，下面哪个说法是错的？

　　a) 他虽然结了婚，但是不能公开
　　b) 他虽然有儿子，但是常常不能跟儿子在一起
　　c) 他没有结婚，因为他怕喜欢他的女孩子们做出傻事
　　d) 他儿子一出生，他就坐飞机离开了

2　关于成龙的工作，下面哪个说法是对的？

　　a) 他的工作朝九晚五，很忙
　　b) 他一工作就会把别的事情都忘掉了
　　c) 他白天不上班，但半夜三更的时候工作
　　d) 他很想放弃工作，陪伴家人

二、填空题 Fill in the blanks, choosing from the words provided.

说不出　　转过脸　　瞪　　看　　打转

他一开门就_____我，然后脸就_____着窗口，我看着他，我也_____话，他_____说："我已经读中学了。"

三、自由回答 Open-ended questions.

1　成龙为了工作，一年半没有见到儿子，你觉得他这样做对不对？为什么？

2　对于成龙和儿子这样的"悲剧"，你认为成龙的影迷有没有责任？请说明。

第十四课 城市夜生活

Chapter 14 Urban nightlife

课文导入 Introduction

都市提供了各种各样的夜生活选择，喝酒、唱歌、跳舞、品茶......还有夜逛书店。你是否想知道，如果身处中国某个城市，可以选择什么样的夜生活？读了下面的文章，你也许对中国城市的夜生活会有所了解。

阅读 A: 都市夜生活：各有所爱 Urban nightlife: To each his own

读前准备 Warm-up

一、选择题 Multiple-choice questions.

1 夜晚的时候，如果你想休息、放松一下，会选择下面哪些方式？

　　a) 去酒吧　　b) 去咖啡馆　　c) 去电影院　　d) 在家看电视、上网

2 下面哪些词可以用来形容(xíngróng: to describe)一座城市的夜生活？

　　a) 多姿多彩　　b) 温馨　　c) 热闹　　d) 光彩鲜亮

课文 Reading

据调查，年轻人最喜欢的夜生活是泡酒吧。酒吧是年轻人的海洋，在那儿可以交友，可以面对陌生人说出一天的不快乐，<u>排解</u>心中的<u>烦闷</u>。酒吧被年轻人当做<u>时尚</u>的一个<u>标志</u>，并成为每周必去的场所。

生词注释 Vocabulary

1. 排解【pái jiě】v.; n. mediate, reconcile

2. 烦闷【fán mèn】煩悶 n.; adj. annoyance; unhappy, uncomfortable

3. 时尚【shí shàng】時尚 n. fashion, vogue

4. 标志【biāo zhì】標誌 v.; n. symbolize, indicate; sign, mark, symbol

但是对年纪<u>稍</u>大一些的人来说, 广场是最好的去处。广场生活越来越<u>多姿多彩</u>。特别是在夏天, 市民们走出家门到广场去, 他们根据自己的爱好, 或双双对对, 或<u>成群结队</u>, 跟着音乐跳交际舞、广场舞*。即使到了冬天, 灯光下的广场甚至街头, 还是能见到聚在一起跳舞的身影。

另一份调查还显示, 如今多数人更爱过休闲、<u>温馨</u>、有<u>人情味</u>的夜生活。一位喜欢去茶吧的林先生说: "那些热闹的娱乐场所很少去, 早几年倒经常去。但现在晚上出来, 一般就是请朋友到茶室喝喝茶、聊聊天。"像林先生这样的人似乎不少, 一位外商告诉记者他和朋友喜欢去音乐茶座这种比较安静的地方, 可以一边享受中国的茶文化和中国音乐, 一边谈生意。

一位出租车司机在接受采访时说: "在我看来, 在高级的娱乐场所花大钱, 把夜生活过得<u>光彩鲜亮</u>的人, 还是很多的, 他们才是夜生活的主角。在家看电视、上网、读读书, 我们一般不把这些叫做夜生活。都市就是个不夜城, 我常常在娱乐场所门口<u>载客</u>、跑夜车。"

(488字)
文: 记者　赵松刚　陈小敏　有删改
原载之一《齐鲁晚报》2011年12月30日
原载之二《温州侨乡报》2001年6月7日
网络来源:

http://sjb.qlwb.com.cn/qlwb/content/20111230/ArticelK24002FM.htm
http://www.zaobao.com/special/newspapers/2001/06/wzqxb070601.html

5. 稍【shāo】adv. a little, a bit, slightly

6. 多姿多彩【duō zī duō cǎi】varied and colorful (成语)

7. 成群结队【chéng qún jié duì】成群結隊 in groups, in crowds (成语)

8. 温馨【wēn xīn】溫馨 adj. warm, cozy

9. 人情味【rén qíng wèi】n. human feelings, human kindness

10. 光彩鲜亮【guāng cǎi xiān liàng】bright, new, cheery (成语)

11. 载客【zài kè】載客 vo. carry passengers

文化/熟语注释 Culture/idiom notes

*广场舞【guǎngchǎng wǔ】二十世纪九十年代以来, 中国的城市建立了许多文化广场。市民们早上或晚上成群结队在广场上跳舞。广场舞既能娱乐, 也能健身, 深受人民群众的喜爱。

After the 1990s, "culture squares" were developed in many cities in China. A "culture square" is a place for local people to engage in cultural activities. People often gather at the culture square and dance in the morning or in the evening. This kind of dance is not only for entertainment but also for exercise, so it is loved by many people.

语法/语言点注释 Grammar/language points

1 被 ...... 当做 ......; be treated as .../be regarded as ...

> 酒吧<u>被</u>年轻人<u>当做</u>时尚的一个标志，并成为每周必去的场所。
> Spending time in bars is regarded by young Chinese people as the fashionable thing to do; for them, a bar has become the "must-visit" place every week.

The word 被 introduces the passive voice in Chinese. In a passive Chinese sentence, the receiver of the action is put at the beginning and the doer is introduced by 被.

Example:

> 电影明星往往被年轻人当做偶像来崇拜。
> Movie stars are often regarded as idols by young people.

2 把 ...... 叫做 ......; ... call ... as ...

> 在家看电视、上网、读读书，我们一般不<u>把</u>这些<u>叫做</u>夜生活。
> We do not usually call (consider) activity such as watching TV, surfing the internet, and reading books as nightlife.

The 把 structure in this sentence is used to introduce the receiver of an action (the object). That is, the object is placed before the verb predicate to emphasize how an effect or consequence has been turned into the object. 叫做 here means "being called," "called as."

Example:

> 中国人常常把没有亲戚关系的熟人也叫做"大姐、妹子、叔叔、阿姨"等。
> The Chinese often refer to their close friends as "sister," "younger sister," "uncle," "aunt," etc., even if there is no kinship between them.

阅读理解 Comprehension

一、对错题 True or false?

1 （　）酒吧对年轻人来说是个时尚的标志。
2 （　）城市广场对年纪稍大一些的人来说是一个好去处。
3 （　）茶吧是一个温馨、有人情味的夜生活场所。
4 （　）出租汽车司机常常去高级娱乐场所过夜生活。
5 （　）一般人认为在家看电视、上网、看书也是夜生活。

二、填空题 List the types of 夜生活 you like or dislike based on the information provided in the chapter and explain why.

夜生活种类	我不喜欢，因为......	我喜欢，因为......

根据提示完成课文结构图 Complete the text structure map according to the clues provided

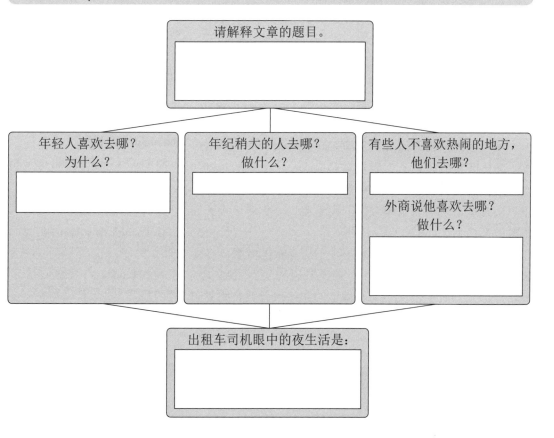

讨论 Discussion

I　　　你认为"在高级的娱乐场所花大钱，把夜生活过得光彩鲜亮的人"是夜生活的主角吗？为什么？

2　在你看来夜生活有什么好处和坏处？怎样的夜生活是健康的？

阅读 B: 都市夜生活飘书香 Urban nightlife with books

课文 Reading

生词注释 Vocabulary

　　晚上9点刚过，上海书城等大大小小的书店关门了，而大众书局这家<u>古色古香</u>的书店内依然<u>灯火通明</u>，室内<u>飘</u>着咖啡和茶的香气。大众书局是一家"24小时书店"，它的<u>首</u>场夜间书友会吸引了很多热爱读书的人，共有近60名彼此陌生的男女老少聚在一起听讲座、交朋友。店内的书架两旁也站着一些读者，他们正在<u>翻阅</u>各类书籍。

　　一名50多岁的书友告诉记者，早上听到广播里介绍了这家新开的"24小时书店"，因为自己家离这儿并不远，晚上就过来看看。另一位女学生模样的读者说，自己刚刚在附近参加完补习班*，再到这家"<u>通宵</u>书店"来"充电"，她笑着告诉记者："虽然不会在这里<u>熬</u>通宵，但体验一下夜里逛书店，很值得。"

　　"今晚雨很大，而且不是周末，居然来了这么多书友，超出了我的预期。"店长高兴地说："上海的年轻人喜欢在餐厅、咖啡馆过夜生活，但'24小时书店'却以'精神餐饮'吸引了年轻的'夜逛族'。你看，今天下大雨都<u>挡</u>不住读书人的热情啊。"

　　开一家"24小时书店"是不少书店老板的梦想。在网络购书越来越普遍的今日，实体书店的生存受到了<u>冲击</u>，但是书店不仅仅是一座城市的文化风景线，更是"文化<u>底线</u>"。夜逛书店，代表了一种文化现象、一种有意义的夜生活方式。

(494字)

文：新华社记者　许晓青　于希旖　有删改
原载《四平日报》2012年3月19日
网络来源：
http://sprbszb.chinajilin.com.cn/html/2012-03/19/content_2500005.htm

1. 古色古香【gǔ sè gǔ xiāng】have an antique flavor, classic beauty（成语）

2. 灯火通明【dēng huǒ tōng míng】燈火通明 ablaze with lights（成语）

3. 飘【piāo】飄 v. blow, drift about, flutter

4. 首【shǒu】n.; adj. head, chief, leader; first, foremost, first of all

5. 翻阅【fān yuè】翻閱 v. browse, look over, glance over

6. 通宵【tōng xiāo】n. through the night, overnight

7. 熬【áo】v. endure, put up with

8. 挡【dǎng】擋 v. keep off, block off

9. 冲击【chōng jī】衝擊 v.; n. pound, assault, impact, affect

10. 底线【dǐ xiàn】底線 n. bottom line, baseline

文化/熟语注释 Culture/idiom notes

*补习班【bǔxí bān】补习班是指以提高学生成绩为目的而设立的课外学习班。他们通常用来训练学生加强某一科目（如英文、数学等）的考试能力。补习班在东亚一些具有严格升学制度的地区很盛行。在中国的大中城市，都设有各种各样的补习班。

补习班 usually refers to all kinds of tutoring class providing extra-curricular study after regular school hours for the purpose of helping students to improve their exam scores. A tutoring class normally concentrates on improving students' exam proficiency in particular subject areas (e.g., English or math). This kind of class is popular in East Asia, where there is a very strict entrance exam system for entering higher level education. Various types of tutoring class are offered in both large- and medium-sized cities in China.

语法/语言点注释 Grammar/language points

1 居然 . . . . . . ; unexpectedly . . .

> 今晚雨很大，而且不是周末，居然来了这么多书友，超出了我的预期。
> It is raining heavily and it is not a weekend night tonight, so it was really unexpected that so many readers should show up (in the bookstore).

The word 居然 is an adverb used to express surprise or that something out of the ordinary happened.

Example:

> 我真没想到，他居然一个人骑着自行车周游了中国。
> I did not imagine that he would cycle around the whole country by himself.

阅读理解 Comprehension

一、选择题 Multiple-choice questions.

1   关于大众书局，下面哪个说法是错的？

    a) 这家书店24小时营业
    b) 在这家书店能买到咖啡和茶
    c) 这是一家古色古香的书店
    d) 喜欢这家店的都是年轻人

2   关于大众书局的首场夜间书友会，下面哪个说法是对的？

    a) 来参加书友会的人互相都认识
    b) 那天是个周末，所以来了很多人
    c) 有人听到了广播里的消息，所以来参加了
    d) 店长早就想到会来这么多书友

二、填空题 Fill in the blanks, choosing from the words provided.

受到　　吸引　　得到

1　这家书店的首场夜间书友会_____了很多热爱读书的人。

2　在网络购书越来越普遍的今日，实体书店的生存_____了冲击。

三、自由回答 Open-ended questions.

1　你喜欢网上购书还是逛书店购书？这两种购书方式各有什么好处和坏处？

2　　　作为读者的你希望自己的城市有一家24小时书店吗？如果你是老板呢，你愿意开一家24小时书店吗？为什么？

第十五课　游山玩水

Chapter 15　Up to the mountains and down to the rivers

课文导入 Introduction

　　旅游是一种了解世界的方法。中国<u>地大物博</u>，<u>气象万千</u>，去中国旅游是一种学习，更是一种享受。无论是在沙漠里，还是在古<u>村落</u>，都有<u>迷人</u>的风景、独特的风情。读一读下面的文章，您也许会感受到在中国旅游的快乐。

生词注释 Vocabulary

1. 地大物博【dì dà wù bó】 vast territory with rich resources（成语）

2. 气象万千【qì xiàng wàn qiān】气象萬千 a spectacular sight, wonderful and mighty panorama（成语）

3. 村落【cūn luò】n. village, town

4. 迷人【mí rén】adj. enchanting, attractive, fascinating

阅读 A: 火焰山 The Flaming Mountain

读前准备 Warm-up

一、填表 Classify the words given into two categories: geography and climate, and then fill in the table provided.

a) 大漠　b) 火焰山　c) 干燥少雨　d) 地表温度　e) 盆地　f) 寒冷　g) 海拔　h) 热

地理		气候	
I _____	2 _____	I _____	2 _____
3 _____	4 _____	3 _____	4 _____

课文 Reading

我根本没有想到，在大漠里能看到日出。

到吐鲁番后的第二天一大早，我和同事乘车向神往已久的火焰(yàn)山驶去。火焰山位于新疆吐鲁番盆地中部，东西长98公里，南北宽9公里，最高处海拔851米。它的北部有海拔5000米以上的天山雪峰，一年四季白雪皑皑。南部盆地中的艾丁湖却低于海平面155米，夏天，盆地内吸收的太阳能久聚不散，加上干燥少雨，地表温度可以高达80℃以上，所以这里被称为是"全国最热的地方"。每当盛夏，山体在烈日的照射下，热气流滚滚上升，赭红色的山体看似烈火在燃烧，火焰山由此而得名。当地人称"克孜勒塔格"，意思是"红山"。

汽车在沙漠公路上开着，看不到人影，更看不到任何绿色植物。忽然，车的前方出现了一团红彤彤的火焰，这团火焰在晨曦中非常耀眼。大约四十分钟后，火焰山到了。我们一下车，一股寒风就迎面扑来，我冻得直打哆嗦，心中不由暗暗叫苦，没想到冬天的火焰山可以这么冷。

不过，即将看到火焰山的兴奋让我忘记了寒冷。在我眼前，茫茫的大漠里出现一大片赭红的山岩，山岩的前面是一块写着"火焰山"字样的标志碑。因为天还没有完全亮，山岩看不大清楚，仿佛蒙着一层面纱。站在火焰山前面，我想起了《西游记》*里孙悟空他们是夏天经过这儿的，孙悟空借了铁扇公主的芭蕉扇扑灭火焰山的熊熊烈火，师徒四人才安全经过了这里，顺利到达西域。

生词注释 Vocabulary

1. 吐鲁番【Tǔ lǔ fān】吐鲁番 pn. Turfan Basin in Xinjiang Province, China

2. 神往【shén wǎng】v. fascinated, longing

3. 已久【yǐ jiǔ】adj. very long

4. 驶【shǐ】駛 v. drive, pilot, sail

5. 位于【wèi yú】位於 vc. located, situated

6. 新疆【Xīn jiāng】pn. Xinjiang Province, China

7. 海拔【hǎi bá】n. height above sea level, elevation

8. 白雪皑皑【bái xuě ái ái】白雪皚皚 phr. an expanse of white

9. 盆地【pén dì】n. basin, plain area skirted by mountains or highland

10. 久聚不散【jiǔ jù bú sàn】pr. collected, could not scatter

11. 气流【qì liú】氣流 n. air current, airflow, airstream

12. 赭红【zhě hóng】n. reddish brown

13. 沙漠【shā mò】n. desert

14. 红彤彤【hóng tōng tōng】紅彤彤 adj. bright pink or red

15. 晨曦【chén xī】n. morning sunlight, first rays of the morning sun

16. 耀眼【yào yǎn】n.; adj. dazzle; dazzling

17. 打哆嗦【dǎ duō suō】vo. tremble, shiver

18. 仿佛【fǎng fú】仿佛 adv. seemingly, as if

19. 蒙【méng】v. cover, encounter, suffer

20. 面纱【miàn shā】面紗 n. veil

21. 芭蕉扇【bā jiāo shàn】n. palm leaf fan

22. 师徒【shī tú】師徒 n. master and apprentice

23. 西域【xī yù】n. western regions in ancient China

就在我们拍照留念时，东方的地平线上露出了<u>太阳</u>红扑扑的<u>脸庞</u>。"日出！"我们惊喜地叫了起来，为能在大漠深处看到这大自然的<u>奇观</u>而欢呼。我和同事不顾寒风，站在火焰山下，看着冉冉升起的红日，由小变大，红得非常亮丽，苍茫的大漠在一刹那忽然就获得了跃动的生命！

24. 太阳【tài yáng】太陽 n. sun

25. 脸庞【liǎn páng】臉龐 n. shape of a face, face

26. 奇观【qí guān】奇觀 n. wonder, spectacle, spectacular sight

(665字)

文：刘蔚报　有删改

原载《新民晚报》2011年12月20日

网络来源：

http://xinmin.news365.com.cn/lycs/201112/t20111220_3209085.htm

文化/熟语注释 Culture/idiom notes

　　*《西游记》【xīyóujì】中国古典四大名著之一，作者是明代小说家吴承恩。此书描写的是孙悟空、猪八戒、沙和尚护送师傅唐僧去西天取经、历经艰难的传奇故事。《西游记》依托的是中国历史上著名的唐代高僧玄奘法师去西域取经的事迹。

Journey to the West is one of the "four great classical novels" in China, written by a novelist called Wu Cheng'en during the Ming Dynasty. The novel describes a legendary pilgrimage of the Buddhist monk master Tang Sanzang to India. Tang was escorted by Sun Wukong, Zhu Baijie, and Sha Wujing. During the journey west, they endured and overcame much hardship. The book is based on the true historical story of the monk Xuanzang, who traveled to the "western regions" during the Tang Dynasty to obtain sacred texts.

语法/语言点注释 Grammar/language points

1 每当......（的时候）; every time when . . .

<u>每当</u>盛夏，山体在烈日的照射下，热气流滚滚上升。
All through mid-summer, the hot sun shone down on the mountain causing hot air to rise up.

This structure is usually used to describe an event or thing that appears regularly under a certain condition or a certain moment in time.

Example:

> 每当我寒暑假回家的时候，我们家的狗都会兴奋地跑过来，围着我不停地摇尾巴。
> Every time I go home during the vacation, the dog runs around excitedly, wags its tail, and wraps itself around me.

2 为......而......; for ... and ...

> 我们惊喜地叫了起来，<u>为</u>能在大漠深处看到这大自然的奇观<u>而</u>欢呼。
> We started to shout cheerfully in surprise, delighted that we were able to see such a natural wonder in the depths of the desert.

In this sentence, 为 is used to introduce a situation or event and 而 is used to indicate the result caused by the situation or event introduced.

Example:

> 　　我住的地方离我工作的地方很远，坐一个小时地铁以后还要走三十分钟路，因此我每天不得不为上班而早起。
> I have to get up early for work every day because I live very far from my workplace, and it takes an hour on the subway and then a 30-minute walk.

阅读理解 Comprehension

一、对错题 True or false?

1 (　)火焰山的北部有一座雪峰，南部有一个湖。
2 (　)火焰山一年四季非常热，是全国最热的地方。
3 (　)火焰山是一座赭红色的山，像烈火在燃烧。
4 (　)火焰山是《西游记》中师徒四人经过的地方。
5 (　)在火焰山下看到日出让作者非常惊喜。

二、填空题 Fill in the blanks, choosing from the words provided.

茫茫　　扑扑　　彤彤　　暗暗　　滚滚　　熊熊　　冉冉　　皑皑

1 白雪___　　2 ___而上　　3 红___　　4 ___叫苦
5 ___大漠　　6 红___　　7 ___烈火　　8 ___升起

三、简答题 Short-answer questions.

1　火焰山为什么叫"火焰山"？这个名字是怎么来的？

2　站在火焰山前，作者想起了什么？

根据提示完成课文结构图 Complete the text structure map according to the clues provided

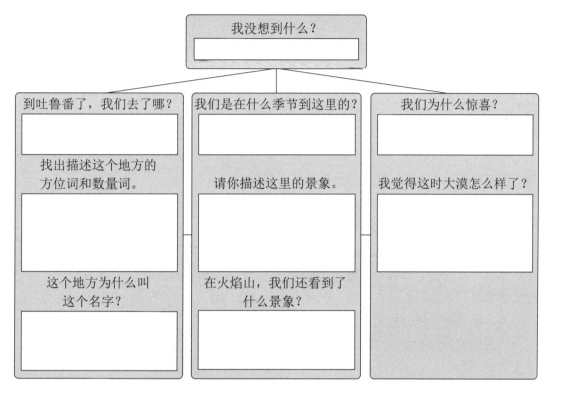

到吐鲁番了，我们去了哪？

找出描述这个地方的
方位词和数量词。

这个地方为什么叫
这个名字？

我们是在什么季节到这里的？

请你描述这里的景象。

在火焰山，我们还看到了
什么景象？

我们没想到什么？

我们为什么惊喜？

我觉得这时大漠怎么样了？

讨论 Discussion

1   读了这篇课文以后，你想起了自己哪一次旅游经历？为什么？
2   你热爱旅行吗？请你谈谈旅行对人生的作用和意义。

阅读 B: 法国女记者眼中的徽州 Huizhou City through the eyes of a female French reporter

课文 Reading

徽州，古称新安，从秦朝开始设置郡县以来，已有 2200多年的历史。古徽州是徽商*的发祥地，明清时期徽商称雄中国商界300多年，有"徽商遍天下"之说。

法国女记者高丽安（Anne Garrigue）是一位中国迷。2006年她对友人说："徽州到处是圆圆的丘陵，到处是茶树，到处雾气迷蒙，景色太美了，仿佛是在一幅中国古画中。这里是中国的普罗旺斯。我要写一本书——为我的同胞描写徽州。"

从此，高丽安十多次走入徽州古村落，与当地建筑师、资料员、手工艺人、艺术家、客栈老板、摄影师建立了友好的关系，她和他们交流并生活在一起。当她的书《石与墨书就的儒商*中国》出版的时候，高丽安已经基本上能用中文与徽州村民直接交流了。

书中的摄影是张建平的作品。除了徽州的自然风光、特色民居，张建平还把更多的镜头给了徽州人民——祠堂前玩耍的孩童、小河边洗衣的妇女、专心致志的手工艺者、祭祀的人们......在这里我们看到了真实的徽州、生活化的徽州。高丽安的文字也描写了这些场景，她说："我写这本书就是要让法国人、让欧洲人了解徽州，所以我不仅写了徽州有特色的建筑、迷人的风景，我还写了人们的生活和他们的文化，我想这才是真正的徽州。"

生词注释 Vocabulary

1. 秦【qín】n. Qin Dynasty (221–206 BC)

2. 郡县【jùn xiàn】郡縣 n. prefecture and county system

3. 发祥地【fā xiáng dì】發祥地 n. cradle, origin

4. 明清【míng qīng】n. Ming and Qing Dynasties

5. 称雄【chēng xióng】稱雄 v. become the ruler, rule the region

6. 丘陵【qiū líng】n. hills, mounds

7. 雾气【wù qì】霧氣 n. fog, mist

8. 迷蒙【mí méng】迷濛 n.; adj. mist; misty

9. 普罗旺斯【Pǔ luó wàng sī】普羅旺斯 pn. Provence (France)

10. 同胞【tóng bāo】n. born of the same parents, fellow citizen or countryman

11. 客栈【kè zhàn】客棧 n. inn, tavern

12. 摄影师【shè yǐng shī】攝影師 n. photographer, cameraman

13. 墨【mò】n. Chinese ink, ink stick, black

14. 儒商【rú shāng】n. Confucian businessman

15. 镜头【jìng tóu】鏡頭 n. camera lens, shot, scene

16. 祠堂【cí táng】n. ancestral hall or temple, memorial temple

17. 专心致志【zhuān xīn zhì zhì】專心致志 concentrate one's attention, thoughts or efforts on one thing（成语）

对于书名中出现的"儒商中国",高丽安解释说:"中国历史上的徽州人,他们不仅有<u>丰厚</u>的文化知识,也有精明的经商头脑,就是中国人所说的徽商、儒商。他们是了解今天中国人的一把<u>钥匙</u>。"对徽州今后的发展,高丽安也有一些<u>忧虑</u>,因为虽然现在中国的经济发展特别快,但是有一部分人却<u>忽视</u>文化的保护,有的建筑和民居缺乏维修。高丽安说:"我希望用我的笔来向全世界的人介绍徽州,<u>呼吁志同道合</u>的人来保护徽州的文化和历史。"

(667字)

文:记者 李芸 有删改

原载《科学时报》2009年12月17日

网络来源:

http://news.sciencenet.cn/sbhtmlnews/2009/12/227008.html

18. 丰厚【fēng hòu】豐厚 adj. rich and thick, rich and generous

19. 钥匙【yào shi】鑰匙 n. key

20. 忧虑【yōu lǜ】憂慮 v.; n. worry, concern; anxiety

21. 忽视【hū shì】忽視 v. ignore, neglect, overlook

22. 呼吁【hū yù】呼籲 v.; n. appeal, call on, plead for, urge; appeal, plea

23. 志同道合【zhì tóng dào hé】share the same ideals and thoughts (成语)

文化/熟语注释 Culture/idiom notes

*儒商【rúshāng】是具有儒家文化精神的商人,既有儒者的道德和才智,又有商人的财富与成功。中国历史上著名的儒商群体有徽商、晋商等。

儒商 refers to a group of businessmen motivated by Confucian ideals. They not only possessed wealth and success, but also Confucian morals and wisdom. Most Confucian merchants in Chinese history came from Anhui and Shanxi.

*徽商【huīshāng】即徽州商人,又称"新安商人",俗称"徽帮"。鼎盛时期徽商曾经占有全国总资产的七分之四。徽州文化发达,徽文化塑造了徽商的品格——儒商,以儒家文化来指导经商。

徽商 refers to a group of businessmen in Anhui, also known as "Xin'an businessmen," but more commonly referred to as "the Hui group." At their most prosperous, the Hui merchant group owned 4/7 of the national asset base. The rich Anhui culture shaped Confucian ideals among the merchants and they conducted their business under Confucian norms.

语法/语言点注释 Grammar/language points

1 从......以来; since...

<u>从</u>秦朝开始设置郡县<u>以来</u>,已有2200多年的历史。

Since the system of prefectures and counties was established in the Qin Dynasty, it is already more than 2,200 years old.

This structure is used to indicate that the time of an action or the continuation of an event is from a certain point in the past until now.

Example:

> 今年本地区从6月下旬以来一直处于多雨天气，这对农作物的生长不利。
> This area has had a lot of rain since the end of last June. It is not at all good for the crops.

2 不仅 ...... 也 ...... ; not only ... but also ...

> 中国历史上的徽州人，他们<u>不仅</u>有丰厚的文化知识，<u>也</u>有精明的经商头脑。
> In the course of Chinese history, people from the Anhui area not only had a rich cultural knowledge, they also possessed sharp business minds.

This structure is to be used in a compound sentence to list two or more things or events related to the topic or subject of the sentence. Here, 不仅 is similar to 不但.

Example:

> 新疆吐鲁番盆地的最低点低于海平面154米，是中国最低地，也是世界第二低地。由于它的特殊的地理环境，不仅吸引了一批批中外游客，也吸引了不少地理学家的到来。
> The Turfan Basin in Xinjiang Province lies at 154 meters below sea level; it is the lowest place in China and the second lowest place in the world. Due to its unique geographic environment, it attracts not only many domestic and foreign tourists, but also many geographers.

阅读理解 Comprehension

一、选择题 Multiple-choice questions.

1   关于徽州，下面哪个说法是错的？

   a) 徽州是一个有2200多年历史的古城
   b) 在中国明清时期，徽州商人非常著名
   c) 徽州到处是平地，到处种着茶树
   d) 徽州的风景很美，像一幅中国古画

2   关于女记者高丽安，下面哪个说法是对的？

   a) 高丽安是法国人，不会说中文
   b) 为了写书，高丽安十多次去徽州古村落
   c) 高丽安的书主要介绍了什么是儒商
   d) 高丽安拍摄了很多徽州照片用在书里

二、填空题 Fill in the blanks, choosing from the words provided.

   志同道合　　专心致志　　迷人　　精明　　丰厚

1　_____的手工艺者
2　_____的知识
3　_____的经商头脑
4　_____的风景

三、简答题 Short-answer questions.

1　对徽州今后的发展，高丽安有哪些忧虑？

2　为什么高丽安说徽州是"中国的普罗旺斯"，你怎么理解？

第十六课　90后年轻一代

Chapter 16　Born in the 1990s – today's younger generation

课文导入 Introduction

　　90后泛指1990年至1999年出生的一代中国人，他们现在二十多岁。90后生长于中国经济高速发展的年代，他们的思想与理念跟老一辈中国人有很大的不同，但他们与国际同龄人语言交流最畅通、文化差异最小。90后被称为"最国际化的一代"、"鼠标一代"。

生词注释 Vocabulary

1. 泛指【fàn zhǐ】v.; n. general reference

2. 畅通【chàng tōng】暢通 adj. unimpeded, unblocked

3. 鼠标【shǔ biāo】鼠標 n. (computer) mouse

阅读 A: 最国际化的一代 The most internationalized generation

读前准备 Warm-up

一、选择题 Multiple-choice questions.

1　你觉得"地球村"这个词的含义是什么？

    a) 地球是个很小的地方，住不下很多人。

    b) 地球上每个国家就是一个村，我们住在不同的村里。

    c) 世界越来越农村化，很多城里人搬到农村去住了。

    d) 高科技缩短了人与人之间的时空距离，所有地球人就像住在一个村子里。

二、简答题 Short-answer question.

你能举几个生活中常见的"全球化"、"国际化"的例子吗？

课文 Reading

近日在西安举行的一场音乐活动中，来自长安大学的90后大学生王小一用一首<u>纯正</u>、地道的英文歌曲，<u>倾倒</u>了一位来自美国肯塔基州的90后。

中文名叫彭家明的美国90后小伙子问主持人，这位<u>一鸣惊人</u>的女孩是在美国长大的留学生吗？他得到<u>否定</u>的答案后惊奇地说，没想到中国90后的英语说得这么地道，英文歌曲唱得这么纯正。

实际上，与60后、70后、80后相比，中国的90后与国际同龄人语言交流最畅通，文化差异最小。中国90后生长的时代背景可谓"<u>得天独厚</u>"。

首先，信息化让全球90后生活在同一个"地球村"，彼此只是<u>隔</u>着一个电脑<u>屏幕</u>。在国内70后、80后成长的年代，美国等发达国家是<u>遥远</u>的，完全属于另一个世界。可对90后来说，尤其是城市中的90后，在他们成长的年代，如果想认识、了解西方社会，那么只需要在网络上<u>输入</u>地址，轻轻一点，各种信息便<u>扑面而来</u>。

其次，经济<u>一体化</u>让很多来自中国城市的90后与美国同龄人共享发达的物质文明。来自美国普通家庭的年轻人彭家明说，中国的90后成长环境与他弟弟一样，<u>享受</u>着发达的物质生活：童年玩的是电子玩具，小学的时候上学、放学坐的是小轿车，中学时代手机不离身，线上聊不完。因此，90后的适应力非常强，对各种新技术非常熟悉。

第三，教育的改革、<u>课程</u>的创新，使英语几乎成为与中文同步进行的第二种语言。中国的90后从小学开始接受英语教育，所以与世界对话，他们没有语言<u>障碍</u>。<u>毫无疑问</u>，90后是现实社会中最国际化的一代，具备了更多的国际<u>视野</u>与思维能力。

虽然如此，90后也被许多年长者认为是不靠谱*的一代，觉得他们<u>叛逆</u>、崇尚自由与享乐。其实我认为90后

生词注释 Vocabulary

1. 纯正【chún zhèng】純正 adj. pure, genuine

2. 倾倒【qīng dǎo】傾倒 v. topple over, greatly admire

3. 一鸣惊人【yì míng jīng rén】一鳴驚人 become famous overnight（成语）

4. 否定【fǒu dìng】v.; n. negate; negation

5. 得天独厚【dé tiān dú hòu】得天獨厚 abound in gifts of nature; unique（成语）

6. 隔【gé】v. separate, cut off, impede, be at a distance from

7. 屏幕【píng mù】n. screen

8. 遥远【yáo yuǎn】遙遠 adj. distant, remote, faraway

9. 输入【shū rù】輸入 v. bring in, import, input

10. 扑面而来【pū miàn ér lái】撲面而來 blow into one's face（成语）

11. 一体化【yì tǐ huà】一體化 v.; n. integrate; integration

12. 享受【xiǎng shòu】v.; n. enjoy (rights, benefits, etc.); pleasure

13. 课程【kèchéng】n. curriculum

14. 障碍【zhàng ài】障礙 n. obstacle, obstruction, barrier

15. 毫无疑问【háo wú yí wèn】毫無疑問 certainty, without a doubt, without question（成语）

16. 视野【shì yě】視野 n. field of vision, perspective

17. 叛逆【pàn nì】v.; n. revolt against; rebel

并没有长辈们想象的那样不靠谱，他们也清楚地知道自己的理想与<u>目标</u>，从来没有放弃自己对社会与家庭所<u>承担</u>的责任。

18. 目标【mù biāo】目標 n. objective, target, goal

19. 承担【chéng dān】承擔 v. undertake

（700字）

文：李剑平　有删改

原载《中国青年报》2011年1月21日

网络来源：

http://zqb.cyol.com/html/2011-01/21/nw.D110000zgqnb_20110121_2-03.htm

文化/熟语注释 Culture/idiom notes

　　*靠谱【kàopǔ】北京方言，现代流行语，成为年青一代的口头语。如果说某人办事情"不靠谱儿"就是说他办事不可靠，让人不放心，靠不住的意思。

The expression 靠谱 is from the Beijing dialect and became a popular slang expression among Chinese youngsters. If someone says that a person is 不靠谱儿 in doing things, it means that he/she is not that reliable or dependable a person.

语法/语言点注释 Grammar/language points

1　与……相比; compared with . . .

　　　<u>与</u>60后、70后、80后<u>相比</u>，中国的90后与国际同龄人语言交流最畅通，文化差异最小。

　　Compared with the generations born in the 1960s, 1970s, and 1980s, the generation born in 1990s China has the most open communication with its international peers, and the fewest cultural differences.

This structure is used to make a comparison among things. It is more formal than 跟/和……相比.

Example:

　　今年受气候影响，蔬菜上市期推迟，而且与去年同期相比，价格上涨。

　　Affected by the weather this year, the vegetables came onto the market late, and the price has risen when you compare it to the price we were paying this time last year.

2　使……几乎……; let (or make) . . . almost . . .

　　课程的创新，<u>使</u>英语<u>几乎</u>成为与中文同步进行的第二种语言。

　　The innovations of the curriculum made English almost as important a language as Chinese.

The word 使 has a similar meaning to 让。

Example:

> 据上海的一家报纸说，忙碌的工作使都市白领几乎没有休闲娱乐的时间。
> According to a Shanghai newspaper, being busy at work means that the urban
>   white-collar workers barely have time for leisure activities and entertainment.

阅读理解 Comprehension

一、选择题 Multiple-choice questions.

1   关于中国大学生王小一，下面哪些说法是对的？

   a) 她出生于1990年代
   b) 她曾去美国留学
   c) 她英文歌唱得非常纯正
   d) 她的歌声让美国小伙子倾倒

2   关于美国小伙子彭家明，下面哪些说法是错的？

   a) 他也出生于1990年代
   b) 他来自美国肯塔基州
   c) 他认为中国的90后跟他的成长环境一样
   d) 他的家庭在美国是一个高收入家庭

二、填空题 Fill in the blanks with the phrases provided.

发达的物质文明　　教材的创新　　时代背景　　信息化　　经济一体化

　　中国90后生长的＿＿＿＿＿可谓"得天独厚"。首先，＿＿＿＿＿让全球90后生活在同
一个"地球村"，彼此只是隔着一个电脑屏幕。其次，＿＿＿＿＿让很多来自中国城市的
90后与美国同龄人共享＿＿＿＿＿。第三，教育的改革、＿＿＿＿＿，使英语几乎成为
与中文同步进行的第二种语言。中国的90后从小学开始接受英语教育。

三、简答题 Short-answer question.

根据课文内容，中国的90后有什么特点？

根据提示完成课文结构图 Complete the text structure map according to the clues provided

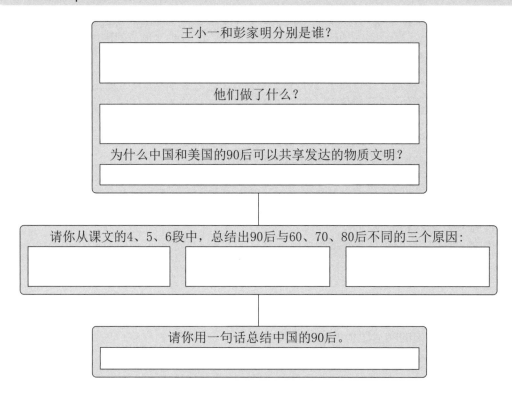

王小一和彭家明分别是谁？

他们做了什么？

为什么中国和美国的90后可以共享发达的物质文明？

请你从课文的4、5、6段中，总结出90后与60、70、80后不同的三个原因：

请你用一句话总结中国的90后。

讨论 Discussion

1 在你的国家，对"90后"这一代年轻人有什么正面和负面的评价？请举例说明。
2 "全球化"和"国际化"给我们的生活带来了哪些改变？请举例说明。

阅读 B: 鼠标一代 The "mouse" generation

课文 Reading

"90后"生长于中国经济高速发展的年代，除了物质生活条件优越以外，他们还享受着高科技数字信息技术。据统计，被称为"鼠标一代"的90后数量约有1.4亿，占全国总人口的11.7%左右。最近做了一项对90后

生词注释 Vocabulary

1. 优越【yōu yuè】優越 adj. superior, advantageous

2. 占【zhàn】佔 v. occupy, take

价值观和消费行为的研究报告。北京、上海、广州、武汉、成都5个城市的2099名90后接受了调查。

在90后眼里，成功的标志首先是"家庭幸福"（17.8%），其次是"事业有成"（16.3%）、"有钱"（14.1%）和"受人尊敬"（12.2%）。

尽管多数90后还没有到参加工作的年龄，但他们却早就支配着很大的金钱数量，并且在家庭消费中拥有决策权。数据显示，90后中学生2010年春节人均收获压岁钱1922.9元，此外每月还能获得平均382.3元的零花钱。90后在家庭里有着高度的消费决策权：84.3%的人坚持认为"买什么衣服要自己决定"。至于房子、车子这样的大宗消费品，有三成左右的90后表示父母会和自己共同决定。有受访者表示："不管是买我个人的东西，还是家里用的东西，一般都听我的。只要我参与了决策，最后往往以我的意见为主。"

调查显示90后有旺盛的消费需求，但是90后具有"买对、不买贵"的消费理念。研究人员总结说，90后并不是人们印象中只会买名牌、追求时尚的"消费动物"，而是精明实在的"经济人"。他们花钱谨慎，消费合理。

90后与父母的关系比其他任何年代的孩子都亲密。约1/3的90后给父母打了满分。虚拟社会成为90后最习惯的生存空间，38.6%的90后称，自己在网络上有5到10个朋友。90后最喜欢的网站中，社交网站（29.5%）排在第三位，前两位是搜索引擎*和门户网站*。

接受调查的近半数90后表示"我喜欢变化，讨厌一成不变"（46.7%）和"我喜欢与众不同"（43%），多数人"希望被他人关注，成为焦点和名人"，男生中这一比例达到40.3%。同时，75.5%的90后相信自己未来成功的可能性比较大或者非常大。调查发现，90后强调个性、寻求自我认同的价值观。

（743字）

文：记者 方奕晗 有删改原载《中国青年报》2011年12月6日
网络来源：

http://zqb.cyol.com/html/2011-12/06/nw.D110000zgqnb_20111206_1-11.htm

3. 尊敬【zūn jìng】v.; adj. respect, honor; honorable

4. 支配【zhī pèi】v.; n. dominate, govern; control, domination

5. 决策权【jué cè quán】決策權 n. decision-making authority

6. 人均【rén jūn】n. capita, per person, average for individuals

7. 平均【píng jūn】v. n. adj.; average; mean, evenness; medium, median

8. 零花钱【líng huā qián】零花錢 n. pocket money

9. 成【chéng】m. one-tenth, percentage

10. 参与【cān yù】參與 v. participate in, take part in, be a part of

11. 旺盛【wàng shèng】adj. vigorous, exuberant, robust

12. 精明【jīng míng】adj. astute, shrewd, skilled

13. 谨慎【jǐn shèn】謹慎 adj. prudent, careful, cautious

14. 搜索引擎【sōu suǒ yǐn qíng】pn. search engine

15. 门户网站【mén hù wǎng zhàn】門戶網站 pn. (website) portals

16. 一成不变【yì chéng bú biàn】一成不變 unchanged, unchangeable（成语）

17. 自我认同【zì wǒ rèn tóng】自我認同 self-agreement, self-identification（成语）

文化/熟语注释 Culture/idiom notes

*搜索引擎【sōusuǒ yǐnqíng】全球最大的中文搜索引擎是百度【bǎidù】baidu.com. 2000年1月创立于北京中关村，创始人是李彦宏。百度是中国人最常使用的中文网站。

The biggest Chinese search engine in the world is baidu.com. It was built in January 2000 in Zhong Guancun, Beijing, by Yanhong Li. It is the most commonly used Chinese website in China.

*门户网站【ménhù wǎngzhàn】中国的新浪网【xīnlàng wǎng】SINA素有"中文第一门户"之称。新浪网下辖北京新浪、香港新浪、台北新浪、北美新浪等，覆盖全球华人社区，新浪网是全球最大的中文门户网站。另外，人人网【rénrén wǎng】renren.com是中国最有人气的社交网站。它刚建立的时候是一个校内网，主要用户是在校大学生，后来向所有互联网用户开放。它是中国最大、最具影响力的SNS网站。

sina.com.cn is known as "China's first portal." Its branches include Beijing Sina, Hong Kong Sina, Taipei Sina, North America Sina, etc., and it connects Chinese communities across the globe. So far, sina.com.cn is the biggest Chinese portal in the world. In addition, renren.com is a major social network site in China and enjoys immense popularity. It was originally built as a campus social website and users were mainly college students. More recently, it has been opened to all web users, and is currently the biggest and most influential SNS site in China.

语法/语言点注释 Grammar/language points

1 尽管......, 但(是)......; despite ... but ...

> 尽管多数90后还没有到参加工作的年龄,但他们却早就支配着很大的金钱数量。
> In spite of the fact that most children born in the 1990s have not yet reached the age at which they may legally work, they have long been in control of vast amounts of family income (at home).

This structure places an emphasis on the situation introduced by the second simple sentence with 但 (是). The first simple sentence with 尽管 states a situation that is inconsistent with the one in the second simple sentence. This pattern is similar to the pattern "虽然......但是......," but 尽管 carries a stronger tone than 虽然.

Example:

> 剧组准备拍一个新电影，但是女主角不好找，尽管已经在全国各地找了三个月，但合适人选还是没有找到。
> The film crew is preparing for a new movie, but has had trouble finding a leading actress. The crew has been searching all over the country for three months, but has still not found the right one.

2 不管......, 还是......, 都......; regardless (no matter) ..., or ..., all ...

<u>不管</u>是买我个人的东西，<u>还是</u>家里用的东西，一般<u>都</u>听我的。

No matter whether the items to be purchased are for my own personal use or for family use, (my family members) usually follow my suggestion.

This compound sentence places an emphasis on the third simple sentence with 都, indicating that the result will be the same regardless of the differences in conditions mentioned in the previous sentences.

Example:

不管你是百万富翁，还是平民百姓，在法律面前都是平等的。

No matter if you are a millionaire or an ordinary civilian, all people are equal under the law.

3 并不是......, 而是......; not really ... but ...

90后<u>并不是</u>人们印象中只会买名牌、追求时尚的"消费动物"，<u>而是</u>精明实在的"经济人"。

Children born in the 1990s are not really label obsessives and slaves to fashion – a sort of "consuming animal" in many people's estimation – but are actually astute and practical "economists."

The pattern 不是A而是B is used to express the idea of "not A but B," while the word 并 used before 不是 is to strengthen the negation in the first simple sentence.

Example:

海马并不是长在海里的马，而是一种形状奇怪的鱼。

A sea horse is not really a horse that has anything to do with the sea at all, but a fish with a rather strange shape.

阅读理解 Comprehension

一、对错题 True or false?

1 (　)在90后眼里，成功的标志首先是"事业有成"。
2 (　)很多90后有很大一笔压岁钱和零花钱。
3 (　)90后只喜欢买贵的东西，追求名牌。
4 (　)90后跟父母关系不错，父母会跟他们商量买房、买车的事。
5 (　)90后喜欢与众不同，强调个性。

二、翻译题 Translate the following sentences into English (pay particular attention to the words in bold).

1   **近半数**90后表示"我喜欢变化"。

2   有**三成**左右的90后表示父母会和自己共同决定。

3   被称为"鼠标一代"的90后**占**全国总人口的11.7%左右。

三、简答题 Short-answer questions.

1   中国的90后成长的时代背景和社会背景是怎样的？

2   根据这份调查，你觉得中国90后哪些行为与价值观令你担忧？

第十七课　外资企业

Chapter 17　Foreign-owned companies

课文导入 Introduction

　　沃尔玛为什么举办"顾客下午茶"活动？餐饮业大王肯德基为什么卖起了豆浆？在星巴克店里喝碧螺春茶，这种过去听上去不太可能的事，现在也变成了现实。让我们来看一看外资企业在中国的经营之道。

生词注释 Vocabulary

1. 沃尔玛【Wò ěr mǎ】pn. Wal-Mart

2. 肯德基【Kěn dé jī】pn. Kentucky Fried Chicken

3. 星巴克【Xīng bā kè】pn. Starbucks

阅读 A: 沃尔玛的"顾客下午茶" Wal-Mart's "afternoon teatime"

读前准备 Warm-up

一、连线题 Draw a line connecting 中文店名 with the corresponding 英文店名 and 经营类别.

中文店名	英文店名	经营类别
沃尔玛	Starbucks	快餐，炸鸡很有名
肯德基	McDonald's	快餐，汉堡包很有名
星巴克	KFC	咖啡等饮料及一些食品
麦当劳	Wal-Mart	百货商品

二、选择题 Multiple-choice question.

你觉得一家店经营得好，下面哪些方法是重要的？

a) 微笑服务，让顾客感到买东西很快乐

b) 多了解顾客对商店的意见和建议

c) 为顾客省钱，让他们少花钱买到跟别的店一样的东西

d) 在电视上、报纸上多做广告

课文 Reading

在2012年"3.15消费者权益日"来临之际，沃尔玛中国140个城市的370家商场推出"诚心倾听，共建幸福商场"计划，邀请顾客参与沃尔玛传统的"顾客下午茶"活动。

据介绍，"顾客下午茶"是沃尔玛特色的商场与顾客之间的交流活动。活动中，商场向消费者发放调查问卷，了解消费者对商品质量、商品价格、商场服务、购物环境等方面的意见，倾听消费者的心声。问卷回收以后，沃尔玛团队进行分析和整理，对一些问题立即处理，满足消费者的期望和需求。

本报记者采访了北京沃尔玛购物广场朝外店的活动。在现场，有10名消费者获得证书，成为这家店的"监督员"。据经理告诉记者说："这些监督员将为我们的服务和商品提出建议和意见，以便我们改进工作。"

记者了解到，为了改进服务，沃尔玛在卖场中设置了呼叫铃。顾客按呼叫铃后，不到1分钟工作人员就会赶到，提供帮助。卖场员工的手臂上有感应手表，顾客一按铃，他们的手表就会震动，显示哪个区域的顾客需要帮助。

北京各家沃尔玛店举办的下午茶活动可以说是丰富多彩。有的店为顾客开设"食品安全"大讲堂，有的店请顾客参观食品加工过程，有的店举办有奖知识问答，有的店为顾客介绍科学小常识，告诉他们怎么辨别真假商品。

沃尔玛中国公司一名高级管理者说："沃尔玛十分关注'消费与安全'话题。我们的工作与消费者的生活息息相关。这次下午茶活动一方面能够更好地了解顾客对商场的意见和建议，帮助改善商场管理。另一方面，这次活动传播了沃尔玛的'三米微笑*'、'盛情服务'等顾客至上的文化，让顾客感受到沃尔玛是一个'幸福商场'。'为顾客省钱，让他们生活得更美好'是沃尔玛的使命。"

(663字)

文：张鑫　有删改

原载《法制晚报》2012年03月14日

网络来源：

http://www.fawan.com/Article/gghz/2012/03/14/134052149034.html

生词注释 Vocabulary

1. 权益【quán yì】權益 n. rights and interests

2. 倾听【qīng tīng】傾聽 v. listen attentively to

3. 幸福【xìng fú】n.; adj. happiness, blessedness; happy, blessed

4. 调查问卷【diào chá wèn juàn】調查問卷 n. questionnaire, survey

5. 消费者【xiāo fèi zhě】消費者 n. consumer

6. 监督员【jiān dū yuán】監督員 n. supervisor, superintendent

7. 呼叫铃【hū jiào líng】呼叫鈴 n. call bell

8. 感应【gǎn yìng】感應 n. induction, response, reaction

9. 震动【zhèn dòng】震動 v. shake, shock, vibrate

10. 丰富多彩【fēng fù duō cǎi】豐富多彩 rich and varied, rich and colorful（成语）

11. 息息相关【xī xī xiāng guān】息息相關 closely interrelated, closely linked（成语）

12. 传播【chuán bō】傳播 v. propagate, broadcast

13. 顾客至上【gù kè zhì shàng】顧客至上 "The customer is always right"（成语）

文化/熟语注释 Culture/idiom notes

　　*三米微笑原则【sānmǐ wēixiào yuánzé】这是由沃尔玛百货有限公司的创始人山姆•沃尔顿先生传下来的。他告诉员工："每当你在三米以内遇到一位顾客时，请看着他的眼睛与他打招呼，同时询问你能为他做些什么。"

"The three-meter rule" was first introduced by Mr. Sam Walton, founder of the Wal-Mart Cooperative. He told the employees to "Greet and make eye contact with every customer who comes within three meters and then ask what you can do for them."

语法/语言点注释 Grammar/language points

ɪ A, 以便 B; (doing) A, so that/so as to B

> 这些监督员将为我们的服务和商品提出建议和意见，以便我们改进工作。
> These inspectors will provide suggestions and advice about our service and products so as to help us improve our work.

The structure is used to express "doing A is for the purpose of B." 以便 is used at the beginning of the second simple sentence to introduce the purpose of doing A.

Example:

> 我喜欢把经常要用的文件放在电脑的"桌面"上，以便很快地打开和查看。
> I like to put the regularly used files on the desktop of my computer, so that (I) can open and check them more conveniently.

阅读理解 Comprehension

一、填空题 Fill in the blanks with the phrases provided.

　　期望和需求　　　调查问卷　　　建议和意见　　　分析和整理

ɪ　活动中，商场向消费者发放_____。
2　问卷回收以后，沃尔玛团队立即进行_____。
3　沃尔玛商场愿意满足消费者的_____。
4　沃尔玛商场请监督员给他们提出_____。

二、填空题 Fill in the blanks based on content from the chapter.

　　北京各家沃尔玛店举办的下午茶活动可以说是丰富多彩。有的店为顾客开设_____，有的店请顾客参观_____，有的店举办_____，有的店为顾客介绍_____，告诉他们怎么辨别真假商品。

三、简答题 Short-answer questions.

1 顾客按呼叫铃后，工作人员为什么会知道？

2 据沃尔玛的一位高级管理者说，"顾客下午茶"活动有什么作用和意义？

根据提示完成课文结构图 Complete the text structure map according to the clues provided

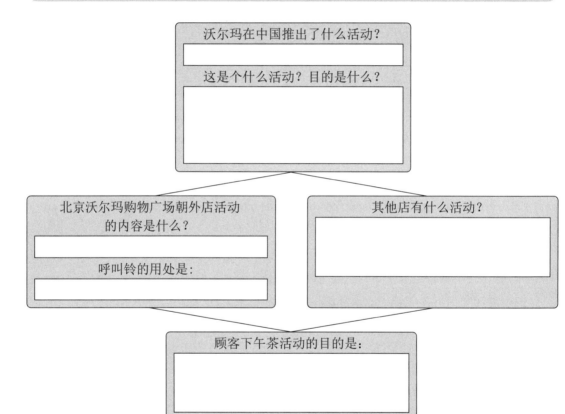

沃尔玛在中国推出了什么活动？

这是个什么活动？目的是什么？

北京沃尔玛购物广场朝外店活动
的内容是什么？

呼叫铃的用处是：

其他店有什么活动？

顾客下午茶活动的目的是：

讨论 Discussion

1 沃尔玛的下午茶活动丰富多彩，如果你是顾客，你想参加哪一项活动，为什么？

2 除了沃尔玛，你最喜欢哪家百货商场？你为什么喜欢那家店？他们的服务有些什么
特色？

阅读 B: 外资餐饮本土化 The localization of foreign-owned restaurants

课文 Reading

昨天早上，记者走访了多家肯德基餐厅，发现肯德基的豆浆比较受欢迎。"平时我早餐吃烧饼加咖啡，但总觉得有点儿不搭调。"肯德基的老顾客小何告诉记者："这次可以把咖啡改成豆浆了。"

肯德基到中国以后，先后推出了老北京鸡肉卷、油条、烧饼等本土化食品。不久前，肯德基在上海还推出了米饭产品。这次肯德基卖豆浆说明了它进一步中国化的努力，因为只有"产品去适应市场，而不是市场去适应产品"。

连锁咖啡业的老大星巴克也开始卖茶了。昨天，美国咖啡连锁企业星巴克正式宣布，在中国推出9款茶品。在星巴克店里喝着碧螺春，这种过去听上去不太可能的事，现在变成了现实。谈到推出茶产品，星巴克的负责人表示，他们做了谨慎的市场调查。

"以前很多顾客到星巴克店里休闲、聊天，他们都喜欢星巴克的环境，但这些顾客不喝咖啡，也不喜欢太甜的饮料。由于缺少可选择的饮品，我们损失了很多顾客。所以经过市场调查，我们推出了能被更多消费者接受的茶。茶是中国的传统饮品，茶在中国有很大的市场潜力。"

肯德基卖豆浆，星巴克卖茶，这并不是说洋餐饮在中国受冷落。采访中，一名在星巴克买茶喝的王小姐告诉记者："听说星巴克卖茶了，就和朋友来尝一尝，味道不错！但是毕竟感觉星巴克不是喝茶的地方，以后还是会选择购买咖啡的。"另一位在肯德基给自己和儿子买早点的女士也说："我肯定不会经常来肯德基买豆浆，因为豆浆并不是非到肯德基才能喝到。"

生词注释 Vocabulary

1. 豆浆【dòu jiāng】豆漿 n. soymilk

2. 烧饼【shāo bǐng】燒餅 n. baked sesame-seed flat cake

3. 搭调【dā diào】搭調 adj. in tune

4. 鸡肉卷【jī ròu juǎn】雞肉卷 n. chicken wrap

5. 油条【yóu tiáo】油條 n. long, deep-fried, twisted dough sticks

6. 连锁【lián suǒ】連鎖 v.; n. chain

7. 款【kuǎn】m. kind, pattern, type

8. 碧螺春【Bì luó chūn】n. Biluochun green tea

9. 损失【sǔn shī】損失 v.; n. lose; loss

10. 潜力【qián lì】潜力 n. latent capability, potential, potentiality

11. 冷落【lěng luò】v.; adj. treat coldly; deserted, desolate

12. 肯定【kěn dìng】v.; adj.; adv. affirm; positive, definite; definitely, undoubtedly

事实上，洋餐饮在中国很受欢迎，拥有大批固定的客户群，以城市白领和中高档收入阶层家庭为主，虽然如此，洋餐的本土化可以吸引那些喜爱中国传统饮食的顾客，使生意<u>更上一层楼</u>*。

(662字)

文：记者　张莹　门莉娜　见习记者　苑冰　有删改

原载之一《每日新报》2010年3月9日

原载之二《每日新报》2010年3月30日

网络来源：

http://epaper.tianjinwe.com/mrxb/mrxb/2010-03/09/content_23157.htm

http://epaper.tianjinwe.com/mrxb/mrxb/2010-03/30/content_37369.htm

13. 批【pī】m. batch

14. 固定【gù dìng】v.; adj. fix; fixed, regular

15. 更上一层楼【gēng shàng yì céng lóu】更上一層樓 scale new heights, attain a yet higher goal（成语）

文化/熟语注释 Culture/idiom notes

*更上一层楼【gèng shàng yì céng lóu】这句话出自唐代诗句"欲穷千里目，更上一层楼"。原意是要想看得更远，就要登得更高。它的引申义是在已经取得的成绩的基础上再进一步提高。

更上一层楼 comes from a line of a Tang poem: "To enjoy a grander sight, climb to a greater height," which means if you want to see farther, you should climb to a higher point up the mountain. The embedded meaning of this expression is that people should always strive to improve on their current achievements.

语法/语言点注释 Grammar/language points

1 非……才……; have to/must ... then ...

豆浆并不是<u>非</u>到肯德基<u>才</u>能喝到。
You do not have to go to KFC to have soymilk.

The word 非 is used to introduce a necessary condition and 才 is used to indicate a result under that condition.

Example:

中国菜并不是非到中国去才能吃到。
You don't have to go to China to enjoy Chinese food.

阅读理解 Comprehension

一、选择题 Multiple-choice questions.

1　根据课文内容，肯德基在中国推出了哪些本土化的食品？

　　a) 豆浆　　　b) 老北京鸡肉卷　　c) 油条　　d) 烧饼　　e) 米饭

2　根据课文内容，星巴克为什么在中国推出了9款茶品？

　　a) 有的中国顾客不喝咖啡
　　b) 茶是中国的传统饮品，有很大的市场潜力
　　c) 星巴克不想损失顾客
　　d) 洋餐饮在中国受冷落，只能卖茶

3　根据课文内容，这位记者采访了以下哪些人物？

　　a) 肯德基的老顾客小何
　　b) 星巴克负责人
　　c) 一位在星巴克买茶喝的王小姐
　　d) 一位在肯德基给自己和儿子买早点的女士

二、填表题 Fill in the blanks based on content from this chapter.

记者采访的人物	被采访人的观点
肯德基的老顾客小何	
星巴克负责人	
一位在星巴克买茶喝的王小姐	
一位在肯德基给自己和儿子买早点的女士	

第十八课　城市在生长

Chapter 18　Urban growth

课文导入 Introduction	生词注释 Vocabulary
据报告，中国是世界上城市化速度最快的国家。可是，当一座座新城崛起的同时，越来越多的"老地方"消失了，传统文化记忆也流失了。那么旧城与新城到底能不能共存呢？	1. 崛起【jué qǐ】v. rise abruptly, rise as a political force 2. 消失【xiāo shī】v. disappear, vanish, dissolve

阅读 A: 郑各庄的城市化进程 The urbanization of Zhengge village

读前准备 Warm-up

一、你知道下面这些词语是什么意思吗？What is the meaning of the following words?

a) 城市　　b) 农村　　c) 工人　　d) 农民　　e) 工业　　f) 农业
g) 市　　　h) 区　　　i) 乡　　　j) 村庄　　k) 城市化　　l) 工业化

二、选择题 Multiple-choice questions.

下面哪三个数字是相同的？Which three of the following list are the same?

a) 13,000　　b) 一万三千　　c) 1.3万　　d) 1,300

三、问答题 Short-answer questions.

1　　你能想象1970年代的中国是什么样的吗？

2　　你喜欢农村还是城市？为什么？

课文 Reading

　　美国东部时间26日下午，哈佛大学肯尼迪政府学院举行了一场特别的讨论课。北京市昌平区郑各庄村委会主任黄福水走进哈佛课堂，讲述郑各庄的城市化进程。

　　学生们首先了解了这样一组数据：郑各庄是典型的城乡结合部，现有568户人家，1500口人。这里1998年开始旧村改造，进入高速发展期。过去13年间，村里自营实体公司由1个发展到35个；产业工人由300多人增至1.3万人；农民人均年收入从3100元提高到4.55万元。

　　黄福水说，郑各庄过去二十年进行了一场"造城运动"，不过不是常见的由房地产商收购土地的模式，而是走"主动城市化"的道路，即在农业办产业，把农村变为产业村，在经济规模达到一定程度后再升级为"服务村"。今后十年，郑各庄希望将养老产业的比重提高到全村产业结构的三分之一，以吸引城里人来农村养老。

　　邀请黄福水来哈佛作报告的是肯尼迪学院的托尼·赛奇先生。他是一个"中国通*"，早在上世纪70年代中期就去过中国，此后一直将中国作为重要研究对象。赛奇先生认为，郑各庄过去二十年的发展案例不但能让学生们了解中国的农村城市化进程，更帮助学生了解中国从一个相对落后的农业国如何一步步实现工业化，并进一步走向服务产业的发展模式。

　　为什么哈佛肯尼迪学院这么重视中国案例研究？赛奇说，十二年前，刚来学院的时候，对中国感兴趣的同事只是少数，但现在大多数人都关注中国的发展，因此有必要主动开展中国案例研究。这些案例不但帮助人们了解"中国模式"，而且在全球化议题上也有重要的研究意义。

（604字）
文：新华社记者孙浩、郭曼桐　有删改
原载《人民日报》海外版　2012年4月28日
网络来源：
http://news.xinhuanet.com/society/2012-04/28/c_123050673.htm

生词注释 Vocabulary

1. 肯尼迪【Kěn ní dí】pn. Kennedy (Harvard John F. Kennedy School of Government)

3. 庄【zhuāng】莊 n. village, town

4. 村委会【cūn wěi huì】村委會 n. village committee

5. 自营【zì yíng】自營 v. self-run, self-support

6. 房地产【fáng dì chǎn】房地產 n. real estate

7. 模式【mó shì】n. model, pattern

8. 即【jí】adv. namely

9. 产业【chǎn yè】產業 n. industry, estate, property

10. 案例【àn lì】n. cases

11. 关注【guān zhù】關注 v.; n. follow (an issue) closely, pay close attention to; concern

文化/熟语注释 Culture/idiom notes

　　*中国通【Zhōngguó tōng】是指称那些能说汉语的非常熟悉中国情况的外国人，特别是那些对中国的政治、文化、经济、生活多方面深入了解的外籍专家、学者。他们也往往也被称为"汉学家"或"中国问题专家"。中国通是一个比较通俗的指称。

中国通 refers to a person who is not Chinese but who, nevertheless, is very familiar with all aspects of Chinese society including the language. And it especially refers to those sinologists or Chinese studies experts who have a good knowledge of Chinese politics, culture, economics, and lifestyle. 中国通 is a colloquial expression.

语法/语言点注释 Grammar/language points

1 以......; in order to (for the purpose of) ...

> 今后十年，郑各庄希望将养老产业的比重提高到全村产业结构的三分之一，以吸引城里人来农村养老。
>
> In the next ten years, Zhengge village wants to increase the local industry of constructing residential homes for senior citizens to be one-third of the entire village's economic base in order to attract city retirees to the village.

The word 将 has a meaning similar to 把. The second simple sentence led by 以 is to introduce a target or a goal.

Example:

> 城市广场上经常有商家举行一些义卖活动，他们将全部收入捐给红十字会，以帮助有困难的家庭。
>
> There is often a charity sale by companies at the city square; the takings are all given to the Red Cross in order to help low-income families.

2 将......作为......; take ... as ...

> 他是一个"中国通"，早在上世纪70年代中期就去过中国，此后一直将中国作为重要研究对象。
>
> He is an expert on China who first visited the country as early as the 1970s and has regarded China as an important subject of study ever since.

The word 将 is a preposition that is similar to 把. 作为 means "regard as," "treat as."

Example:

> 我的导师建议我将中国的城市化问题作为我的毕业论文研究方向。
>
> My adviser suggests that I consider the issue of Chinese urbanization as my dissertation topic.

阅读理解 Comprehension

一、选择题 Multiple-choice questions.

1 关于郑各庄，下面哪些说法是对的？

    a) 郑各庄在北京市昌平区   b) 郑各庄位于城乡结合部

    c) 房地产商收购了郑各庄的土地   d) 郑各庄走了主动城市化的道路

2 关于托尼·赛奇先生，下面哪些说法是错的？

    a) 他邀请黄福水来哈佛作报告

    b) 他1970年就去过中国

    c) 他把中国作为重要研究对象，他是一个"中国通"

    d) 他和他的同事十二年前并不关注中国

二、翻译题 Translate the following sentence into English (pay particular attention to the underlined words).

过去13年间，村里自营实体公司<u>由</u>1个发展<u>到</u>35个；产业工人<u>由</u>300人增<u>至</u>1.3万人；农民人均年收入<u>从</u>3100元提高<u>到</u>4.55万元。

三、简答题 Short-answer questions.

1 赛奇先生认为郑各庄的发展案例能给学生提供哪方面的知识？

2 赛奇先生认为研究中国案例有什么重要的意义？

根据提示完成课文结构图 Complete the text structure map according to the clues provided

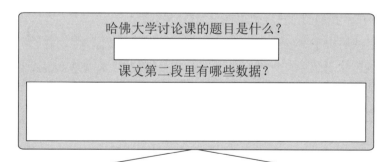

讨论 Discussion

1   郑各庄希望发展养老产业，吸引城里人来农村养老。请问你觉得像郑各庄这样的农村，有哪些方面能吸引城里人来养老？

2   在你的国家有没有一个地方像郑各庄一样，发生了很大的变化？请举例说明。

阅读 B: 保持住老城 Maintaining the Old Town

课文 Reading

近年来，在快速城市化的过程中，越来越多的"老地方"开始在人们眼前消失。有时和朋友们聊天时说起一些小时候常去的地方，就会发现，这些地方好像都不在了，只存在于我们的记忆里了。那时候就特别惆怅。

北京是一座有800年历史的古城，然而现在古都风貌已越来越难看到了。我从小在北京的胡同*里长大，可是小时候印象中的高台阶、守门石狮、影壁*、四合院*、木地板屋，很多都消失了，连老邻居也都不见了。

现在人们的居住条件、生活条件比以前有了很大的改善，但许多人几十年前的生活印迹却只能在老照片中看到，只能在梦境和记忆中重现。"旧城改造"太快了啊，再过二三十年，我们的子孙后代也许只能在博物馆、教科书中了解老城历史了。

在飞快的城市化进程中，一个个老城区、古乡镇被一座座现代化的新城代替了。可是在我看来，老城区、古乡镇，是古老文明的重要载体，它们的消失，对我们民族的历史文化甚至人类文明来说都是一种巨大的损失。

城市现代化和传统文化形成了矛盾，怎么解决这个问题呢？其实，旧城与新城之间并不矛盾，它们完全可以共存。在一些欧洲发达国家，大城市中都完好地保留着传统的街道与建筑。这些传统街区与建筑的保留，并不妨碍这些城市成为国际化都市，外地游客来这些城市

生词注释 Vocabulary

1. 惆怅【chóu chàng】惆悵 adj. disconsolate, melancholy

2. 风貌【fēng mào】風貌 n. style and features, manner

3. 胡同【hú tòng】衚衕 n. lane, alley, bystreet

4. 台阶【tái jiē】臺階 n. staircase, steps

5. 石狮【shí shī】石獅 n. stone lions

6. 影壁【yǐng bì】n. screen wall

7. 印迹【yìn jì】印跡 n. mark, print

8. 梦境【mèng jìng】夢境 n. dream, dreamland

9. 载体【zǎi tǐ】載體 n. carrier, knowledge or information

10. 妨碍【fáng'ài】妨礙 v.; n. hinder, hamper, obstruct; hindrance, obstruction

旅游看的正是传统的街道与建筑，而不是<u>摩天大楼</u>。一座城市，如果都是<u>高楼大厦</u>，传统文化记忆就会失去很多。可以这么说，许多传统文化里的风俗习惯都是在老城区里保留下来的，老城区不在了，这些东西就难以保留下来。所以，我们在现代化进程中，应该注意保持城市的传统特色。

11. 摩天大楼【mó tiān dà lóu】
摩天大樓 n. skyscraper

12. 高楼大厦【gāo lóu dà shà】
高樓大廈 high buildings and large mansions（成语）

（635字）

编写：虞农

参考材料来源：

1. 《人民日报》2011年1月18日《保卫老城》作者赵蓓蓓
2. 《人民日报》2011年1月18日《忧伤的旧城 呼和浩特旧城改造很"彻底"》作者张宏
3. 《新华日报》2008年10月23日《记忆定格怀旧影像》
   记者 伍巧玲 董晨

文化/熟语注释 Culture/idiom notes

*胡同【hútòng】胡同，是北京的一大特色。"胡同"即小巷，南方人称为"弄堂"。胡同是指主要街道之间的比较小的街道，住着一户户人家。

胡同 are a feature of Beijing residential housing areas meaning "alleys." In southern China, people call them 弄堂【lòngtáng】. It mainly refers to the small alleys in which households sit cheek by jowl on both sides.

*影壁【yǐngbì】影壁，也称照壁，古称萧墙，影壁的作用既是遮挡外人视线，也是阻挡鬼怪。它立于大门内，也可位于大门外。影壁上有很多精巧的吉祥图样的雕饰，是北京四合院大门内外的重要装饰壁面。

影壁 is also known as 照壁【zhàobì】, or 萧墙【xiāoqiáng】in ancient times. It is a type of wall used as a means of keeping away from other people's prying eyes and warding off attacks of ghosts or evil spirits. It usually stands inside or outside the courtyard house. 影壁 is usually decorated with elaborate paintings or murals, so it is the main decorative wall of the 四合院.

*四合院【sìhéyuàn】四合院是中国华北地区的民用住宅，是一种四四方方或者是长方形的院落，一家一户，住在一个封闭式的院子里。北京的胡同中有数不清的四合院建筑。

四合院 is a type of residential house in north China; it consists of a square or rectangular courtyard surrounded by a house in which one family lives. There are innumerable courtyard houses all connected by alleys in Beijing.

语法/语言点注释 Grammar/language points

1 在......过程中......; in the process of...

近年来，在快速城市化的过程中，越来越多的"老地方"开始在人们眼前消失。
In recent years, during the process of rapid urbanization, more and more old places
    have started to disappear.

This pattern is used to describe the process or scope of an event or a situation.

Example:

科学研究表明，动物在进化过程中，大脑的重量不断增加。
Studies in science have indicated that, during the process of animal evolution, the
    weight of the brain has been increasing.

2 对......来说; as far as.../as for.../to...

它们的消失，对我们民族的历史文化甚至人类文明来说都是一种巨大的损失。
Their disappearance is a great loss to our nation's history and culture, and perhaps
    even to the civilization of the whole world.

This structure is used to introduce a certain or particular situation/event relevant to
the topic.

Example:

对一个用惯了左手写字的人来说，用右手写字很难。
It is hard for a habitual left-handed writer to write with their right hand.

3 正是A, 而不是B; it is (precisely) A, but not B

外地游客来这些城市旅游看的正是传统的街道与建筑，而不是摩天大楼。
It is precisely the traditional streets and architecture that the tourists come to see;
    definitely not the skyscrapers.

This structure is used to confirm the information introduced by 正是. The emphasis is
placed on the first simple sentence. 正 as an adverb in the sentence is used for emphasis.

Example:

这个电影吸引人的正是演员真实自然的表演，而不是那些用现代技术合成的
特技效应。
It is precisely the real and natural performance of the actors that attracted the
    audience, not the special effects synthesized by modern technology.

阅读理解 Comprehension

一、选择题 Multiple-choice questions.

1　根据课文内容，作者感到惆怅是什么原因？

　　a) 他不想长大，因为小时候的生活很美好
　　b) 朋友越来越少了，只有老邻居还在
　　c) 往事越来越模糊，在记忆中消失了
　　d) "城市化" 太快了，一些 "老地方" 都消失了

2　根据课文内容，下面哪个观点作者不会同意？

　　a) 老城区、古乡镇，是古老文明的重要载体
　　b) 老城区保留了传统文化里的风俗习惯
　　c) 老城的消失，对一个民族的历史文化来说是一种巨大的损失
　　d) 建设国际化现代大都市，不得不拆除旧的街区和建筑

二、填空题 Fill in the blanks, choosing from the words provided.

保持　　摩天大楼　　街道　　建筑　　特色　　消失

　　外地游客来这些城市旅游看的正是传统的____与____，而不是_____。一座城市，如果都是高楼大厦，传统文化记忆就会失去很多。我们在现代化进程中，应该注意____城市的传统_____。

三、自由回答 Open-ended question.

你去过北京吗？你听说过北京吗？请你用下面的词汇来谈谈北京。

古城　　古都　　老城区　　胡同　　四合院　　街道　　建筑　　高楼大厦

第十九课　改变中的农村

Chapter 19　Villages undergoing change

课文导入 Introduction

　　中国的农村在环境上、经济上都发生着巨大的变化，这些变化靠农民自己的劳动，也靠新一代有知识有才能的<u>村官</u>做出的努力。农村的<u>深刻</u>变化，还表现在农村的习俗、人们<u>精神面貌</u>、思想观念上的改变。

生词注释 Vocabulary

1. 村官【cūn guān】n. village official

2. 深刻【shēn kè】adj. deep, profound

3. 精神面貌【jīng shén miàn mào】phr. spiritual outlook

阅读 A: 我见证了农村新变化 My witnessing of the changes in the village

读前准备 Warm-up

一、选择题 Multiple-choice questions

1　"农村热闹的场景与城市广场上出现的几乎没两样"，你认为没两样是什么意思？

　　a) 一样　　b) 不一样

2　大学生放弃在大城市找工作而回到农村老家，你认为可能是什么原因？

　　a) 大城市生活压力太大了，没有农村好
　　b) 农村虽然比城市落后，可是有自己的家人，有亲情
　　c) 回农村老家的大学生是为了用自己的知识与才能改变农村，让农村更美好
　　d) 农村村官这个队伍非常需要年轻的大学生

课文 Reading

2008年7月，我从一名大学生成为一名大学生村官。三年过去了，我不仅亲身感受到农村各方面发生的巨大变化，也为我们大学生村官这个群体在这些变化中做出的努力感到骄傲。

这些年农村在经济上发生了翻天覆地的变化。如今的农民不再只是种地了，而是到企业上班，甚至自己创业。经济宽裕了，房子也建得越来越好，有线电视、热水器、电脑，这些城里人家中有的，现在农民家里也都有了。

经济宽裕了，随之而来的，就是农民们有了新的精神文化需求。如今，一到下午，老人们就自发地聚在一起，唱唱扬州小调，或者下两盘棋；夜晚，找块空地，放个录音机，大妈们也开开心心地跳起舞来，热闹的场景，与城市广场上出现的几乎没两样。

"路更通畅了，水更清了，环境卫生更好了"成为这些年农民们的切身感受。"雨天一身泥，晴天一身灰"，过去，农村交通十分不方便。但现在，硬质化道路几乎通到了家家户户门口，农民不仅出行方便了，不少人家还开起了小汽车。

垃圾问题在农村曾经是个老大难*问题，以前没有垃圾池，有了垃圾就往家附近的小塘小沟里一扔，而现在村里建起了供村民使用的垃圾池，我们村还摆放了垃圾桶，每天有人清理。同时，各村都搞起了河塘清淤工程，河塘里的水又变得像我们小时候那样清澈了。

作为一名大学生村官，我不仅亲身感受到这些年农村的变化，更亲身参与到整个农村面貌的改变之中。三年前，我放弃在省城找工作，回老家当了一名村官，当时很多人不理解。但现在，我们这个队伍越来越壮大。我们这些年轻的大学生村官，不仅改变了农村干部的知识层次和年龄结构，还努力给农村带来了良好的变化，让更多的农民走上富裕之路。

(661字)

文：何瑞琳　有删改

原载《扬州日报》2011年8月11日

网络来源：

http://www.yznews.com.cn/yzwzt/2011-08/11/content_3687972.htm

生词注释 Vocabulary

1. 骄傲【jiāo ào】驕傲 v.; n.; adj. be proud of; pride; arrogant, conceited

2. 翻天覆地【fān tiān fù dì】enormous changes（成语）

3. 宽裕【kuān yù】寬裕 adj. well-to-do, be comfortably off, plenty

4. 随之而来【suí zhī ér lái】phr. 隨之而來 following upon

5. 小调【xiǎo diào】小調 n. ditty, tune, minor (for music)

6. 通畅【tōng chàng】通暢 adj. unobstructed, easy and smooth

7. 切身【qiè shēn】adj. personal (experience/understanding)

8. 感受【gǎn shòu】v.; n. feel; experience

9. 泥【ní】n. wet mud

10. 灰【huī】n.; adj. ash, dust

11. 硬质化【yìng zhì huà】硬質化 v.; adj. harden, stiffen; hard, stiff

12. 垃圾【lā jī】n. garbage, junk, trash

13. 塘【táng】n. pool, pond

14. 沟【gōu】溝 n. ditch, waterway

15. 清淤【qīng yū】清淤 vo. desilt, desilting

16. 清澈【qīng chè】adj. limpid, crystal clear

17. 层次【céng cì】層次 n. level (of knowledge); levels

文化/熟语注释 Culture/idiom notes

*老大难【lǎo dà nán】是一个俗语。原指大龄青年男女找不到对象，婚姻成为问题。现在也泛指任何棘手的事情，形容问题长期存在而难以解决。

老大难 is an idiom. It originally referred to young people who were having problems finding a date or getting married. Nowadays it is also used as a general reference to any issue that is tough to handle, or a problem that has existed for a while and is difficult to resolve.

语法/语言点注释 Grammar/language points

1 不仅......，更......; not only ..., even ...

> 作为一名大学生村官，我<u>不仅</u>亲身感受到这些年农村的变化，<u>更</u>亲身参与到整个农村面貌的改变之中。
>
> As a village official with a college degree, I didn't merely experience the changes in the village through these years, but, more important, I also took part in the reformation of the whole village.

The structure 不仅......，更...... is a progressive pattern placing emphasis on the part introduced by 更, which means "even more."

Example:

> 作为一个企业的管理者，他不仅仅要了解员工的情况，更要随时掌握市场的信息。
>
> As the manager of the company, not only does he need to know the employee situation; more important, he has to keep track of market information.

阅读理解 Comprehension

一、选择题 Multiple-choice questions.

1 根据课文内容，以前的农村是怎样的？

   a) 交通十分不方便
   b) 坏境很不好，雨天一身泥，晴天一身灰
   c) 垃圾就往家附近的小塘小沟里一扔
   d) 农村干部的知识层次很高

2 根据课文内容，现在的农村是怎样的？

   a) 交通很方便，道路几乎通到家门口
   b) 农村建了垃圾池，有的村摆了垃圾桶
   c) 房子建得越来越好，农民家中的设备跟城里人一样
   d) 夜晚，农村人到城市广场上去跳舞

二、填空题 Fill in the blanks, choosing from the words provided.

改变　　变化　　富裕　　宽裕　　面貌　　场景

1　年轻的大学生当村官，＿＿＿了农村干部的知识层次和年龄结构。

2　改革开放以后中国很多农民走上了＿＿＿之路。

3　以前农村的道路和环境卫生都比较落后，而现在农村的＿＿＿完全不一样了。

三、简答题 Short-answer questions.

1　经济宽裕以后，农民们有了哪些文化活动？

2　根据课文内容，你觉得为什么三年前"我"回老家当村官，很多人不理解？

根据提示完成课文结构图 Complete the text structure map according to the clues provided

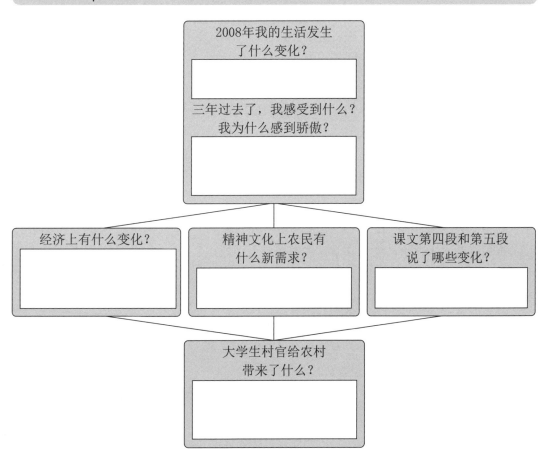

讨论 Discussion

I 　　　课文中这名大学生，毕业的时候放弃在省城找工作，回老家当了一名村官，他的做法跟一般人很不一样。那么你呢？你大学毕业后找工作，有什么跟一般人不同的就业想法吗？

阅读 B: 农村习俗的变迁 Changes to countryside customs

课文 Reading

　　前几日，空闲时间回农村老家看了看，和村里的百姓一聊天，感觉自己像老外*似的，农村现在的习俗已经变得越来越陌生了。

　　一是农村问候语的变迁。过去的农村人早上一见面，会问你一句：吃饭了没？晚上见了你，会问一句：喝汤了没？吃，对于当时的农村太重要了，早上能够吃上饭的人家，说明这个家庭生活是有保障的。晚上问喝汤了没有，是因为晚上不干农活，一般的家庭就吃汤汤水水的东西，节省粮食。现在的农村人见了面，问候语变成了：在哪儿做生意？赚钱不？因为现在农民根本不愁吃饭，农村人进城赚钱的很多，只要人勤快、能干，不愁挣不到钱。

　　二是农村人办喜事*的变迁。过去农村年轻人办喜事，那可真是"大"事。女方家常常希望嫁闺女多挣点礼品，要求男方送见面礼、看好礼、定亲礼、要亲礼、娶亲礼。男方家一般来说都得费很大的力气才能娶亲。现在的情况怎样呢？无论是同学之间，还是外出打工时认识的朋友，如果喜欢上对方，双方就会选个时间把婚礼办了。有的富裕一些的男方会给女方家人一张存款单，女方经济条件好的也会陪嫁一些电器和生活用品。

　　三是农民处理家庭关系方式的变迁。过去农村家庭子女比较多，而且多数不富裕，父母的养老问题常常在

生词注释 Vocabulary

1. 老外【lǎo wài】 n. foreigner

2. 保障【bǎo zhàng】 v.; n. protect (life, property, rights, etc.) from damage or violation; guarantee

3. 节省【jié shěng】節省 v. economize, save

4. 勤快【qín kuài】 adj. diligent, hard working

5. 愁【chóu】 v.; n. worry; sorrow

6. 嫁【jià】 v. (a woman) marry to (a man)

7. 闺女【guī nü】閨女 n. girl, daughter

8. 娶【qǔ】 v. (a man) marry to (a woman), take a wife

9. 富裕【fù yù】 adj. well-to-do, well off, rich and prosperous

10. 存款单【cún kuǎn dān】存款單 n. deposit slip, certificate of deposit

几个子女之间推来推去。当时农村最流行的办法是每个儿子家<u>轮流</u>负责父母的吃饭、穿衣问题。女儿一般都是一年给父母做几件衣服。

现在的农村年轻人结婚后，少则生一个，多则生两个孩子。他们自己外出打工、做生意，家中的一切就交给了农村的父母。他们在城市挣了钱寄给父母，让老人好好照顾家和<u>抚养</u>孩子。

农村老家的这些习俗变迁，让我感受到了农村改革开放三十年来的深刻变化。

(661字)

文：华安 有删改

原载《天中晚报》2008年12月29日

网络来源：

http://www.zmdnews.cn/Info.aspx?ModelId=1&Id=237313

11. 轮流【lún liú】輪流 v. rotate, do sth in turn, take turns, alternate

12. 抚养【fǔ yǎng】撫養 v.; n. foster, raise, bring up; fostering, raising, bringing up

文化/熟语注释 Culture/idiom notes

*老外【lǎowài】是对外国人的通称。中国人习惯称呼朋友同事为老张、老王、老李、老赵等。改革开放后，中国人与外国人的接触越来越多，就按中国人的习俗，称他们为"老外"。

老外 is a general term used to refer to a foreigner, meaning "elder foreigner." Chinese people used to call friends and colleagues elder Zhang, elder Wang, elder Li, elder Zhao, etc. After opening up to the outside world, Chinese people started to contact people in foreign countries more and more. They followed the Chinese tradition and referred to foreigners as 老外.

*办喜事【bànxǐshì】办喜事是中国的传统和民俗。中国传统思想认为婚姻是人生的头等大事。在农村，历来一家办喜事，全村都出动。大红双喜字是办喜事的象征，门上、窗上、树上、墙上以及接送新娘的车上，处处贴满了大红双喜字，象征着双喜临门，成双成对。

Traditionally, wedding preparations must follow certain procedures stipulated by local customs. Chinese people regard marriage as the most important event in one's life. In rural areas and the countryside, it is a tradition that if there is a wedding in one family, the whole village will come out to help and celebrate. The double happiness character 囍 is the symbol for "happy wedding" and is pasted on doors, windows, trees, walls, and the cars that come to pick up the bride. It symbolizes the arrival of a doubly joyful event.

语法/语言点注释 Grammar/language points

1 像 . . . . . . 似的; like . . .

> 感觉自己像老外似的，农村现在的习俗已经变得越来越陌生了。
> I feel like a foreigner. The traditions of the village are becoming more and more unfamiliar to me.

This structure is normally used in a figurative sentence meaning "like/similar to."

Example:

> 我的哥哥是个温和的人，可最近他竟然喝酒闹事，像换了个人似的。
> My elder brother is a gentle person, but recently he has been drinking and fighting; he is like a totally different person.

2 . . . . . . 则 . . . . . . 则 . . . . . . ; . . . (then) . . . (then) . . .

> 现在的农村年轻人结婚后，少则生一个，多则生两个孩子。
> For married young people nowadays in the village, at the least they (then) give birth to one child, and at the most they (then) give birth to two children.

The word 则 here is a conjunction, i.e. it connects the subject and predicate in the sentence.

Example:

> 如果违反交通规则，轻则罚款，重则吊销驾照，你就不能开车了。
> If you violate traffic regulations and it is not too serious, you (then) get a ticket issuing a fine; if it is a serious offense, your driver's license (then) is revoked; you may no longer drive.

阅读理解 Comprehension

一、填表题 Fill in the blanks based on content from the chapter.

问候语的变迁 change of greeting custom	办喜事的变迁 change of wedding custom	处理家庭关系的变迁 change of handling family issues custom
以前 　1. 早上问_____。 　2. 晚上问_____。	以前 男方得_____ _____。	以前 　1. 父母的养老问题常常_____。 　2. 最流行的做法是_____。
现在 　见面了问_____。	现在 　1. 男方会_____ 　2. 女方会_____	现在 　1. 现在的农村年轻人_____。 　2. 农村的父母在家_____。

二、填空题 Fill in the blanks, choosing from the words provided.

新郎　　新娘　　订婚　　结婚　　嫁　　娶　　婚礼

　　今天晚上我跟朋友去参加了一场_____。主持人热情地请____和____介绍了相识、相爱的过程。主持人问新郎：“你愿意_____她吗？”然后又问新娘：“你愿意_____给他吗？”大家高声大笑，真诚地祝这对新人_____以后生活幸福美满。

第二十课　中国少数民族风采

Chapter 20　Fascinating Chinese minorities

课文导入 Introduction	生词注释 Vocabulary
中国有55个少数民族。藏族主要居住在青藏高原*，这些年很多藏民从事旅游业，接待来自全国各地的游客。在中国，有一首人人会唱的歌，"高高的兴安岭，一片大森林，森林里住着勇敢的鄂伦春……"。现代的藏人和鄂伦春人的生活会有什么样的变化呢？请大家读一读下面的课文吧。	1. 藏族【Zàng zú】pn. Tibetan minority group 2. 鄂伦春【È lún chūn】鄂倫春 pn. Oroqen minority group

阅读 A: 藏民家庭旅馆 The Tibetan family inn

读前准备 Warm-up

一、简答题 Short-answer questions.

1　Tibet（西藏），你一定听说过吧？请你谈谈你对西藏的了解。

2　比较下面三种旅游住宿方式，请谈谈你去不同地方旅游的时候将怎么选择不同的住宿方式？为什么？

　　a) 住酒店客房　　b) 住家庭旅馆　　c) 住野外帐篷

课文 Reading

官方统计显示，2010年，来西藏林芝地区这个藏语中的"太阳宝座"旅行的人已达152万人次。老藏民唐次仁的家就在林芝地区的扎西岗村。

2001年的"五一"长假，唐次仁第一次在自住的藏式老房里接待了一批从内地来的游客。这位藏族农民敏锐地感到"家庭旅馆"是生财之道，从此他就做起了这一行。到2010年，唐次仁一年就接待六、七百位客人，收入约人民币六、七万元。

这个新兴的产业得到了政府在政策上和资金上的扶持。唐次仁2003年从县政府得到4万元的资助，在老房里装修起一个有现代生活被褥、床铺的标准化房间。后来，扎西岗村22户经营家庭旅馆的农户得到总共98万人民币的贴息贷款，用于改建卫浴设备。扎西岗村成为远近闻名的家庭旅馆村。

唐次仁带记者参观2006年在自家院内加建的一栋两层高的小楼。传统木石结构的藏式房屋非常透亮、干净。接待客人的数目从4人增加到24人。这个满脸皱纹的藏族大叔微笑着说："10多万元的本钱，只用两、三年就都回来了"。虽然旅馆里能做排骨炖土豆等菜，但只要客人愿意，唐次仁更希望能跟客人分享当地香浓的酥油茶*和地道的藏餐。

生词注释 Vocabulary

1. 官方【guān fāng】n. official, of the government

2. 统计【tǒng jì】統計 v.; n. count, compute; statistics, census

3. 达【dá】達 v. reach, attain, amount to

4. 人次【rén cì】m. sum of people participating, visitor count

5. 内地【nèi dì】內地 n. inland, interior

6. 敏锐【mǐn ruì】敏銳 adj. quick, sharp (eyes), acute (sense)

7. 生财之道【shēng cái zhī dào】生財之道 methods to gain money（成语）

8. 新兴【xīn xīng】新興 adj. new and developing, rising, newly developing

9. 扶持【fú chí】v.; n. give aid to, support, hold up; aid, support

10. 被褥【bèi rù】n. bedding, bedclothes

11. 贴息【tiē xī】貼息 v.; n. discount; subsidized interest

12. 贷款【dài kuǎn】貸款 v.; n. grant a loan, provide a loan; loan, credit

13. 卫浴【wèi yù】衛浴 n. bathroom

14. 设备【shè bèi】設備 n. equipment, facilities

15. 栋【dòng】棟 m. measure word (for buildings, houses)

16. 皱纹【zhòu wén】皺紋 n. wrinkle, furrow, lines (facial)

17. 排骨【pái gǔ】n. spareribs, steak, rib

18. 炖【dùn】燉 v. stew slowly, braise

19. 土豆【tǔ dòu】n. potato

20. 香浓【xiāng nóng】香濃 adj. aromatic and concentrated (smell)

21. 酥油茶【sū yóu chá】n. buttered tea

副镇长告诉记者，唐次仁三、四十岁的时候<u>走遍</u>西藏各地，到过成都。他<u>见多识广</u>，是村里最早投资家庭旅馆的两户村民之一。这些年更多村民跟随他们，经营起家庭旅馆。这位副镇长说，扎西岗村的藏民<u>纯朴</u>热情，而这里的村庄和山水风景特别美。因此，"<u>生态</u>旅游"作为未来发展方向之一，已经确定下来。

请记者喝过自家做的香甜酥油茶*后，唐次仁客气地问记者是否还有别的问题，他还要赶到村里去听垃圾处理<u>培训</u>。<u>互道</u>"亚姆"（康区藏语"再见"的意思）后，老人笑眯眯地转身走向他的培训课堂。

22. 走遍【zǒu biàn】v. go over, travel across

23. 见多识广【jiàn duō shí guǎng】見多識廣 wisdom comes from extensive observation（成语）

24. 纯朴【chún pǔ】純樸 adj. honest and pure

25. 生态【shēng tài】生態 n. ecology, habits, way of life

26. 培训【péi xùn】培訓 v.; n. train; training

27. 互道【hù dào】v. say to each other, greet each other

（667字）

文：中新社记者　刘舒凌　有删改

原载中国新闻网2011年6月28日

网络来源：

http://www.chinanews.com/gn/2011/06-28/3142054.shtml

文化/熟语注释 Culture/idiom notes

*青藏高原【qīngzàng gāoyuán】青藏高原是中国最大、世界海拔最高的高原，有"世界屋脊"之称，著名的喜马拉雅山脉即位于青藏高原。青藏高原也是亚洲许多大河的发源地。藏族是居住在这里的一个主要的和历史悠久的民族。

The Qinghai-Tibet plateau is the biggest plateau in China and is also the highest altitude plateau in the world. Hence, it is referred to as "the roof of the world," and is where the Himalayas lie. 青藏高原 is also the source of many of the big rivers in Asia. The Tibetans are the major ethnic group in this area and they have a long history.

*酥油茶【sūyóu chá】酥油茶，是藏族民众每日必不可少的饮料。青藏高原气候寒冷，蔬菜不宜生长，但茶叶却容易保存。藏民懂得蔬菜所含有的营养成分，可以通过茶叶来补充。制作酥油茶的酥油是从牛、羊奶中提炼出来的。自制酥油茶是一种很费力的工作。

Buttered tea is an essential drink for the Tibetans. The weather on the Qinghai-Tibet plateau is very cold and is not suitable for growing vegetables, but tea leaves are easy to preserve. The Tibetans know that the same nutrition that is found in vegetables can be obtained from tea leaves. The butter that they use to make the tea is extracted from cows' and goats' milk. Producing homemade buttered tea is quite a labor-intensive activity, however.

语法/语言点注释 Grammar/language points

1 是……之一; one of . . .

他见多识广，<u>是</u>村里最早投资家庭旅馆的两户村民<u>之一</u>。
He is knowledgeable and experienced, and was one of the first two villagers to make an investment in the family inn business in the village.

This pattern is used to name one thing of many from the same group or category.

Example:

龙是中华民族的图腾，也是中国的12生肖之一。
The dragon is the national totem of China, and is also one of the 12 zodiac animals.

2 作为……之一; as one of . . .

"生态旅游" <u>作为</u>未来发展方向<u>之一</u>，已经确定下来。
"Ecotourism" has already been determined as one of the items for future development.

The word 作为 here is a preposition, introducing a certain identity or property of the subject in the sentence. The word 之一 means it is one of a kind.

Example:

电脑作为现代生活必需品之一，为人们带来了极大的方便。
As a necessity in modern daily life, the computer has brought great convenience to people.

阅读理解 Comprehension

一、对错题 True or false?

1 （　）老藏民唐次仁第一次在家接待游客是2001年的时候。
2 （　）县政府支持扎西岗村的农民经营家庭旅馆。
3 （　）排骨炖土豆是地道的藏餐。
4 （　）老藏民唐次仁去过西藏以外的地方。
5 （　）老藏民唐次仁要去村里培训村民怎么处理垃圾。

二、填空题 Fill in the blanks, choosing from the words provided.

栋　　批　　户　　个　　位

1 2001年，唐次仁在自己家接待了一___从内地来的游客。
2 2003年，唐次仁在老房里装修起一___标准化房间。
3 2006年，唐次仁在自家院内加建了一___两层高的小楼。
4 扎西岗村发展生态旅游，有很多___村民经营家庭旅馆。

根据提示完成课文结构图 Complete the text structure map according to the clues provided

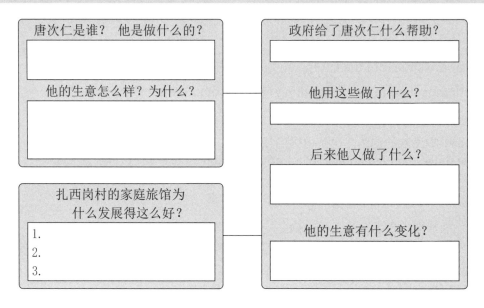

讨论 Discussion

1   你认为扎西岗村的藏民除了经营家庭旅馆以外，还可以开发哪些与旅游相关的生财之道？

2   请用中文解释"生态旅游"是什么意思？为了发展"生态旅游"，你对扎西岗村的旅游业有哪些建议？

阅读 B: 鄂伦春人新生活 The new life of the Oroqen minority group

课文 Reading

　　鄂伦春族主要<u>分布</u>在中国东北的内蒙古和黑龙江两省，有自己的语言——鄂伦春语，但没有本民族文字。"鄂伦春"一词有两种含义，即"使用驯鹿的人"和"山岭上的人"。

生词注释 Vocabulary

1. 分布【fēn bù】v.; n. distribute; distribution

六十年前，鄂伦春人还过着<u>原始游猎</u>生活。他们靠<u>狩猎</u>为生，打来的猎物在部族内平均分配，老、<u>弱</u>、<u>伤</u>、<u>残</u>者还要多分一些。鄂伦春族的男人几乎个个都是好骑手和好射手，他们一个人、一匹马、一杆枪在大兴安岭的密林深处狩猎。住的一般是用几个木杆搭成的<u>圆锥形</u>的房子，夏天围上<u>桦树</u>皮，冬天围上<u>兽皮</u>，当地人叫"撮罗子"。

1951年，鄂伦春自治旗宣告成立，鄂伦春人<u>陆续</u>下山定居。1996年，为了保护大兴安岭的生态，鄂伦春人放下了手中的猎枪，从狩猎转变为<u>农耕</u>。这六十年间，鄂伦春人发生了翻天覆地的变化。政府为他们建起了猎民新村，不但通了自来水，冬天还有暖气。以前长期生活在深山老林，生活艰苦，没有医疗，鄂伦春人一般只能活到三、四十岁，而现在，鄂伦春人同时享受城镇和农村医疗双保险，老人年过70也不稀奇。

如今，鄂伦春民族的传统兽皮制作技艺、桦树皮制作技艺以及原创鄂伦春歌舞，都已被列入国家级非物质文化<u>遗产</u>保护名录*。<u>流散</u>民间的鄂伦春原创歌曲，也被整理成《鄂伦春原创歌曲80首》出版<u>发行</u>。

为保护只有口语，没有文字的鄂伦春民族语言，自治旗政府制定了鄂伦春语言保护计划，最近出版了一本鄂伦春语典籍，收录了近3万条鄂伦春语<u>词条</u>，完整地保留了狩猎环境下<u>原生态</u>的鄂伦春族语言。《鄂伦春研究》等书籍也<u>相继</u>出版。同时，鄂伦春民族博物馆、文化生态保护园区等文化保护项目也一批批展开。

(635字)

原载中国广播网　2011年9月3日
责编：时晨　有删改
网络来源：
http://news.cnr.cn/gnxw/201109/t20110903_508455005_1.shtml

2. 原始【yuán shǐ】adj. original, firsthand, primitive

3. 游猎【yóu liè】游獵 v.; n. travel to hunt; hunting trip

4. 狩猎【shòu liè】狩獵 v.; n. hunt, go hunting; hunt, hunting

5. 弱【ruò】v.; adj. weaken; weak, feeble, young

6. 伤【shāng】傷 v.; n.; adj. wound; injury; wounded

7. 残【cán】殘 v.; adj. injure, damage; incomplete

8. 圆锥形【yuán zhuī xíng】圓錐形 n. cone

9. 桦树【huà shù】樺樹 n. birch

10. 兽皮【shòu pí】獸皮 n. animal skin

11. 陆续【lù xù】陸續 adv. constantly, continually

12. 农耕【nóng gēng】農耕 n. farming, agriculture

13. 遗产【yí chǎn】遺產 n. legacy, inheritance, heritage

14. 流散【liú sàn】v. wander, scatter, drift

15. 发行【fā xíng】發行 v. issue, distribute

16. 词条【cí tiáo】詞條 n. vocabulary entry, lexical item

17. 原生态【yuán shēng tài】n. primeval ecology

18. 相继【xiāng jì】相繼 adv. in succession, one after another

文化/熟语注释 Culture/idiom notes

*非物质文化遗产【fēi wùzhì wénhuà yíchǎn】非物质文化遗产包括口头传统和表述、表演艺术、社会风俗、礼仪、节庆等。截至2009年，中国共有昆曲、古琴艺术等26个项目入选联合国教科文组织"人类非物质文化遗产代表作名录"，成为世界上入选项目最多的国家。

The term "intangible cultural heritage" refers to oral legends and stories, performing arts, social customs, etiquette, and festivals, etc. By 2009, 26 treasures including Kun opera and Guqin (music performed on this ancient stringed instrument) had been recorded on the UNESCO "List of Intangible Cultural Heritage," thereby making China the country with the greatest number of intangible cultural heritages.

语法/语言点注释 Grammar/language points

1   以及......，都......; as well as . . . all . . .

    鄂伦春民族的传统兽皮制作技艺、桦树皮制作技艺<u>以及</u>原创鄂伦春歌舞，<u>都</u>已被列入国家级非物质文化遗产保护名录。
    The traditional Oroqen techniques for processing hides and making artifacts and crafts from birch bark, as well as the traditional dances of the Oroqens, have all been included on the List of Intangible Cultural Heritage.

The word 以及 is a conjunction used to include additional items in the same category. 都 means "all" and is used for inclusive purposes. That is, all the information mentioned in the previous parallel structure is included.

Example:

听音乐、打高尔夫球、看电影以及旅游，都是我喜欢的业余活动！
Listening to music, playing golf, watching movies, and traveling are all activities that I love to do in my spare time!

2   近 + number; nearly . . .

最近出版了一本鄂伦春语典籍，收录了<u>近</u>3万条鄂伦春语词条。
There is a recently published Oroqen dictionary that has a collection of nearly 30,000 Oroqen entries.

The word 最近 in the first part of this compound sentence means "recently," while the word 近 placed before "3万条" is an adverb used before numbers or numeric expressions meaning "nearly" or "approximately."

Example:

这次学校的留学生部组织去大兴安岭旅游，有近200个留学生报名参加了。
The International Student Office has made an arrangement for students to travel to the Daxing'an Mountains; nearly 200 students have signed up for the trip.

阅读理解 Comprehension

一、选择题 Multiple-choice questions.

I   关于以前的鄂伦春人，下面哪些说法是对的？

   a) 他们过着原始游猎生活
   b) 他们住在深山老林里
   c) 他们夏天穿桦树皮，冬天穿兽皮
   d) 他们身体很好，寿命很长

2   关于现在的鄂伦春人，下面哪些说法是错的？

   a) 他们过着农耕生活
   b) 他们自己建了猎民新村
   c) 他们享受城镇和农村医疗双保险
   d) 他们有了自己的文字

二、填空题 Fill in the blanks, choosing from the words provided.

分配   享受   过着   靠   放下   保护

   六十年前，鄂伦春人还____原始游猎生活。他们____狩猎为生，打来的猎物在部族内平均____。1996年，为了____大兴安岭的生态，鄂伦春人____了手中的猎枪，从狩猎转变为农耕。

三、简答题 Short-answer questions.

I   鄂伦春族有哪三项国家级非物质文化遗产？

2   鄂伦春自治旗政府开展了哪些语言和文化保护项目？

Answer key

Chapter 1

阅读 A: Warm-up

答案: N/A

Comprehension

一、

中国的校园文化	美国的校园文化
没有学生会在学校里直呼老师的名字	学生可以直呼老师的名字
中国的高中是三年制	有的高中是三年制，有的是四年制，跟大学一样
男女学生不能过分亲热；学校对待"早恋"现象非常严格	男生、女生的交往很开放
报考大学只要有高考成绩就行了	在美国，既要有一份良好的个人简历又要请老师写推荐信。当然，SAT 考试成绩是每个人都必须的。
申请者只能被一所大学录取	能同时被好几所大学录取

二、

1 In China, many high schools are very strict in dealing with the teenage "puppy love" phenomenon.
2 In America, it is more open: male and female students' close interaction is only lightly punished, if at all.

Text structure map

找出中美校园文化差别的两个原因。

中美文化不同	中美教育体制不同

第一个差别是什么方面的？

师生关系

中美有什么不一样？

在中国，师生关系比较正式，但在美国学生把老师当朋友。

第四个差别是什么方面的？

男女关系

中美有什么不一样？

在中国，男生和女生在老师面前，一定要保持距离。在美国，男生、女生的交往开放多了。

第二个差别是什么方面的？

学制

中美有什么不一样？

中国小学六年，初中三年，高中三年。美国小学六年包括幼儿园，初中和高中根据学区不同，年数不同。

第五个差别是什么方面的？

报考大学

中美有什么不一样？

中国的学生只要有高考成绩就可以了。在美国，要有简历、SAT 成绩和其他资料。

第三个差别是什么方面的？

计分方式

中美有什么不一样？

中国用数字计分，60分及格，100分满分。而美国，成绩是用 A、B、C、D 来分等级的。

第六个差别是什么方面的？

大学的选择

中美有什么不一样？

中国的高考生只能填三所大学，被一所大学录取。在美国，你能同时被好几所大学录取，然后挑选一所。

阅读 B: Comprehension

一、

1 a), c), d); 2 a), c), d); 3 b), c).

二、

1   从我的窗户 <u>望</u> 下去可以看到一个学校的操场和校园。
2   除了这些以外，我也 <u>观察</u> 到他们生活中的另一面。
3   男孩、女孩们一起走着，甜蜜的小情侣们随处可 <u>见</u>。
4   他们精彩的生活在我面前一一 <u>展现</u>。

Chapter 2

阅读 A: Warm-up

一、

1   答案: N/A
2   答案: N/A
3   "把脉、看舌苔"用在中医; "喝药、诊断、复查、服药"用在中医、西医都可以。

Comprehension

一、

1 c); 2 b), c); 3 a); 4 c).

二、

1   朋友对这位老中医十分佩服,一丝不苟地按照他的话去做。
2   什么时候服药,什么时候复查,都被他仔仔细细写在了每天的日程表上。

Text structure map

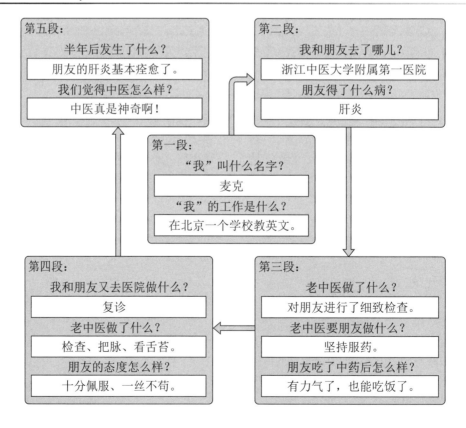

阅读 B: Comprehension

一、

1   上个月，我在一位中国朋友的陪同_下_到一家医院看病。
2   从进医院大门开始已经30分钟了，居然还没看_上_病。
3   医生只用了3分钟的时间就开_出_处方让我们去拍片子。
4   拍完片，又_被_告知得等两小时才能回来拿片子。

二、

1 F, 2 T, 3 T, 4 T, 5 F, 6 T.

Chapter 3

阅读 A: Warm-up

一、

答案: N/A

二、

a), b), c).

Comprehension

一、

1 d); 2 d).

二、

1   夏亮组织乐队很不容易，他们没有钱，也没有排练的地方。
2   答案: N/A

Text structure map

夏亮的摇滚乐队

第一支乐队

| 时间：2008年9月/大二刚开学 | 地点：山东大学宿舍楼下的地下室 |

| 成员：两名室友、另外两名大学生、夏亮。 | 活动：凑钱买音响、贝司、二手架子鼓，排练。 |

结果：
两名成员毕业，两名成员退出，只剩下夏亮一个。

第二支乐队

| 时间：2009年9月/大三 | 地点：山东大学 |

| 成员：三位热爱摇滚的同校学生，外校一名热爱摇滚的女同学，夏亮。 | 活动：在圣诞晚会上演唱，2010年6月10日在大学生活动中心搞暑假专场演出。 |

结果：
夏亮回老家西安实习，乐队将再一次变得残缺。

阅读 B: Comprehension

一、

1 T, 2 F, 3 T, 4 T, 5 F.

二、

1 <u>吹</u> 葫芦丝   2 <u>拉</u> 二胡   3 <u>弹</u> 琵琶
4 <u>拉</u> 小提琴   5 <u>弹</u> 钢琴   6 <u>敲</u> 大鼓

三、

西洋乐器：钢琴、小提琴、吉他、萨克管、小号、大鼓
中国民族乐器：笛子、葫芦丝、二胡、琵琶、古筝、长笛、扬琴

Chapter 4

阅读 A: Warm-up

一、

1   答案: N/A
2   答案: N/A

二、答案: N/A

Comprehension

一、1 d); 2 a), b), c); 3 d); 4 a), b), d).

二、

1   I had been wondering why she was never in the dorm on Thursday evenings; I have just found out today that she has been out taking a yoga class every Thursday evening.
2   With regard to my relationship with Lao Zhang, we are more like friends than a student–teacher relationship.

Text structure map

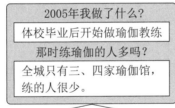

阅读 B: Comprehension

一、

1 T, 2 T, 3 T, 4 T, 5 F, 6 T.

二、

1　成都话"耍"用普通话说就是"玩"，用流行语说就是"休闲"。
2　文化休闲可以去影院、音乐厅、歌厅、KTV等场所，也就是看电影、听音乐会、唱歌等。
3　健身美容休闲就是健身（比方说练瑜伽）、美容美发、洗浴按摩等。
4　"农家乐"有丰富多彩的休闲项目，如：赏花、品果、垂钓、麻将、棋牌、乒乓、桌球、篝火等。呼吸着清新的空气，闻着花香果香，吃着农家风味的饭菜。

Chapter 5

阅读 A: Warm-up

一、

1　答案: N/A
2　答案: N/A

二、

轻食主义: light-meal philosophy　　少食多餐: eat little and often
素食主义: vegetarianism　　　　　　节食:　　on a diet

Comprehension

一、

1 c); 2 a), b), c); 3 d).

二、

1　"三低一高"的意思是低 糖分 、低 脂肪 、低 盐分 和高 纤维 。
2　轻食主义者喜欢的烹饪方式是 蒸 、 炖 、 煮 ，避免 煎 和 炸 。

三、

1　因为轻食主义者认为适当的肉类脂肪、蛋白质是人体需要的。
2　因为点心类的食物分量少、品种多、有营养，吃一份轻食点心，可以有效地增加饱腹感，在正餐的时候不会因为太饿而吃得过多。

Text structure map

什么是轻食主义？

来源于 <u>欧洲，</u> _____
意味着 <u>吃清淡、热量低的食物。</u>

轻食主义和素食主义、节食主义有什么不同？

轻食主义提倡 <u>少吃，</u> _____
　　　不禁止 <u>吃肉。</u>
　　　　喜欢 <u>各种有色蔬菜、</u>
　　　　　　<u>新鲜菌类、海鲜和鱼类。</u>

如何吃得少而又让人感到满足？

小技巧1: <u>先喝汤。</u> _____
小技巧2: <u>放慢进食速度，细嚼慢咽。</u>
小技巧3: <u>下午茶。</u> _____

请你找出四个关键词总结轻食主义的理念。
简单、适量、健康、均衡

阅读 B: Comprehension

一、

1 T, 2 F, 3 T, 4 T, 5 T, 6 T.

二、

1 年轻的丈夫居然有了"三高"：高<u>血压</u>、高<u>血脂</u>、高<u>血糖</u>。
2 女儿吃饭的时候挑食，喜欢吃<u>荤</u>菜，不喜欢吃<u>素</u>菜。
3 <u>适</u>量是营养，<u>过</u>量是毒物。请别用"腻爱"害了自己的亲人。
4 吃饭要养成好习惯，<u>荤素</u>搭配，<u>营养</u>均衡才能更健康。

Chapter 6

阅读 A: Warm-up

一、

1 答案: N/A
2 答案: N/A

二、

1 b); 2 c); 3 c).

Comprehension

一、

1 他们学_成_后会带着和以前有很大不同的价值观回国。
2 这项调查是_由_中国和英国两所大学共同进行的。
3 越多中国人出国，_并_重新审视自己，中国与外部世界的关系就会越正常。

二、

1 b); 2 a), b), c).

三、

1 一些家长以前认为女孩子不能出远门，但现在观念变了。有一位父亲准备送女儿去美国沃顿商学院留学。
2 出国前这些学生生活在单一文化背景中，出国留学帮助他们了解生活在其他文化背景下的人，然后发现彼此的共性。出国留学改变了年轻人的价值观。

Text structure map

第一段

这篇文章的主要观点是什么？

出国留学的中国年青人越来越多，他们学成后会带着和以前有很大不同的价值观回国。

第二段

在过去两年中，有多少中国学生出国留学？

62万，是1978年中国恢复留学以来的留学生总数的四分之一。

为什么中国有这么多的留学生？

原因1：在中国，绝大多数家庭只有一个孩子。

原因2：在中国家长看来，孩子现在的最好前途就是出国留学。

原因3：许多中国家庭现在也负担得起送孩子留学的学费。

第四段

中国在英留学生的调查显示了什么？

中国留学生刚开始时不习惯西方的生活和教育方式，但是几年之后承认，出国永远改变了他们的人生。

接受调查的学生是怎么说的？

出国留学帮助他们了解生活在其他文化背景下的人，然后发现彼此的共性。

第三段

石家庄第42中学有什么变化？

毕业班学生中，有10%已经出国留学，学校为希望毕业后出国留学的学生成立了一个班。

关于留学，中国家长的观点有什么变化？

中国人以前都认为女孩子不能出远门，但现在女孩子也可以出国留学。

第五段

找出文章最后一段的关键句。

越多中国人出国，并重新审视自己，中国与外部世界的关系就会越正常。

阅读 B: Comprehension

一、

1 T, 2 F, 3 F, 4 F, 5 T.

二、

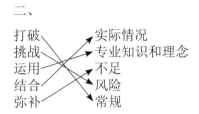

打破　　　　实际情况
挑战　　　　专业知识和理念
运用　　　　不足
结合　　　　风险
弥补　　　　常规

Chapter 7

阅读 A: Warm-up

答案: N/A

Comprehension

一、

1 F, 2 F, 3 F, 4 T, 5 F.

二、

1 我从某网站上看到一则招聘启事，跟我的专业很符合，<u>于是</u>我想去应聘。
2 这是我第一次参加工作面试，尽管有些紧张，<u>但</u>我回答得还可以。
3 虽然我自己觉得面试的时候表现不错，结果却<u>还</u>是没有通过。
4 我给面试官写了一封信去，我不是想请他重新考虑我，<u>只是</u>想咨询一下。
5 我在信上问了面试官<u>对</u>我整个面试过程的看法和建议，我想在以后的面试中改正缺点。

三、

1 因为晚上7点20分是所有参加面试的人集合的时间，而"我"迟到了10分钟，我感到非常过意不去，所以向考官道歉。（你认为这位面试者迟到了吗？N/A）
2 "我"个人认为整个过程很严谨，考试方式很科学。考试的环节一步接一步，效率很高。

Text structure map

我应聘的是什么工作？

我应聘的是咨询师，负责解答客户的来电问题，处理投诉，类似于客户服务。

下午有几轮考试？

两轮

找出说明我通过考试的关键词。

简单、轻松、过关、顺利、通过

什么事让我没吃晚饭？

我是外地人，晚上还有面试，回不去家了，所以赶紧去公司附近找旅馆。

我迟到了吗？

我在所有参加面试的人集合的时候迟到了10分钟，但是面试的时候没迟到。

见到面试官我为什么要道歉？

我为了迟到的10分钟过意不去，所以见到面试官的第一反应就是鞠躬道歉。

用一句话总结这次面试的过程与结果。

整个过程很严谨、科学、高效，结果我得到了这份工作。

阅读 B: Comprehension

一、

1 b); 2 a), b), d).

二、

　　苏小姐一开始想不通为什么自己努力工作却被 裁员 ，她不知道以后怎么办，是不是能找到工作，她还觉得被裁员很 丢人 ，怕朋友笑话自己。在职业规划专家的开导下，苏小姐在空闲时间积极地给自己 充电 ，考出了一个 证书 ，找到了新的工作。苏小姐重新找回了 自信 ，走出了裁员的 阴影 。

三、

假如是自己能力不够　　　　　　　　那么可以看看同行的公司有没有机会

假如是你的公司单个企业不景气　　　也许就要做转行的准备了

假如是整个行业不景气　　　　　　　应该去请教职业规划专家

　　　　　　　　　　　　　　　　　那就通过各种方法增强竞争力

四、

1   If you feel it is a problem with your own ability, you should seek ways to improve your competitiveness.

2   When you have just been laid off, you feel frustrated, and such a negative mood can affect your performance in applying for a new job, and so finding another job doesn't go smoothly.

Chapter 8

阅读 A: Warm-up

一、

1   答案: N/A
2   答案: N/A

二、1 c); 2 b); 3 b); 4 c).

Comprehension

一、1 c); 2 c); 3 a); 4 c); 5 c).

Text structure map

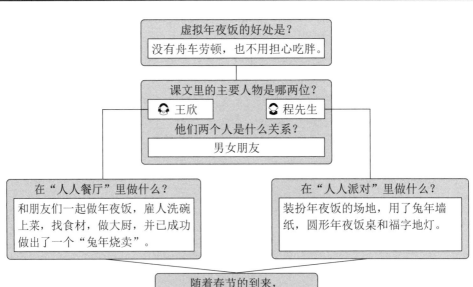

阅读 B: Comprehension

一、

1 F, 2 T, 3 F, 4 T, 5 F, 6 T.

二、

1　马晓天　从事　网络广播剧制作已经好几年了。
2　网络广播剧听起来画面感很强，因为剧中加入了不少　现场　音效。
3　网络广播剧社团的成员并不是专业制作者，而是　业余　爱好者。
4　一部网络广播剧的制作　周期　在三个月到半年。

Chapter 9

阅读 A: Warm-up

一、

1　中国的春节是农历的正月初一。中国人过春节有贴春联、放鞭炮、舞龙舞狮等习俗。
2　中国的清明节在4月5日这一天。清明节的传统习俗是扫墓。
3　端午节、中秋节、重阳节等。

Comprehension

一、

1 F, 2 F, 3 F, 4 F, 5 F, 6 T.

二、

1　课文介绍了三种过年新习俗：多喝饮料少喝酒、晚辈给长辈发红包、QQ视频里拜年。
2　今年春节期间宋先生宴请同学，但大家都不怎么喝酒，而喝牛奶、果汁。
　　今年春节期间小涛拿出两个红包，给了爷爷、奶奶。以前都是长辈给晚辈红包。
　　今年春节期间小荣没能回家过年，小荣通过QQ视频跟父母拜年。

Text structure map

这篇文章的题目是什么？
不一样的过年

第一部分的人物有：	第二部分的人物有：	第三部分的人物有：
宋先生、母亲、同学	小涛、父母、爷爷奶奶、记者	小荣、父母
第一部分说的变化是什么？	**第二部分说的变化是什么？**	**第三部分说的变化是什么？**
喝白酒的人在减少，喝酒的数量也在减少。	以前长辈给晚辈红包，如今晚辈给长辈红包。给长辈红包的现象很普遍。	许多年青人没时间回家和父母过年，用QQ视频和父母团圆。

阅读 B: Comprehension

一、

1 d); 2 c).

二、

1　很多人在清明节扫墓时习惯烧纸，而在中国历史上，大家采用的最原始的祭扫办法是 把纸钱向空中扬去 ，或者在先人墓前用砖头 压住一张纸钱 。不过，现在较好的办法是 买一束鲜花 ，祭拜过后 将花瓣撒在墓前 。

2　过去清明节有个习俗就是 折柳枝，编成花环戴在头上 。但这种做法破坏环境，如今大家可以 结伴郊游 ，还可以进行 植树 活动。古时的人们过清明节还开展各种户外活动，文人则聚在一起作诗、画画、写书法。现代人的生活太忙了，清明节可以举办 放风筝、诗歌朗诵 等活动。

Chapter 10

阅读 A: Warm-up

一、

答案: N/A

Comprehension

一、

1 a), b), d); 2 b), d); 3 a), b).

二、

1　小媛家说"我"学历不高，工作也不稳定，所以他们反对"我"和小媛结婚。
2　小媛在一家百货商场的专柜卖衣服，工作很辛苦，业绩却不大好。丈夫那个时候工作已经干得不错了，他就不让小媛出去工作了，怕她太辛苦。
3　这个丈夫带小媛出席一些工作场合，还让她在公司里做一些事情。小媛有了这些机会，就变得闪亮动人。这位丈夫的行动证明了他真的很爱她。

Text structure map

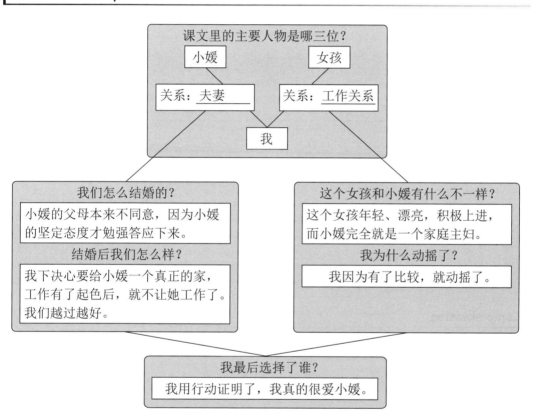

阅读 B: Comprehension

一、

1　网恋：男女双方足不出户通过网络谈恋爱。他们往往缺乏面对面的接触和了解。
2　闪婚：就是闪电式结婚，从认识到结婚时间相当短。婚前双方可能了解不够。
3　闪离：进入婚姻生活时间不长就草草离婚。闪离的原因常常是因为婚前双方了解不够。
4　裸婚：指的是不买房、不买车、不办婚礼、不买婚戒，直接登记结婚的一种节俭的结婚方式。
5　婚姻包办：指的是婚事由男女双方的父母决定，自己没有追寻爱情的自由。

二、

1 T, 2 T, 3 F, 4 T.

三、

1 婚后，他们一直恩爱如 初 ，生活幸福。
2 然而事实上，据我所 知 ，我们并没有完全摒弃传统。
3 我们常说婚姻是人生的 头 等大事。
4 白头偕 老 的爱情是人生最理想和完美的境界。
5 你父母的爱情同样 令 人羡慕！

Chapter 11

阅读 A: Warm-up

一、

答案： N/A

二、

美国（c) 鹰）
英国（b) 狮子）
中国（a) 龙）
法国（d) 公鸡）

Comprehension

一、

1 T, 2 T, 3 F, 4 T.

二、

1 d); 2 d).

三、

1 "望子成龙"的"龙"代表的是成功人士。
2 因为他说画了眼睛龙就会飞走。
3 这个成语表示一件事情的前后关系、来历和发展。

Text structure map

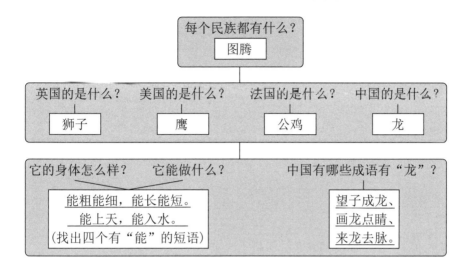

阅读 B: Comprehension

一、

I d); 2 c); 3 a), b), c); 4 b), c), d).

二、

1 土家族的晒龙袍节是为了 纪念 土王，而普米族的祭龙潭节是为了感谢龙神 保佑 了普米人。在少数民族中，还有很多与龙有关的 节日 和 民俗 。

2 在我看来，晒龙袍节和祭龙潭节都跟 战争 有关系。土家族的土王战败时，身上穿着战袍。普米族人则为了 躲避 战争而 逃 到外乡去，回来的时候发现井里的碗还是好的，没有被 毁掉 。

三、

1 龙舟，是一条长十四、五米，形状像龙的木船。船头做成龙头的样子。每条船的颜色都不一样，龙头的样子也不同。这些龙舟看起来就像一条条帅气的龙。

2 是一条非常鲜艳的大龙。这条舞动的大龙，是人们手工制作的，用了草、竹、木纸、布等材料。龙身上的节数有九节、十一节、十三节，最多可达二十九节。

3 因为中国人崇拜龙，认为龙是神。在土家族人心目中，土王是至高无上的，土王就是"龙"，他穿的衣服就是"龙袍"。

Chapter 12

阅读 A: Warm-up

一、答案: N/A

二、答案: N/A

Comprehension

一、

1 c); 2 b).

二、

1　小明擦_掉_了一个朋友的名字。黑板上只剩_下_了父母和伴侣。
2　我忽然认识_到_，父母也要学_会_独立生活。

三、答案: N/A

Text structure map

中国家庭的传统观念是什么？

养儿防老，父母在，不远游。

本文的第一个人物是谁？

小琳

本文的第二个人物是谁？

姓钮的母亲

她现在有工作吗？ 为什么？

没有，因为她是即将毕业正在找工作的大四学生。

以前的想法是：

把希望寄托在孩子身上，希望将来父母老了，子女能照顾与陪伴。

毕业后她打算在哪儿工作，为什么？

她打算在离家较近的地方工作，可以照顾父母。

现在的想法是：

认为父母也要学会独立生活，要让自己充实起来。

为什么改变了？

听到同事讲的一个故事，发现自己的想法太陈旧了。

阅读 B: Comprehension

一、

1 T, 2 T, 3 T, 4 T, 5 T.

二、

1 现代年轻人家庭 观念 不强，逐渐失去了中国文化的特质。
2 中西方是不同的，中国是一种家庭文化，西方则是一种 宗教 文化。
3 中国人认为血浓于水，血缘关系不可 割裂 。
4 对于西方人来说，成熟的标志之一是 脱离 父母，可以晚上不回家了。
5 如果不能 辨别 这些亲属关系，那么就会看不懂中国的传统古籍。

Chapter 13

阅读 A: Warm-up

一、

答案: N/A

二、

答案: N/A

Comprehension

一、

1 T, 2 T, 3 F, 4 F, 5 T.

二、

婚礼请柬已经发出，如果 被 媒体知道婚礼延期，一定会有很多 猜测 ，这 对 我产生什么后果，不言而喻。母亲 以 婚礼延期对我不利为由，坚持要我先回香港。三个哥哥也让我以 公众信誉 为重。

三、

答案: N/A

Text structure map

```
家对我有什么影响？
家已深深扎根在我的心里，作为一
种力量支撑我、伴随我。
```

第一件事 我遇到了什么问题？	第二件事 母亲做了什么？	第三件事 母亲让我做什么？
我结婚前才得知母亲患了重病。我既想照顾母亲，又怕婚礼延期对我产生影响。	母亲穿旧毛衣不方便，我想给她买件开衫，她却把旧毛衣变成了开衫。	母亲总是让我把吃不完的饭菜打包带回家。

第一件事

我的家人是怎么做的？

母亲坚持要我先回香港，三个哥哥也让我以公众信誉为重。

这件事对我有什么影响？

亲人的理解让我觉得我不是孤单的，我代表着巩家。

第二件事

在这件事上，母亲对我有什么影响？

母亲的观念和精神都影响着我。

第四件事
母亲对我的生活有什么影响？

我愿意过着朴素（simple）的生活，比如到地摊买便宜的衣服，不戴首饰。

阅读 B: Comprehension

一、

1 c); 2 b).

二、

　　他一开门就 瞪 我，然后脸就 看 着窗口，我看着他，我也 说不出 话，他 转过脸 说："我已经读中学了。"

Chapter 14

阅读 A: Warm-up

一、

1 答案: N/A

2 a), b), c), d)

Comprehension

一、

1 T, 2 T, 3 T, 4 F, 5 F.

二、(The answers given serve as an example, for your reference only.)

夜生活种类	我不喜欢，因为⋯⋯	我喜欢，因为⋯⋯
泡酒吧	我不喜欢，因为酒吧里音乐太吵，而且有人吸烟，我觉得在这样的环境里对健康很不好。	
去城市广场		我喜欢，因为去城市广场跳舞是免费的。我很喜欢这种不花钱却又开心、热闹的活动。
去茶室喝茶、聊天		我喜欢，因为在茶吧里一边听中国音乐，一边喝中国茶，让我体验到中国文化。而且我喜欢茶吧优雅、安静的氛围。
在家看电视、上网		我喜欢，因为在学习和工作之余，我很希望能一个人安安静静的，看看电视、上上网很好。
去逛通宵书店	我不喜欢，因为要是在书店看书看到很晚，怎么回家？坐出租车回家的话就太贵了。	

Text structure map

```
请解释文章的题目。
都市夜生活，各有所爱，意思是
都市里的娱乐活动丰富多彩，不
同的人喜欢不同的夜生活方式。
```

```
年轻人喜欢去哪？
为什么？
酒吧，可以交友，可以排
解烦闷。
```

```
年纪稍大的人去哪？
做什么？
广场，可以跳舞。
```

```
有些人不喜欢热闹的地方，
他们去哪？
去茶室喝茶、聊天。
外商说他喜欢去哪？
做什么？
音乐茶座，一边享受中国
的茶文化和中国音乐，一
边谈生意。
```

```
出租车司机眼中的夜生活是：
在家看电视、上网、读读书不
是夜生活，在高级娱乐场所花
大钱才是光鲜亮丽的夜生活。
```

阅读 B: Comprehension

一、 1 d); 2 c).

二、

1   这家书店的首场夜间书友会 _吸引_ 了很多热爱读书的人。

2   在网络购书越来越普遍的今日，实体书店的生存 _受到_ 了冲击。

Chapter 15

阅读 A: Warm-up

一、

地理		气候	
1 大漠	2 火焰山	1 干燥少雨	2 地表温度
3 盆地	4 海拔	3 寒冷	4 热

Comprehension

一、

I T, 2 F, 3 T, 4 T, 5 T.

二、

1 白雪__皑皑__   2 __滚滚__而上   3 红__扑扑__   4 __暗暗__叫苦

5 __茫茫__大漠   6 红__彤彤__   7 __熊熊__烈火   8 __冉冉__升起

三、

1 每当盛夏，山体在烈日的照射下，热气流滚滚上升，赭红色的山体看似烈火在燃烧，火焰山由此而得名。

2 站在火焰山前面，我想起了《西游记》里孙悟空他们师徒四人夏天经过这里的故事。

Text structure map

我没想到什么？

在大漠里能看到日出。

到吐鲁番了，我们去了哪？

火焰山

找出描述这个地方的方位词和数量词。

中部、东西、98公里、南北、9公里、851米、北部、5000米、南部、155米、80℃

这个地方为什么叫这个名字？

盛夏山体在烈日的照射下，像烈火在燃烧，由此得名。

我们是在什么季节到这里的？

冬天

请你描述这里的景象。

沙漠里没有人也没有绿色植物，只见一团红彤彤的火焰在晨曦中非常耀眼。

在火焰山，我们还看到了什么景象？

大漠里出现了一大片赭红的山岩，天还没有完全亮，山岩仿佛蒙着面纱。

我们为什么惊喜？

在大漠深处看到了日出。

我觉得这时大漠怎么样了？

大漠在日出时好像获得了生命。

阅读 B: Comprehension

一、

ɪ c); 2 b).

二、

1 <u>专心致志</u> 的手工艺者
2 <u>丰厚</u> 的知识
3 <u>精明</u> 的经商头脑
4 <u>迷人</u> 的风景

三、

1 高丽安忧虑的是，现在中国的经济发展特别快，但是有一部分人却忽视文化的保护，有的建筑和民居缺乏维修。
2 答案: N/A

Chapter 16

阅读 A: Warm-up

一、ɪ d)

二、答案: N/A

Comprehension

一、

ɪ a), c), d); 2 c), d).

二、

中国90后生长的 <u>时代背景</u> 可谓"得天独厚"。首先， <u>信息化</u> 让全球90后生活在同一个"地球村"，彼此只是隔着一个电脑屏幕。其次， <u>经济一体化</u> 让很多来自中国城市的90后与美国同龄人共享 <u>发达的物质文明</u> 。第三，教育的改革、 <u>教材的创新</u> ，使英语几乎成为与中文同步进行的第二种语言。中国的90后从小学开始接受英语教育。

三、

中国的90后与国际同龄人语言交流最畅通，文化差异最小。他们的适应力非常强，对各种新技术非常熟悉。他们也清楚地知道自己的理想与目标，从来没有放弃自己对社会与家庭所承担的责任。

Text structure map

王小一和彭家明分别是谁？

王小一是长安大学的90后大学生。彭家明是一位来自美国肯塔基州的90后小伙子。

他们做了什么？

王小一用一首纯正、地道的英文歌倾倒了彭家明，彭家明没想到中国90后的英语说得这么好。

为什么中国和美国的90后可以共享发达的物质文明？

因为生长的时代背景 "得天独厚"。

请你从课文的4、5、6段中，总结出90后与60、70、80后不同的三个原因：

| 信息化让90后了解世界很方便。 | 经济的发展让中国的90后享受丰富的物质生活。 | 教育的进步使90后更早学习英语。 |

请你用一句话总结中国的90后。

90后是中国最国际化的一代。

阅读 B: Comprehension

一、

1 F, 2 F, 3 F, 4 T, 5 T.

二、

1 Almost half of young people born in the 1990s said: "I like change."
2 Thirty per cent of young people born in the 1990s said that their parents will make decisions jointly with them.
3 Young people born in the 1990s, also known as the "mouse" generation, account for 11.7% of the total population of China.

Chapter 17

阅读 A: Warm-up

一、

中文店名	英文店名	经营类别
沃尔玛	Starbucks	快餐，炸鸡很有名
肯德基	McDonald's	快餐，汉堡包很有名
星巴克	KFC	咖啡等饮料及一些食品
麦当劳	Wal-Mart	百货商品

二、

答案: N/A

Comprehension

一、

1   活动中，商场向消费者发放 <u>调查问卷</u> 。
2   问卷回收以后，沃尔玛团队立即进行 <u>分析和整理</u> 。
3   沃尔玛商场愿意满足消费者的 <u>期望和需求</u> 。
4   沃尔玛商场请监督员给他们提出 <u>建议和意见</u> 。

二、

　　北京各家沃尔玛店举办的下午茶活动可以说是丰富多彩。有的店为顾客开设"食品安全"大讲堂 ，有的店请顾客参观 <u>食品加工过程</u> ，有的店举办 <u>有奖知识问答</u> ，有的店为顾客介绍 <u>科学小常识</u> ，告诉他们怎么辨别真假商品。

三、

1   因为卖场员工的手臂上有感应手表，顾客一按铃，他们的手表就会震动，显示哪个区域的顾客需要帮助。
2   据沃尔玛的一位高级管理者说，下午茶活动一方面能够更好地了解顾客对商场的意见和建议，帮助改善商场管理。另一方面，下午茶活动传播了沃尔玛的"三米微笑"、"盛情服务"等顾客至上的文化，让顾客感受到沃尔玛是一个幸福商场。

Text structure map

沃尔玛在中国推出了什么活动？

> 顾客下午茶活动

这是个什么活动？目的是什么？

> 这是个商场与顾客之间的交流活动。它的目的是为了了解消费者对商品质量、价格、商场服务、环境等方面的意见。

北京沃尔玛购物广场朝外店活动的内容是什么？

> 请十名消费者成为沃尔玛的监督员。

呼叫铃的用处是：

> 让商场很快地找到顾客，快速提供服务。

其他店有什么活动？

> "食品安全"大讲堂，请顾客参观食品加工过程，举办有奖知识问答，为顾客介绍科学小常识。

顾客下午茶活动的目的是：

> 帮商场更好地了解顾客对商场的意见和建议，让顾客感受到沃尔玛是一个'幸福商场'。

阅读 B: Comprehension

一、

1 a), b), c), d), e); 2 a), b), c); 3 a), b), c), d).

二、

记者采访的人物	被采访人的观点
肯德基的老顾客小何	烧饼加咖啡有点儿不搭调，应该把咖啡改成豆浆。
星巴克负责人	很多顾客喜欢星巴克的环境，但有的顾客不喝咖啡，也不喜欢太甜的饮料。经过市场调查，我们推出了能被更多消费者接受的茶。
一位在星巴克买茶喝的王小姐	毕竟感觉星巴克不是喝茶的地方，以后还是会选择购买咖啡的。
一位在肯德基给自己和儿子买早点的女士	肯定不会经常来肯德基买豆浆，因为豆浆并不是非到肯德基才能喝到。

Chapter 18

阅读 A: Warm-up

一、

a) city   b) countryside   c) worker   d) farmer   e) industry   f) agriculture   g) city   h) district
i) township   j) village   k) urbanization   l) industrialization

二、a), b), c)

三、答案: N/A

Comprehension

一、1 a), b), d); 2 b), d).

二、In the past 13 years, the number of self-supported companies in the village has increased from one to 35, with an increase of the number of workers from 300 to 13,000, and farmers' average annual income has increased from ￥3,100 to ￥45,500.

三、

1   不但能让学生们了解中国的农村城市化进程，更帮助学生了解中国从一个相对落后的农业国如何一步步实现工业化，并进一步走向服务产业的发展模式。

2   这些案例不但帮助人们了解"中国模式"，而且在全球化议题上也有重要的研究意义。

Text structure map

哈佛大学讨论课的题目是什么？

> 郑各庄的城市化进程

课文第二段里有哪些数据？

> 568户人家，1500口人，1998年，13年间，1 个自营实体公司，35个自营实体公司，300多产业工人，1.3万产业工人，3100元年收入，4.55万年收入。

请你解释"造城运动"。

> 即"主动城市化"，在农业办产业，然后再升级为"服务村"。

郑各庄的一个大产业是什么？

> 养老产业

赛奇先生为什么请黄福水来哈佛作报告？

> 让学生们了解中国的城市化。

哈佛肯尼迪学院为什么重视对中国的学习？

> 现在大多数人都关注中国的发展。

阅读 B: Comprehension

一、

1 d); 2 d).

二、

外地游客来这些城市旅游看的正是传统的 街道 与 建筑 ，而不是 摩天大楼 。一座城市，如果都是高楼大厦，传统文化记忆就会失去很多。我们在现代化进程中，应该注意 保持 城市的传统 特色 。

Chapter 19

阅读 A: Warm-up

一、

1 a); 2 答案: N/A

Comprehension

一、

1 a), b), c); 2 a), b), c).

二、

1　年轻的大学生当村官， 改变 了农村干部的知识层次和年龄结构。
2　改革开放以后中国很多农民走上了 富裕 之路。
3　以前农村的道路和环境卫生都比较落后，而现在农村的 面貌 完全不一样了。

三、

1　一到下午，老人们就自发地聚在一起，唱唱扬州小调，或者下两盘棋；夜晚，找块空地，放个录音机，大妈们也开开心心地跳起舞来，热闹的场景，与城市广场上出现的几乎没两样。
2　答案: N/A

Text structure map

```
┌─────────────────────────────┐
│    2008年我的生活发生         │
│    了什么变化？              │
├─────────────────────────────┤
│ 我从一名大学生成为了一名      │
│ 大学生村官。                │
├─────────────────────────────┤
│ 三年过去了，我感受到什么？    │
│ 我为什么感到骄傲？           │
├─────────────────────────────┤
│ 我感受到农村的巨大变         │
│ 化，也为我们大学生村官做出的  │
│ 努力感到骄傲。              │
└─────────────────────────────┘
```

┌──────────────────┐ ┌──────────────────┐ ┌──────────────────┐
│ 经济上有什么变化？ │ │ 精神文化上农民有   │ │ 课文第四段和第五段 │
│   │ │ 什么新需求？   │ │ 说了哪些变化？   │
├──────────────────┤ ├──────────────────┤ ├──────────────────┤
│ 农民到企业上班和自己创 │ │ 自发地一起唱小调、下棋、│ │ 交通和环境方面的变化。│
│ 业，经济和生活条件都好 │ │ 跳舞。   │ └──────────────────┘
│ 了。   │ └──────────────────┘
└──────────────────┘

┌──────────────────┐
│ 大学生村官给农村   │
│ 带来了什么？   │
├──────────────────┤
│ 大学生村官年轻、有知识，│
│ 给农村带来了良好的变化，│
│ 帮农民走向富裕。   │
└──────────────────┘

阅读 B: Comprehension

一、

问候语的变迁 change of greeting custom	办喜事的变迁 change of wedding custom	处理家庭关系的变迁 change of handling family issues custom
以前 1. 早上问吃饭了没？ 2. 晚上问喝汤了没？	以前 男方得送见面礼、看好礼、定亲礼、要亲礼、娶亲礼。 男方家一般来说都得费很大的力气才能娶亲。	以前 1. 父母的养老问题常常在几个子女之间推来推去。 2. 最流行的做法是每个儿子家轮流负责父母的吃饭、穿衣问题。女儿一般都是一年给父母做几件衣服。
现在 见面了问在哪儿做生意？赚钱不？	现在 1. 男方会给女方家人一张存款单。 2. 女方会陪嫁一些电器和生活用品。	现在 1. 现在的农村年轻人外出打工、做生意，他们在城市挣了钱寄给父母。 2. 农村的父母在家照顾一切和抚养孩子。

二、

今天晚上我跟朋友去参加了一场 婚礼 。主持人热情地请 新郎 和 新娘 介绍了相识、相爱的过程。主持人问新郎："你愿意 娶 她吗？"然后又问新娘："你愿意 嫁 给他吗？"大家高声大笑，真诚地祝这对新人 结婚 以后生活幸福美满。

Chapter 20

阅读 A: Warm-up

一、

1　答案: N/A

2　(The answer given serves as an example, for your reference only.)

如果是去大城市旅游、购物、参观博物馆和美术馆，我会选择住在酒店客房，我觉得这样比较安全，而且酒店附近一般来说交通方便。如果是到一个安静、美丽的小岛或小镇旅游，我会选择住家庭旅馆，因为我很想体验当地人的生活。如果去森林、草原、沙漠这样的地方旅游，我最愿意住野外的帐篷，因为我想倾听大自然的声音，感受远离人类社会的难得的悠然。

Comprehension

一、

1 T, 2 T, 3 F, 4 T, 5 F.

二、

1　2001年，唐次仁在自己家接待了一 批 从内地来的游客。
2　2003年，唐次仁在老房里装修起一 个 标准化房间。
3　2006年，唐次仁在自家院内加建了一 栋 两层高的小楼。
4　扎西岗村发展生态旅游，有很多 户 村民经营家庭旅馆。

Text structure map

唐次仁是谁？ 他是做什么的？ 唐次仁是个老藏民，是做家庭旅馆生意的。	**政府给了唐次仁什么帮助？** 政策上的扶持和经济上的资助。
他的生意怎么样？ 为什么？ 他的生意很好，因为来西藏旅游的内地游客很多。	**他用这些做了什么？** 修标准化房间。
	后来他又做了什么？ 他建了一栋两层高的小楼，接待游客。
扎西岗村的家庭旅馆 为什么发展得这么好？ 1. 有唐次仁这样有见识的藏民。 2. 村民们纯朴、热情。 3. 这个地方的山水风景很美。	**他的生意有什么变化？** 接待客人的数目增加了，本钱两三年就回来了。

阅读 B: Comprehension

一、

1 a), b); 2 b), d).

二、

六十年前，鄂伦春人还 过着 原始游猎生活。他们 靠 狩猎为生，打来的猎物在部族内平均 分配 。1996年，为了 保护 大兴安岭的生态，鄂伦春人 放下 了手中的猎枪，从狩猎转变为农耕。

三、

1 鄂伦春民族有三项国家级非物质文化遗产：兽皮制作技艺，桦树皮制作技艺，以及原创鄂伦春歌舞。

2 鄂伦春原创歌曲被整理成《鄂伦春原创歌曲80首》出版发行；另外，最近出版了一本鄂伦春语典籍，还有《鄂伦春研究》等书籍也相继出版了。同时，鄂伦春民族博物馆、文化生态保护园区等文化保护项目也一批批展开了。

Pinyin–English glossary

Pinyin	Simplified characters	Traditional characters	English translation	Word class	Chapter
Āěrjílìyà	阿尔及利亚	阿爾及利亞	People's Democratic Republic of Algeria	pn.	6
àn	按		press (with the hand); according to, in accordance with	v.; prep.	2
ànlì	案例		cases	n.	18
ànmó	按摩		massage	v.; n.	4
áo	熬		endure, put up with	v.	14
báhé	拔河		play tug-of-war; game of tug-of-war (a Chinese sports game)	v.; n.	9
bǎi	摆	擺	put, place	v.	4
báilǐng	白领		white collar	n.	8
báitóuxiélǎo	白头偕老	白頭偕老	remain married until old age	成语	10
báixuě áiái	白雪皑皑	白雪皚皚	snow capped	phr.	15
bājiāoshàn	芭蕉扇		palm leaf fan	n.	15
bǎmài	把脉	把脈	feel (take) somebody's pulse	vo.	2
bànlǚ	伴侣	伴侶	companion, partner, husband or wife	n.	12
bànyèsāngēng	半夜三更		late at night	成语	13
bǎofùgǎn	饱腹感	飽腹感	sense of satiety	n.	5
bàoqiàn	抱歉		sorry, regret	n.	7
bǎoyòu	保佑		bless and protect; blessings	v.; n.	11
bǎozhàng	保障		protect (life, property, rights, etc.) from damage or violation; guarantee	v.; n.	19
bēijù	悲剧	悲劇	tragedy	n.	13
bèirù	被褥		bedding, bedclothes	n.	20

bēishāng	悲伤	悲傷	sorrow; sad, sorrowful	n.; adj.	9
bēnbō	奔波		be busy running about, rush about	v.	7
bēnfàng	奔放		bold and unrestrained	adj.	3
biànbié	辨别	辨別	differentiate, distinguish	v.	12
biānjù	编剧		write a play; playwright, screenwriter	vo.; n.	8
biànqiān	变迁	變遷	change; change of situation	v.; n.	9
biǎnsǔn	贬损	貶損	disparage, derogate	v.	13
biāozhì	标志	標誌	symbolize, indicate; sign, mark, symbol	v.; n.	14
biāozhǔn	标准	標準	standard, norm, criterion	n.	4
bǐcǐ	彼此		each other, one another	pr.	6
biéwúxuǎnzé	别无选择	別無選擇	no other choice	成语	13
bìjìng	毕竟	畢竟	after all, all in all	adv.	4
Bìluóchūn	碧螺春		Biluochun green tea	n.	17
bìngqì	摒弃	摒棄	discard, abandon	v.	10
bìrán	必然		inevitability; inevitably	n.; adv.	3
búduàn	不断	不斷	uninterruptedly, continuously, constantly	adv.	1
bùjīn	不禁		cannot help (doing something)	adv.	2
bùluò	部落		tribe	n.	11
bùrán	不然		(it) is not so; otherwise	v.; conj.	12
bùyán'éryù	不言而喻		it goes without saying, it is self-evident	成语	13
bùyuē'értóng	不约而同	不約而同	take the same action or view without prior consultation	成语	2
cādiào	擦掉		wipe out, scrub off	v.	12
cǎifǎng	采访	採訪	have an interview with; interview	v.; n.	9
cáiyuán	裁员	裁員	lay off employees	vo.	7
cán	残	殘	injure, damage; incomplete	v.; adj.	20
cáng	藏		hide, conceal, store away	v.	13
cánquē	残缺	殘缺	incomplete (with parts missing)	v.	3
cānyù	参与	參與	participate in, take part in, be a part of	v.	16
cǎocǎo	草草		careless, hasty	adv.	10
cèhuà	策划		plot, plan	v.	8
cèmù	侧目	側目	glance	vo.	3
céngcì	层次	層次	level (of knowledge); levels	n.	19

cèshì	测试	測試	test; testing	v.; n.	7
chānfú	搀扶	攙扶	support gently by the hand or arm	v.	2
cháng	尝	嘗	taste, try	v.	3
chàngtōng	畅通	暢通	unimpeded, unblocked	adj.	16
chǎnyè	产业	產業	industry, estate, property	n.	18
cháo	潮		tide, current, trend	n.	6
cháyuè	查阅	查閱	read, look up	v.	9
chéng	成		one-tenth, percentage	m.	16
chéngdān	承担	承擔	undertake	v.	16
chéngqúnjiéduì	成群结队	成群結隊	in groups, in crowds	成语	14
chēngwèi	称谓	稱謂	appellation, title	n.	12
chēngxióng	称雄	稱雄	become the ruler, rule the region	v.	15
chéngzài	承载	承載	bear the weight of, load	v.	9
chénjiù	陈旧	陳舊	old, outdated, old fashioned	adj.	12
chénxī	晨曦		morning sunlight, first rays of the morning sun	n.	15
chímíng	驰名	馳名	renowned, famous	adj.	4
chīqíng	痴情		unreasoning passion; be infatuated	n.; adj.	13
chóngbài	崇拜		worship	v.; n.	11
chōngjī	冲击	衝擊	pound, assault, impact, affect	v.; n.	14
chōngmǎn	充满	充滿	filled with	v.	3
chóngshàng	崇尚		uphold, advocate	v.	12
chōngshí	充实	充實	enrich; rich, abundant	v.; adj.	12
chóu	愁		worry; sorrow	v.; n.	19
chóubèi	筹备		prepare, arrange, plan	v.	8
chóuchàng	惆怅	惆悵	disconsolate, melancholy	adj.	18
chuánbō	传播	傳播	propagate, broadcast	v.	17
chuǎngdàng	闯荡	闖蕩	leave home to make a living	v.	13
chuǎngjìn	闯进	闖進	intrude into, suddenly get in	v.	4
chuàngzào	创造	創造	create, produce	v.	5
chuàngzuò	创作	創作	create, produce; work of literature or art	v.; n.	3
chuánjiàoshì	传教士	傳教士	missionary	n.	11
chuánshuō	传说	傳說	pass from mouth to mouth; legend	v.; n.	11
chǔfāng	处方	處方	prescription	n.	2
chǔfèn	处分	處分	take disciplinary action against, punish; punishment	v.; n	1
chuídiào	垂钓	垂釣	fish; fishing	v.; n.	4

chǔlǐ	处理	處理	handle, deal with; disposal	v.; n.	6
chún	纯	純	pure; purely	adj.; adv.	9
chúnpǔ	纯朴	純樸	honest and pure	adj.	20
chúnzhèng	纯正	純正	pure, genuine	adj.	16
chúyì	厨艺	廚藝	culinary skill	n.	5
cíjiùyíngxīn	辞旧迎新	辭舊迎新	farewell to the old year and welcome to the new	成语	9
cítáng	祠堂		ancestral hall or temple, memorial temple	n.	15
cítiáo	词条	詞條	vocabulary entry, lexical item	n.	20
còuqián	凑钱	湊錢	pool money	vo.	3
cūnguān	村官		village official	n.	19
cúnkuǎndān	存款单	存款單	deposit slip, certificate of deposit	n.	19
cūnluò	村落		village, town	n.	15
cūnwěihuì	村委会	村委會	village committee	n.	18
cùqiú	蹴球	蹴球	ancient type of Chinese football	n.	9
dá	达	達	reach, attain, amount to	v.	20
dǎbāo	打包		pack	v.	13
dādiào	搭调	搭調	in tune	adj.	17
dǎduōsuō	打哆嗦		tremble, shiver	vo.	15
dàikuǎn	贷款	貸款	grant a loan, provide a loan; loan, credit	v.; n.	20
dànbáizhì	蛋白质	蛋白質	protein	n.	5
dǎng	挡	擋	keep off, block off	v.	14
dàng'ànguǎn	档案馆	檔案館	archives	n.	9
dānwù	耽误	耽誤	delay, hold up	v.	7
dàoqiàn	道歉		apologize; apology	vo.; n.	7
dǎorù	导入	導入	introduce to	vc.	1
dǎpái	打牌		play mahjong or cards	vo.	12
dǎzhuàn	打转	打轉	spin, rotate	v.	13
dèng	瞪		stare at, glare with displeasure	v.	13
dēnghuǒtōngmíng	灯火通明	燈火通明	ablaze with lights	成语	14
détiāndúhòu	得天独厚	得天獨厚	abound in gifts of nature; unique	成语	16
déxīnyìngshǒu	得心应手	得心應手	do with high proficiency, handy	成语	10
diǎnjí	典籍		classical books or records	n.	12
diàocháwènjuàn	调查问卷	調查問卷	questionnaire, survey	n.	17
dìdàwùbó	地大物博		vast territory with rich resources	成语	15
dìlǐ	地理		geography	n.	11

dīngzhǔ	叮嘱	叮囑	exhort; exhortation	v.; n.	9
díshìní	迪士尼		Disney, Disneyland	pn.	13
dìtān	地摊	地攤	street stall	n.	13
dǐxiàn	底线	底線	bottom line, baseline	n.	14
dòng	栋	棟	measure word (for buildings, houses)	m.	20
dòngrén	动人	動人	moving, charming	adj.	10
dòngyáo	动摇	動搖	vacillate, wave, shake	v.	10
dōu	兜		wrap up; bag, sack	v.; n.	13
dōufēng	兜风	兜風	ride, going out for a drive	v.; n.	13
dòujiāng	豆浆	豆漿	soymilk	n.	17
duàn	段		section, part	m. n.	12
dúbái	独白		monologize; monolog	v.; n.	8
duī	堆		pile up; pile	v.; m. n.	13
dùn	炖	燉	stew slowly, braise	v.	20
duǒbì	躲避		hide, avoid	v.	11
duōzīduōcǎi	多姿多彩		varied and colorful	成语	14
Èlúnchūn	鄂伦春	鄂倫春	Oroqen minority group	pn.	20
ēn'àirúchū	恩爱如初	恩愛如初	love and respect like before	成语	10
fān	番		kind, sort, for counting occurrences	m.	7
fáng'ài	妨碍	妨礙	hinder, hamper, obstruct	v.; n.	18
fángdìchǎn	房地产	房地產	real estate	n.	18
fǎngfú	仿佛	仿佛	seemingly, as if	adv.	15
fàngqì	放弃	放棄	abandon, give up	v.	3
fánmáng	繁忙		busy, bustling	adj.	4
fánmèn	烦闷	煩悶	annoyance; unhappy, uncomfortable	n.; adj.	14
fāntiānfùdì	翻天覆地		enormous changes	成语	19
fǎnyìng	反映		reflect	v.	4
fǎnyìng	反应	反應	react, respond; reaction	v.; n.	7
fānyuè	翻阅	翻閱	browse, look over, glance over	v.	14
fànzhǐ	泛指		general reference	v.; n.	16
fātiě	发帖		post (a thread, message, advertisement)	vo.	8
fāxiàn	发现	發現	notice, find out, discover; discovery	v.; n.	1
fāxiángdì	发祥地	發祥地	cradle, origin	n.	15
fāxíng	发行	發行	issue, distribute	v.	20
féinì	肥腻	肥膩	rich, greasy	adj.	5
fēnbù	分布		distribute; distribution	v.; n.	20
fēngfùduōcǎi	丰富多彩	豐富多彩	rich and varied, rich and colorful	成语	17

fēnghòu	丰厚	豐厚	rich and thick, rich and generous	adj.	15
fēngmào	风貌	風貌	style and features, manner	n.	18
fēngshōu	丰收	豐收	harvest	n.	11
fēngxiǎn	风险	風險	risk, danger	n.	6
fēngyǔwúzǔ	风雨无阻	風雨無阻	go as planned regardless of the weather	成语	4
fēngzhēng	风筝	風箏	kite	n.	9
fěnsī	粉丝	粉絲	fans	n.	8
fēnxiǎng	分享		share	v.	8
fǒudìng	否定		negate; negation	v.; n.	16
fù	赴		go to, attend	v.	13
fùchá	复查	復查	reexamine; reexamining	v.; n.	2
fúchí	扶持		give aid to, support, hold up	v.; n.	20
fùdān	负担	負擔	bear or shoulder (responsibility); burden	v.; n.	6
fúdǎo	辅导	輔導	guide, coach; guidance, coaching	v.; n.	3
fǔyǎng	抚养	撫養	foster, raise, bring up	v.; n.	19
fúyào	服药	服藥	take medicine	vo.	2
fùyù	富裕		well-to-do, well off, rich and prosperous	adj.	19
fùzá	复杂	複雜	complicated, complex	adj.	3
gàiniàn	概念		concept, notion	n.	5
gǎn	敢		dare, have courage to (do things)	v.	2
gāndèngyǎn	干瞪眼		stand by anxiously	ci	3
gāngà	尴尬	尷尬	awkward, embarrassed	adj.	2
gǎngwèi	岗位	崗位	post, position	n.	7
gǎnqíng	感情		feeling, emotion, affection	n.	10
gǎnshòu	感受		feel; experience	v.; n.	19
gānyán	肝炎		hepatitis	n.	2
gǎnyìng	感应	感應	induction, response, reaction	n.	17
gǎnyú	敢于	敢於	dare to	adv.	6
gàofā	告发	告發	report (an offender), lodge an accusation against	v.	3
gāolóudàshà	高楼大厦	高樓大廈	high buildings and large mansions	成语	18
gé	隔		separate, cut off, impede, be at a distance from	v.	16

gèhánggèyè	各行各业	各行各業	all professions	成语	6
gēliè	割裂		cut, sever	v.	12
gèngshàngyìcénglóu	更上一层楼	更上一層樓	scale new heights, attain a yet higher goal	成语	17
gètǐ	个体	個體	individuality	n.	1
gōu	沟	溝	ditch, waterway	n.	19
gōuhuǒ	篝火		campfire	n.	4
guàhào	挂号	掛號	register at a hospital	vo.	2
guānfāng	官方		official, of the government	n.	20
guǎngbōjù	广播剧		radio play	n.	8
guāngcǎixiānliang	光彩鲜亮		bright, new, cheery	成语	14
guāngróng	光荣	光榮	honor, glory; honorable, glorious	n.; adj.	9
guānjiàn	关键	關鍵	key point, crucial importance	n.	11
guānzhù	关注	關注	follow (an issue) closely, pay close attention to; concern	v.; n.	18
gùdìng	固定		fix; regular, fixed	v.; adj.	17
guīnü	闺女	閨女	girl, daughter	n.	19
gǔkē	骨科		orthopedics	n.	2
gùkèzhìshàng	顾客至上	顧客至上	customers come first	成语	17
gǔsègǔxiāng	古色古香		have an antique flavor, classic beauty	成语	14
gùyōng	雇佣	雇傭	employ, hire	v.	8
hǎibá	海拔		height above sea level, elevation	n.	15
hǎibào	海报	海報	poster	n.	3
hǎiguī	海归	海歸	return from overseas; returnees	v.; n.	6
hánlèi	含泪	含淚	with tears, in tears	vo.	12
háowúyíwèn	毫无疑问	毫無疑問	certainty, without a doubt, without question	成语	16
héng	横	橫	cross; horizontal	v.; adj.	1
héqún	合群		get along well with others; gregarious	vo.; adj.	1
hóngtōngtōng	红彤彤	紅彤彤	bright pink or red	adj.	15
hǒu	吼		roar, growl, shout	v.	3
hū	呼		exhale, cry out, call	v.	1
huābàn	花瓣		pedal	n.	9
huānshēng	欢声	歡聲	cheerful sound	n.	11
huàshù	桦树	樺樹	birch	n.	20
hùdào	互道		say to each other, greet each other	v.	20
huī	灰		ash, dust	n.; adj.	19
huǐdiào	毁掉		damage, ruin	v.	11

huīfù	恢复	恢復	recover, restore	v.	6
huíguī	回归	回歸	return to original place; regression	v.; n.	3
hūjiàolíng	呼叫铃	呼叫鈴	call bell	n.	17
hūlüè	忽略		ignore, neglect	v.	6
húlusī	葫芦丝	葫蘆絲	cucurbit flute (or hulusi)	n.	3
húntun	馄饨	餛飩	wonton	n.	4
hūnyīnbāobàn	婚姻包办	婚姻包辦	marriage is arranged	phr.	10
huòdé	获得	獲得	obtain, acquire	v.	11
hūshì	忽视	忽視	ignore, neglect, overlook	v.	15
hútòng	胡同	衚衕	lane, alley, bystreet	n.	18
hūyù	呼吁	呼籲	appeal, call on, plead for, urge	v.; n.	15
jí	即		namely	adv.	18
jià	嫁		(a woman) marry to (a man)	v.	19
jiān	兼		double; simultaneously, concurrently	v.; adv.	3
jiān	兼		do concurrently	v.; adv.	10
jiānchí	坚持	堅持	persist in; persistence	v.; n.	4
jiǎndiào	剪掉		cut off	v.	3
jiànduōshíguǎng	见多识广	見多識廣	wisdom comes from extensive observation	成语	20
jiāndūyuán	监督员	監督員	supervisor, superintendent	n.	17
jī'áng	激昂		excited and indignant	adj.	1
jiànxíngjiànyuǎn	渐行渐远	漸行漸遠	go far gradually, get apart gradually	成语	10
jiànyì	建议	建議	propose, suggest; suggestion	v.; n.	9
jiānzhá	煎炸		fry and deep fry (cooking method)	v.	5
jiāo'ào	骄傲	驕傲	be proud of; pride; arrogant, conceited	v.; n.; adj.	19
jiāoqū	郊区	郊區	suburb, outskirts	n.	4
jiāotì	交替		supersede; alternately	v.; adv.	1
jiàzhíguān	价值观	價值觀	values	n.	6
jiàzigǔ	架子鼓		drum set	n.	3
jìdiàn	祭奠		hold a memorial ceremony for	v.; n.	9
jiēduàn	阶段	階段	stage, phase, period	n.	6
jiégòu	结构	結構	structure	n.	2
jiēnà	接纳	接納	accept (into an organization), admit (as a member)	v.	4
jiépāi	节拍	節拍	time, beat, tempo	n.	1

jiéshěng	节省	節省	economize, save	v.	19
jiéshí	节食	節食	diet	v.; n.	5
jiēwěn	接吻		kiss, give a kiss	vo.	1
jiézòu	节奏	節奏	rhythm	n.	3
jígé	及格		pass a test or examination; a pass grade	v.; n.	1
jíjiāng	即将	即將	soon, upcoming	adv.	12
jìlǜ	纪律	紀律	rules, regulations	n.	4
jǐng	井		well	n.	11
jīngcǎi	精彩		brilliant, splendid, wonderful	adj.	1
jǐnggào	警告		warn; warning	v.; n.	1
jīngmíng	精明		astute, shrewd, skilled	adj.	16
jìngrán	竟然		unexpectedly, to one's surprise	adv.	2
jīngshénmiànmào	精神面貌		spiritual outlook	phr.	19
jīngsuàn	精算		actuarial science	n.	6
jīngtàn	惊叹	驚嘆	exclaim with admiration, marvel at	v.	2
jìngtóu	镜头	鏡頭	camera lens, shot, scene	n.	15
jīngyíng	经营	經營	manage, run; operation	v.; n.	4
jīnróng shíbào	金融时报	金融時報	*Financial Times*	pn.	6
jǐnshèn	谨慎	謹慎	prudent, careful, cautious	adj.	16
jǐnzhāng	紧张	緊張	nervous, intense	adj.	7
jìnzhǐ	禁止		prohibit	v.	5
jīròujuǎn	鸡肉卷	雞肉卷	chicken wrap	n.	17
jìshén	祭神		offer sacrifice to gods, worship	vo.; n.	11
jítǐ	集体	集體	collective team, collectivity	n.	1
jìtuō	寄托	寄託	place (one's hope, feeling, etc.) on	v.	9
jiūjìng	究竟		outcome; actually, after all	n.; adv.	12
jiǔjùbúsàn	久聚不散		collected, could not scatter	pr.	15
juécè	决策	決策	make policy; policy decision	v.; n.	6
juécèquán	决策权	決策權	decision-making authority	n.	16
juéqǐ	崛起		rise abruptly, rise as a political force	v.	18
jūgōng	鞠躬		bow (to show respect)	vo.	7
jùjué	拒绝	拒絕	refuse; rejection	v.; n.	9
jùlèbù	俱乐部	俱樂部	club	n.	4
jùlí	距离	距離	distance, interval; be apart from	n.; v.	6

jūnhéng	均衡		balance; balanced	v.; n.; adj.	5
jūnlèi	菌类	菌類	fungus	n.	5
jùnxiàn	郡县	郡縣	prefecture and county system	n.	15
jūrán	居然		unexpectedly, to one's surprise	adv.	5
kàozhěn	靠枕		supporting pillow	n.	4
kèchéng	课程	課程	curriculum	n.	16
Kèláiméngfēilǎng	克莱蒙费朗	克萊蒙費朗	Clermont-Ferrand	pn.	6
Kěndéjī	肯德基		Kentucky Fried Chicken	pn.	17
kěndìng	肯定		affirm; positive, definite; definitely, undoubtedly	v.; adj.; adv.	17
Kěnnídí	肯尼迪		Kennedy (Harvard John F. Kennedy School of Government)	pn.	18
kěxiǎng'érzhī	可想而知		one can well imagine	成语	10
kèzhàn	客栈	客棧	inn, tavern	n.	15
kuàguógōngsī	跨国公司	跨國公司	international corporation	n.	7
kuǎn	款		kind, pattern, type	m.	17
kuānróng	宽容	寬容	show forebearing; tolerant	v.; adj.	10
kuānyù	宽裕	寬裕	well-to-do, be comfortably off, plenty	adj.	19
kǔmèn	苦闷	苦悶	depressed, downhearted	adj.	7
kǔxiào	苦笑		make a wry smile; forced smile	v.; n.	2
lǎba	喇叭		brass wind instrument, trumpet	n.	1
làcháng	腊肠		Chinese sausage	n.	8
láiyuán	来源	來源	originate; origin, source	v.; n.	5
lājī	垃圾		garbage, junk, trash	n.	19
lǎn	揽	攬	seize, grasp, take (into one's arms)	v.	4
làngmàn	浪漫		romantic	adj.	10
lǎowài	老外		foreigner	n.	19
lǎoyítào	老一套		conventional (things), conventionality	n.	1
lěngluò	冷落		treat coldly; deserted, desolate	v.; adj.	17
liánluò	联络	聯絡	contact, communicate; liaison	v.; n.	12
liǎnpáng	脸庞	臉龐	shape of a face, face	n.	15
liánsuǒ	连锁	連鎖	chain	v.; n.	17
lièduì	列队	列隊	line up, form into lines	vo.	1
línghuāqián	零花钱	零花錢	pocket money	n.	16

lǐniàn	理念		idea	n.	5
línyīn	林荫	林蔭	tree shade	n.	4
lǐsuǒdāngrán	理所当然	理所當然	take for granted; it goes without saying	成语	1
liúsàn	流散		wander, scatter, drift	v.	20
liúyán	留言		leave comments, leave a message; message	vo.; n.	8
lóngpáo	龙袍	龍袍	dragon robe, imperial robe	n.	11
lún	轮	輪	take turns; round	v.; m.; n.	2
lúnliú	轮流	輪流	rotate, do sth in turn, take turns, alternate	v.	19
lùntán	论坛		forum, tribune, place to express oneself in public	n.	8
luòwǔ	落伍		fall behind; out of date	vo.; adj.	3
lùxù	陆续	陸續	constantly, continually	adv.	20
mài	脉	脈	pulse	n.	11
májiàng	麻将	麻將	mahjong	n.	4
mǎnyì	满意	滿意	satisfy; satisfaction	v.; n.	2
máodùn	矛盾		contradiction	n.	3
máosèdùnkāi	茅塞顿开	茅塞頓開	suddenly enlightened	成语	7
méitǐ	媒体	媒體	news media	n.	13
méng	蒙		cover, encounter, suffer	v.	15
měng	懵		muddled	adj.	5
mèngjìng	梦境	夢境	dream, dreamland	n.	18
ménhùwǎngzhàn	门户网站	門戶網站	(website) portals	pn.	16
miǎnqiǎng	勉强	勉強	force sb to do sth; reluctant; reluctantly	v.; adj.; adv.	10
miànshā	面纱	面紗	veil	n.	15
miànshìguān	面试官	面試官	interviewer	n.	7
míbǔ	弥补	彌補	compensate, make up for	v.	6
mìjué	秘诀	秘訣	secret (of success)	n.	10
míméng	迷蒙	迷濛	mist; misty	n.; adj.	15
mínglìngjìnzhǐ	明令禁止		prohibit by explicit order	成语	1
míngqīng	明清		Ming and Qing Dynasties	n.	15
mǐnruì	敏锐	敏銳	quick, sharp (eyes), acute (sense)	adj.	20
mínsú	民俗		folk custom	n.	9
mínzú	民族		ethnic group, nation	n.	9
mírén	迷人		enchanting, attractive, fascinating	adj.	15
míshàng	迷上		fascinated by, crazy about	v.	3
mò	墨		Chinese ink, ink stick, black	n.	15

mòjìng	墨镜	墨鏡	sunglasses	n.	13
mòqì	默契		tacit understanding	n.	10
móshì	模式		model, pattern	n.	18
mótiāndàlóu	摩天大楼	摩天大樓	skyscraper	n.	18
mǒu	某		certain (refer to a certain person or thing)	pr.	11
mùbiāo	目标	目標	objective, target, goal	n.	16
nèidì	内地	内地	inland, interior	n.	20
nèihán	内涵	内涵	connotation, implied meaning	n.	9
ní	泥		wet mud	n.	19
niàntou	念头	念頭	thought, idea, intention	n.	10
niǔ	扭		turn round, twist, sprain	v.	2
nónggēng	农耕	農耕	farming, agriculture	n.	20
Nuòdīnghàndàxué	诺丁汉大学	諾丁漢大學	University of Nottingham	pn.	6
ǒurán	偶然		accidental, unusual; accidentally	adj.; adv.	7
pāi	拍		take (an X-ray examination)	v.	2
páichì	排斥		reject, exclude	v.	4
páigǔ	排骨		spareribs, steak, rib	n.	20
páijiě	排解		mediate, reconcile	v.; n.	14
pángbái	旁白		say as an aside; aside (in a play)	v.; n.	8
pángdà	庞大	龐大	big, huge, enormous	adj.	6
pángxì	旁系		collateral	adj.	12
pànnì	叛逆		revolt against; rebel	v.; n.	16
pào	泡		soak, immerse	v.	4
pèifú	佩服		admire, think highly of	v.	2
péixùn	培训	培訓	train; training	v.; n.	20
pèiyīn	配音		dub (a film, etc.); dubbing	vo.; n.	8
péndì	盆地		basin, plain area skirted by mountains or highland	n.	15
pèngdào	碰到		run into, bump into	v.	3
pēngrèn	烹饪	烹飪	culinary art; cook, cooking	v.; n.	5
pī	批		batch	m.	17
piànzi	片子		film, movie	n.	2
piāo	飘	飄	blow, drift about, flutter	v.	14
piāopiāoyùxiān	飘飘欲仙	飄飄欲仙	feeling as if in paradise, "in heaven"	成语	4

píng	凭	憑	rely on, depend on	v.	10
píngjūn	平均		average; mean, evenness; medium, median	v.; n.; adj.	16
píngmù	屏幕		screen	n.	16
pǔbiàn	普遍		universal, general	adj.	4
Pǔluówàngsī	普罗旺斯	普羅旺斯	Provence (France)	pn.	15
pūmiànérlái	扑面向来	撲面而來	blow into one's face	成语	16
Pǔmǐzú	普米族		Pumi minority	pn.	11
qiān	牵	牽	lead along	v.	13
qiángdào	强盗	強盜	bandit, robber	n.	1
qiángliè	强烈	強烈	strong, powerful, intense	adj.	10
qiángzhǐ	墙纸		wallpaper	n.	8
qiānjiāwànhù	千家万户	千家萬戶	thousands of families and households	成语	8
qiánlì	潜力	潛力	latent capability, potential, potentiality	n.	17
qiánxī	前夕		eve, on the eve of	n.	8
qiányímòhuà	潜移默化	潛移默化	imperceptibly influence, influence unconsciously	成语	13
qiāoluódǎgǔ	敲锣打鼓	敲鑼打鼓	beat drums and gongs	成语	11
qièshēn	切身		personal (experience/ understanding)	adj.	19
qìfēn	气氛		surrounding feeling, atmosphere	n.	8
qǐfú	起伏		rise and fall; rising and falling	v.; adj.	11
qíguān	奇观	奇觀	wonder, spectacle, spectacular sight	n.	15
qìliú	气流	氣流	air current, airflow, airstream	n.	15
qín	秦		Qin Dynasty (221–206 BC)	n.	15
qíngbùzìjīn	情不自禁		cannot help doing	成语	10
qīngchè	清澈		limpid, crystal clear	adj.	19
qīngdǎo	倾倒	傾倒	topple over, greatly admire	v.	16
qǐngjiǎn	请柬	請柬	invitation card, written invitation	n.	13
qínglǚ	情侣	情侶	sweethearts, lovers	n.	1
qīngtīng	倾听	傾聽	listen attentively to	v.	17
qíngtóuyìhé	情投意合		find one another congenial, hit it off perfectly	成语	10
qīngxī	清晰		clear, explicit	adj.	9
qíngxù	情绪	情緒	emotion, feeling, mood	n.	7

qīngyū	清淤	清淤	desilt, desilting	vo.	19
qínháng	琴行		music instrument company	n.	3
qínkuài	勤快		diligent, hard working	adj.	19
qīnshǔ	亲属	親屬	relatives, kinship	n.	12
qípái	棋牌		chess, board or card game	n.	4
qìpài	气派	氣派	imposing manner; dignified	n.; adj.	2
qǐsè	起色		improvement, sign of recovery	n.	10
qiūlíng	丘陵		hills, mounds	n.	15
qiūqiān	秋千	鞦韆	swing	n.	9
qìxiàngwànqiān	气象万千	氣象萬千	spectacular sight, wonderful and mighty panorama	成语	15
qǐyè	企业	企業	enterprise, company	n.	7
qǔ	娶		(a man) marry to (a woman), take a wife	v.	19
quān	圈		circle	v.; n.	13
quánqiúhuà	全球化		globalize; globalization	v.; n.	1
quányì	权益	權益	rights and interests	n.	17
quányù	痊愈	痊癒	completely cured or recovered (from an illness)	v.	2
quánzhí	全职	全職	full time	n.; adj.	4
rǎomín	扰民	擾民	disturb residents	vo.	3
ráomìng	饶命	饒命	spare one's life	vo.	2
réncì	人次		sum of people participating, visitor count	cm.	20
réngrán	仍然		still, yet	adv.	3
rénjūn	人均		capita, per person, average for individuals	n.	16
rénlìzīyuánbù	人力资源部	人力资源部	human resources department	n.	7
rénqíngwèi	人情味		human feelings, human kindness	n.	14
rěntòng	忍痛		bear and suffer pain, reluctantly give up	vo.	3
rónghé	融合		mix together, fuse, merge	v.; n.	11
ruò	弱		weaken; weak, feeble, young	v.; adj.	20
rúshāng	儒商		Confucian businessman	n.	15

sài	赛	賽	compete; contest	v.; n.	11
sǎomù	扫墓	掃墓	sweep a grave, pay respect to the dead people	vo.	9
sēngrén	僧人		shaman, monk	n.	9
shài	晒	曬	be exposed to the sun	v.	11
shāixuǎn	筛选	篩選	filter	v.	10
shāmò	沙漠		desert	n.	15
shānchú	删除	刪除	delete	v.	10
shàndài	善待		be kind to	v.	10
shāng	伤	傷	wound; injury; wounded	v.; n.; adj.	20
shǎnliàng	闪亮	閃亮	twinkle, brilliant, shiny	adj.	10
shānliáng	山梁		ridge (of a mountain or hill)	n.	11
shānluán	山峦	山巒	chain of mountains	n.	11
shànyǎngfèi	赡养费	贍養費	alimony	n.	10
shāo	稍		a little, a bit, slightly	adv.	14
shāobǐng	烧饼	燒餅	baked sesame-seed flat cake	n.	17
shāomài	烧卖		Cantonese steamed dumpling (a type of dimsum)	n.	8
shǎshì	傻事		silly things	n.	13
shāshǒu	杀手	殺手	professional killer, hitman	n.	5
shèbèi	设备	設備	equipment, facilities	n.	20
shèjiāo	社交		social contact, social life	n.	8
shēngcáizhīdào	生财之道	生財之道	methods to gain money	成语	20
shēngtài	生态	生態	ecology, habits, way of life	n.	20
shēngyá	生涯		career, profession, livehood	n.	7
shēnkè	深刻		deep, profound	adj.	19
shénqí	神奇		magical	adj.	2
shēnqǐng	申请	申請	apply for, make an official request; application	v.; n.	1
shěnshì	审视	審視	look at carefully, examine	v.	6
shèntòu	渗透	滲透	permeate, infiltrate; infiltration	v.; n.	13
shénwǎng	神往		fascinated, longing	v.	15
shèrù	摄入	攝入	absorb, ingest	v.	5
shétāi	舌苔		coated tongue	n.	2
shèyǐngshī	摄影师	攝影師	photographer, cameraman	n.	15
shǐ	驶	駛	drive, pilot, sail	v.	15

shíchéndàhǎi	石沉大海		never seen or heard again (like a stone dropped into the sea)	成语	7
shìfǒu	是否		whether or not, is it so or not	adv.	13
shìpín	视频	視頻	video	n.	9
shíshàng	时尚	時尚	fashion, vogue	n.	14
shíshī	石狮	石獅	stone lions	n.	18
shītú	师徒	師徒	master and apprentice	n.	15
shìyě	视野	視野	field of vision, perspective	n.	16
shīyèzhě	失业者	失業者	unemployed person	n.	7
shǒu	首		head, chief, leader; first, foremost, first of all	n.; adj.	14
shǒuduàn	手段		means, method	n.	4
shōugōng	收工		stop work for the day	vo.	13
shòuliè	狩猎	狩獵	hunt, go hunting; hunt, hunting	v.; n.	20
shòupí	兽皮	獸皮	animal skin	n.	20
shòuquán	授权		empower, authorize, license	v.	8
shuǎ	耍		play, play with	v.; n.	4
shǔbiāo	鼠标	鼠標	(computer) mouse	n.	16
shùjù	数据	數據	data	n.	6
shùjùkù	数据库	數據庫	database	n.	6
shūrù	输入	輸入	bring in, import, input	v.	16
sōusuǒyǐnqíng	搜索引擎		search engine	pn.	16
suízhī'érlái	随之而来	隨之而來	following upon	phr.	19
sǔnshī	损失	損失	lose; loss	v.; n.	17
sūyóuchá	酥油茶		buttered tea	n.	20
tái	抬		lift, raise	v.	13
táijiē	台阶	臺階	staircase, steps	n.	18
tàiyáng	太阳	太陽	sun	n.	15
tán	潭		deep pool, pond	n.	11
táng	塘		pool, pond	n.	19
táo	逃		escape, flee, run away	v.	11
tāo	掏		pull out, dig	v.	4
tàotóu	套头	套頭	turtleneck, pullover	adj.	13
tèshū	特殊		special, particular, exceptional	adj.	6
tiāoxuǎn	挑选	挑選	pick, choose, select	v.	1
tiǎozhàn	挑战	挑戰	challenge; contest	vo.; n.	7
tíchàng	提倡		advocate, promote	v.	5
tiēxī	贴息	貼息	discount, subsidized interest	v.; n.	20
tíhúguàndǐng	醍醐灌顶	醍醐灌頂	realize suddenly, be enlightened	成语	12
tǐzhì	体制	體制	system, organization	n.	1

tóngbāo	同胞		born of the same parents, fellow citizen or countryman	n.	15
tōngchàng	通畅	通暢	unobstructed, easy and smooth	adj.	19
tōngguò	通过	通過	pass through; by means of	v.; prep.	8
tǒngjì	统计	統計	count, compute; statistics, census	v.; n.	20
tōngxiāo	通宵		through the night, overnight	n.	14
tóusù	投诉	投訴	complain; complaint	v.; n.	7
tǔdòu	土豆		potato	n.	20
tuīérguǎngzhī	推而广之	推而廣之	apply broadly	成语	12
tuījiàn	推荐	推薦	recommend; recommendation	v.; n.	1
tuìxiū	退休		retire	v.	4
tūjī	突击	突擊	make a sudden attack, make a concentrated effort	v.	3
Tǔlǔfān	吐鲁番	吐魯番	Turfan Basin in Xinjiang Province, China	pn.	15
tuōlí	脱离	脫離	separate oneself from, away from, out of	v.	12
túténg	图腾	圖騰	totem	n.	11
wàijí	外籍		foreign nationality, non-local residents	n.	1
wǎn	挽		draw, pull, retrieve	v.	1
wǎngluò	网络	網絡	network	n.	8
wàngshèng	旺盛		vigorous, exuberant, robust	adj.	16
wēibó	微博		microblog	n.	8
wéichí	维持	維持	maintain, keep, support	v.	10
wèikǒu	胃口		appetite	n.	2
wèiyú	位于	位於	located, situated	vc.	15
wèiyù	卫浴	衛浴	bathroom	n.	20
wēnxīn	温馨	溫馨	warm, cozy	adj.	14
Wòdùnshāng xuéyuàn	沃顿商学院	沃頓商學院	Wharton School of the University of Pennsylvania	pn.	6
Wòěrmǎ	沃尔玛		Wal-Mart	pn.	17
wùhuì	误会	誤會	misunderstand; misunderstanding	v.; n.	5
wùqì	雾气	霧氣	fog, mist	n.	15
xiàhuài	吓坏	嚇壞	scared, frighten	v.	5
xiàjuéxīn	下决心	下决心	make up one's mind	vo.	10

xián	弦		string (of a musical instrument)	n.	3
xiáncài	咸菜	鹹菜	pickled vegetables	n.	13
xiāngguān	相关	相關	related, interrelated	adj.	6
xiāngjì	相继	相繼	in succession, one after another	adv.	20
xiāngnóng	香浓	香濃	aromatic and concentrated (smell)	adj.	20
xiǎngshòu	享受		enjoy (rights, benefits, etc.); pleasure	v.; n.	16
xiāngyù	相遇		meet	v.	10
xiàngzhēng	象征		symbolize, signify, stand for; symbol	v.; n.	8
xiànmù	羡慕		admire; admiration	v.; n.	10
xiānqǐ	掀起		lift, surge	v.	3
xiànrù	陷入		sink into, get caught up in	v.	4
xiānyàn	鲜艳	鮮艷	brightly colored	adj.	11
xiǎodiào	小调	小調	ditty, tune, minor (for music)	n.	19
xiāofèizhě	消费者	消費者	consumer	n.	17
xiāojí	消极	消極	negative, passive, dispirited	adj.	7
xiāoshī	消失		disappear, vanish, dissolve	v.	18
xiāoxiàng	肖像		portrait	n.	3
xǐchūwàngwài	喜出望外		overjoyed, happy beyond expectations	成语	2
xiépō	斜坡		slope	n.	13
xìjiáomànyàn	细嚼慢咽	細嚼慢咽	chew well and swallow slowly	成语	5
Xīngbākè	星巴克		Starbucks	pn.	17
xìngfú	幸福		happiness, blessedness; happy, blessed	n.; adj.	17
xìngfúzhīyuán	幸福之源		source of happiness	phr.	10
xíngróng	形容		describe	v.	10
xíngxiàng	形象		image	n.	11
xíngzhèng	行政		administration	n.	1
Xīnjiāng	新疆		Xinjiang Province, China	pn.	15
xīnxīng	新兴	新興	new and developing, rising, newly developing	adj.	20
xìnyù	信誉	信譽	prestige, credit, reputation	n.	13
xiūxián	休闲	休閑	have a leisure time activity; leisure	v.; adj.	4
xīxīxiāngguān	息息相关	息息相關	closely interrelated, closely linked	成语	17

xīyù	西域		western regions in ancient China	n.	15
xìzhì	细致	細緻	intricate, precise about details	adj.	2
xuānchuán	宣传		propagate, disseminate; propaganda	v.; n.	8
xuǎnzé	选择		choose, select; selection, option	v.; n.	8
xuèguǎn	血管		blood vessel	n.	11
xuènóngyúshuǐ	血浓于水	血濃於水	blood is thicker than water	成语	12
xuéqū	学区	學區	school district	n.	1
xūnǐ	虚拟	虛擬	virtual, fictitious	adj.	8
xùnsù	迅速		rapid, prompt	adj.	3
yǎngshēng	养生	養生	keep in good health, care for life	v.	5
yǎngwòqǐzuò	仰卧起坐	仰臥起坐	sit-ups	phr.	4
yánjǐn	严谨	嚴謹	rigorous, strict, precise	adj.	7
yǎnkuàng	眼眶		eye socket, rim of the eye	n.	13
yánqī	延期		postpone, put off, delay, extension	v.	13
yànqǐng	宴请	宴請	invite (someone to a banquet)	v.	9
yǎnshì	掩饰	掩飾	cover up, conceal; dissimulation	v.; n.	1
yánsù	严肃	嚴肅	strictly enforce; serious (attitude), solemn	v.; adj.	7
yáogǔnyuè	摇滚乐	搖滾樂	rock and roll music	pn.	3
yáokòng	遥控		control remotely; remote control	v.; n	8
yàoshi	钥匙	鑰匙	key	n.	15
yàoyǎn	耀眼		dazzle; dazzling	n.; adj.	15
yáoyuǎn	遥远	遙遠	distant, remote, faraway	adj.	16
yǎxìng	雅兴	雅興	aesthetic mood, refined interest	n.	9
yíchǎn	遗产	遺產	legacy, inheritance, heritage	n.	20
yíchànà	一刹那	一刹那	in a flash, a very short time, in the twinkling of an eye	phr.	13
yìchéngbúbiàn	一成不变	一成不變	unchanged, unchangeable	成语	16
yīcì	依次		progress in proper order; sequencially	v.; adv.	1
yìguótāxiāng	异国他乡	異國他鄉	foreign country	成语	6
yíjiànzhōngqíng	一见钟情	一見鐘情	fall in love at first sight	成语	10
yǐjīng	已经	已經	already	adv.	2

yǐjiǔ	已久		very long	adj.	15
yījù	依据	依據	judging by; basis	v.; n.	6
yìmíngjīngrén	一鸣惊人	一鳴驚人	become famous overnight	成语	16
yǐncáng	隐藏	隱藏	hide, conceal, keep out of sight	v.	10
yīng	鹰	鷹	eagle	n.	11
yǐngbì	影壁		screen wall	n.	18
yìngchou	应酬	應酬	socialize with; social engagement	v.; n.	13
yìngpìnzhě	应聘者	應聘者	job applicant	n.	7
yíngxiāo	营销	營銷	marketing	n.	7
yíngyǎng	营养	營養	nutrition	n.	5
yìngzhìhuà	硬质化	硬質化	harden, stiffen	v.; adj.	19
yìnjì	印迹	印跡	mark, print	n.	18
yīnrén'éryì	因人而异	因人而異	vary with each individual, different from person to person	成语	5
yīnyǐng	阴影	陰影	shadow	n.	7
yīrán	依然		still, as before	adv.	4
yìrújìwǎng	一如既往		just as before, in the past or as always	成语	12
yìsībùgǒu	一丝不苟	一絲不苟	conscientiousness and meticulousness about every detail	成语	2
yìtǐhuà	一体化	一體化	integrate; integration	v.; n.	16
yìwèi	意味		mean; meaning	v.; n.	5
yǒngxiàn	涌现	涌現	emerge in a large number, spring up	v.	9
yòuéryuán	幼儿园	幼兒園	kindergarten, nursery	n.	1
yóuliè	游猎	游獵	travel to hunt; hunting trip	v.; n.	20
yōulǜ	忧虑	憂慮	worry, concern; anxiety	v.; n.	15
yóutiáo	油条	油條	long, deep-fried, twisted dough sticks	n.	17
yōuxiù	优秀	優秀	excellent, outstanding	adj.	1
yōuyǎ	优雅	優雅	beautiful and elegant, graceful	adj.	1
yōuyuè	优越	優越	superior, advantageous	adj.	16
yuánshēngtài	原生态		primeval ecology	n.	20
yuánshǐ	原始		original, firsthand, primitive	adj.	20
yuánzhù	援助		help, support; assistance	v.; n.	12
yuánzhuīxíng	圆锥形	圓錐形	cone	n.	20
yújiā	瑜伽		yoga	n.	4
yùjiǎn	预检	預檢	pre-examine; initial inspection	v.; n.	2
yūn	晕	暈	pass out; dizzy	v.; adj.	2
yùnàn	遇难	遇難	killed, die in an accident	vo.	11

zàikè	载客	載客	carry passengers	vo.	14
zàitǐ	载体	載體	carrier, knowledge or information	n.	18
zàiyì	在意		care about, mind	v.	12
Zàngzú	藏族		Tibetan minority group	pn.	20
zēngguāng	增光		dignify, add to the prestige of	v.	3
zhāduī	扎堆		gather sb/sth round	vo.	1
zhāgēn	扎根		rooted in	vo.	13
zhàn	占	佔	occupy, take	v.	16
zhànbài	战败	戰敗	lose a battle or war, be defeated	v.	11
zhàng'ài	障碍	障礙	obstacle, obstruction, barrier	n.	16
zhǎngwò	掌握		grasp; mastery	v.; n.	5
zhǎnlǎn	展览	展覽	display, show; exhibition	v.; n.	9
zhànzhēng	战争	戰爭	war	n.	11
zhāojiǔwǎnwǔ	朝九晚五		work from nine to five every day	成语	13
zhāopìn	招聘		invite applications, give public notice of vacancies to be filled	v.	7
zhèbèizi	这辈子	這輩子	this life	n.	10
zhěhóng	赭红		reddish brown	n.	15
zhèndòng	震动	震動	shake, shock, vibrate	v.	17
zhěnduàn	诊断	診斷	diagnose; diagnosis	v.; n.	2
zhènghǎo	正好		just right, just enough, happen to	adv.	12
zhèngquè	正确	正確	correct, right, proper	adj.	2
Zhèngzhōu	郑州	鄭州	Zhengzhou (capital of Henan Province, China)	pn.	6
zhèntiān	震天		shake (the air), shock	vo.	11
zhēzhù	遮住		shut up, blot out	v.	1
zhī	织	織	knit, weave	v.	13
zhīchēng	支撑	支撐	hold up, sustain, support	v.	13
zhīfáng	脂肪		fat	n.	5
zhīmíngdù	知名度		popularity, fame	n.	13
zhīpèi	支配		dominate, govern; control, domination	v.; n.	16
zhìtóngdàohé	志同道合		share the same ideals and thoughts	成语	15
zhíxì	直系		immediate (family members)	adj.	12
zhìyuàn	志愿	志願	volunteer to do something; wish, will	v.; n.	1
zhízé	职责	職責	duty, obligation, responsibility	n.	7

zhōngguī	终归	終歸	eventually, in the end, after all	adv.	12
zhòngsuǒzhōuzhī	众所周知	眾所周知	known to all	成语	4
zhōuchēláodùn	舟车劳顿		fatigued by a long journey	成语	8
zhòuwén	皱纹	皺紋	wrinkle, furrow, lines (facial)	n.	20
zhuāng	庄	莊	village, town	n.	18
zhuāngbàn	装扮		dress up, attire, decorate	v.	8
zhuāngzuò	装作	裝作	act, pretend to	v.	12
zhuānxīnzhìzhì	专心致志	專心致志	concentrate one's attention, thoughts or efforts on one thing	成语	15
zhuīpěng	追捧		follow, pursue, admire	v.	13
zìbēi	自卑		having low self-esteem	adj.	4
zìháo	自豪		take pride in oneself	v.	8
zīshēn	资深	資深	senior	adj.	3
zìwǒrèntóng	自我认同	自我認同	self-agreement, self-identification	成语	16
zīxúnshī	咨询师	諮詢師	consultant, counselor	n.	7
zìyíng	自营	自營	self-run, self-support	v.	18
zōnghé	综合	綜合	synthesize; synthesis	v.; n.	11
zōngjiào	宗教		religion	n.	12
zǒubiàn	走遍		go over, travel across	v.	20
zǒudòng	走动	走動	walk about, (of relatives and friends) visit each other	v.	12
zú	族		nationality, class or group of things or people with common features	n.	8
zúbùchūhù	足不出户		keep to the house, stay home	成语	10
zuì'ègǎn	罪恶感	罪惡感	guilty feeling	n.	10
zuìzhōng	最终	最終	ultimate, final	n.	7
zūnjìng	尊敬		respect, honor; honorable	v.; adj.	16
zuòdiàn	座垫	座墊	seat cushion	n.	4
zuòwúxūxí	座无虚席	座無虛席	packed to capacity, full house	成语	4

English–Pinyin glossary

English translation	Simplified characters	Traditional characters	Pinyin	Word class	Chapter
a little, a bit, slightly	稍		shāo	adv.	14
abandon, give up	放弃	放棄	fàngqì	v.	3
ablaze with lights	灯火通明	燈火通明	dēnghuǒtōngmíng	成语	14
abound in gifts of nature; unique	得天独厚	得天獨厚	détiāndúhòu	成语	16
absorb, ingest	摄入	攝入	shèrù	v.	5
accept (into an organization), admit (as a member)	接纳	接納	jiēnà	v.	4
accidental, unusual; accidentally	偶然		ǒurán	adj.; adv.	7
act, pretend to	装作	裝作	zhuāngzuò	v.	12
actuarial science	精算		jīngsuàn	n.	6
administration	行政		xíngzhèng	n.	1
admire, think highly of	佩服		pèifú	v.	2
admire; admiration	羡慕		xiànmù	v.; n.	10
advocate, promote	提倡		tíchàng	v.	5
aesthetic mood, refined interest	雅兴	雅興	yǎxìng	n.	9
affirm; positive, definite; definitely, undoubtedly	肯定		kěndìng	v.; adj.; adv.	17
after all, all in all	毕竟	畢竟	bìjìng	adv.	4
air current, airflow, airstream	气流	氣流	qìliú	n.	15
alimony	赡养费	贍養費	shànyǎngfèi	n.	10
all professions	各行各业	各行各業	gèhánggèyè	成语	6
already	已经	已經	yǐjīng	adv.	2
ancestral hall or temple, memorial temple	祠堂		cítáng	n.	15
ancient type of Chinese football	蹴球	蹴球	cùqiú	n.	9
animal skin	兽皮	獸皮	shòupí	n.	20
annoyance; unhappy, uncomfortable	烦闷	煩悶	fánmèn	n.; adj.	14

apologize; apology	道歉		dàoqiàn	vo.; n.	7
appeal, call on, plead for, urge	呼吁	呼籲	hūyù	v.; n.	15
appellation, title	称谓	稱謂	chēngwèi	n.	12
appetite	胃口		wèikǒu	n.	2
apply broadly	推而广之	推而廣之	tuīérguǎngzhī	成语	12
apply for, make an official request; application	申请	申請	shēnqǐng	v.; n.	1
archives	档案馆	檔案館	dàng'ànguǎn	n.	9
aromatic and concentrated (smell)	香浓	香濃	xiāngnóng	adj.	20
ash, dust	灰		huī	n.; adj.	19
astute, shrewd, skilled	精明		jīngmíng	adj.	16
average; mean, evenness; medium, median	平均		píngjūn	v.; n.; adj.	16
awkward, embarrassed	尴尬	尷尬	gāngà	adj.	2
baked sesame-seed flat cake	烧饼	燒餅	shāobǐng	n.	17
balance; balanced	均衡		jūnhéng	v.; n.; adj.	5
bandit, robber	强盗	強盜	qiángdào	n.	1
basin, plain area skirted by mountains or highland	盆地		péndì	n.	15
batch	批		pī	m.	17
bathroom	卫浴	衛浴	wèiyù	n.	20
be apart from; distance, interval	距离	距離	jùlí	v.; n.	6
be busy running about, rush about	奔波		bēnbō	v.	7
be exposed to the sun	晒	曬	shài	v.	11
be kind to	善待		shàndài	v.	10
be proud of; pride; arrogant, conceited	骄傲	驕傲	jiāo'ào	v.; n.; adj.	19
bear and suffer pain, reluctantly give up	忍痛		rěntòng	vo.	3
bear or shoulder (responsibility); burden	负担	負擔	fùdān	v.; n.	6
bear the weight of, load	承载	承載	chéngzài	v.	9
beat drums and gongs	敲锣打鼓	敲鑼打鼓	qiāoluódǎgǔ	成语	11
beautiful and elegant, graceful	优雅	優雅	yōuyǎ	adj.	1
become famous overnight	一鸣惊人	一鳴驚人	yìmíngjīngrén	成语	16
become the ruler, rule the region	称雄	稱雄	chēngxióng	v.	15

bedding, bedclothes	被褥		bèirù	n.	20
big, huge, enormous	庞大	龐大	pángdà	adj.	6
Biluochun green tea	碧螺春		Bìluóchūn	n.	17
birch	桦树	樺樹	huàshù	n.	20
bless and protect; blessings	保佑		bǎoyòu	v.; n.	11
blood is thicker than water	血浓于水	血濃於水	xuènóngyúshuǐ	成语	12
blood vessel	血管		xuèguǎn	n.	11
blow into one's face	扑面而来	撲面而來	pūmiànérlái	成语	16
blow, drift about, flutter	飘	飄	piāo	v.	14
bold and unrestrained	奔放		bēnfàng	adj.	3
born of the same parents, fellow citizen or countryman	同胞		tóngbāo	n.	15
bottom line, baseline	底线	底線	dǐxiàn	n.	14
bow (to show respect)	鞠躬		jūgōng	vo.	7
brass wind instrument, trumpet	喇叭		lǎba	n.	1
bright pink or red	红彤彤	紅彤彤	hóngtōngtōng	adj.	15
bright, new, cheery	光彩鲜亮		guāngcǎixiānliang	成语	14
brightly colored	鲜艳	鮮艷	xiānyàn	adj.	11
brilliant, splendid, wonderful	精彩		jīngcǎi	adj.	1
bring in, import, input	输入	輸入	shūrù	v.	16
browse, look over, glance over	翻阅	翻閱	fānyuè	v.	14
busy, bustling	繁忙		fánmáng	adj.	4
buttered tea	酥油茶		sūyóuchá	n.	20
call bell	呼叫铃	呼叫鈴	hūjiàolíng	n.	17
camera lens, shot, scene	镜头	鏡頭	jìngtóu	n.	15
campfire	篝火		gōuhuǒ	n.	4
cannot help (doing something)	不禁		bùjīn	adv.	2
cannot help doing	情不自禁		qíngbùzìjīn	成语	10
Cantonese steamed dumpling (a type of dimsum)	烧卖		shāomài	n.	8
capita, per person, average for individuals	人均		rénjūn	n.	16
care about, mind	在意		zàiyì	v.	12
career, profession, livelihood	生涯		shēngyá	n.	7
careless, hasty	草草		cǎocǎo	adv.	10
carrier, knowledge or information	载体	載體	zàitǐ	n.	18
carry passengers	载客	載客	zàikè	vo.	14
cases	案例		ànlì	n.	18

certain (refer to a certain person or thing)	某		mǒu	pr.	11
certainty, without a doubt, without question	毫无疑问	毫無疑問	háowúyíwèn	成语	16
chain	连锁	連鎖	liánsuǒ	v.; n.	17
chain of mountains	山峦	山巒	shānluán	n.	11
challenge; contest	挑战	挑戰	tiǎozhàn	vo.; n.	7
change; change of situation	变迁	變遷	biànqiān	v.; n.	9
cheerful sound	欢声	歡聲	huānshēng	n.	11
chess, board or card game	棋牌		qípái	n.	4
chew well and swallow slowly	细嚼慢咽	細嚼慢咽	xìjiáomànyàn	成语	5
chicken wrap	鸡肉卷	雞肉卷	jīròujuǎn	n.	17
Chinese ink, ink stick, black	墨		mò	n.	15
Chinese sausage	腊肠		làcháng	n.	8
choose, select; selection, option	选择		xuǎnzé	v.; n.	8
circle	圈		quān	v.; n.	13
classical books or records	典籍		diǎnjí	n.	12
clear, explicit	清晰		qīngxī	adj.	9
closely interrelated, closely linked	息息相关	息息相關	xīxīxiāngguān	成语	17
club	俱乐部	俱樂部	jùlèbù	n.	4
coated tongue	舌苔		shétāi	n.	2
collateral	旁系		pángxì	adj.	12
collected, could not scatter	久聚不散		jiǔjùbúsàn	pr.	15
collective team, collectivity	集体	集體	jítǐ	n.	1
companion, partner, husband or wife	伴侣	伴侶	bànlǚ	n.	12
compensate, make up for	弥补	彌補	míbǔ	v.	6
compete; contest	赛	賽	sài	v.; n.	11
complain; complaint	投诉	投訴	tóusù	v.; n.	7
completely cured or recovered (from an illness)	痊愈	痊癒	quányù	v.	2
complicated, complex	复杂	複雜	fùzá	adj.	3
concentrate one's attention, thoughts or efforts on one thing	专心致志	專心致志	zhuānxīnzhìzhì	成语	15
concept, notion	概念		gàiniàn	n.	5
cone	圆锥形	圓錐形	yuánzhuīxíng	n.	20

Confucian businessman	儒商		rúshāng	n.	15
connotation, implied meaning	内涵	內涵	nèihán	n.	9
conscientiousness and meticulousness about every detail	一丝不苟	一絲不苟	yìsībùgǒu	成语	2
constantly, continually	陆续	陸續	lùxù	adv.	20
consultant, counselor	咨询师	諮詢師	zīxúnshī	n.	7
consumer	消费者	消費者	xiāofèizhě	n.	17
contact, communicate; liaison	联络	聯絡	liánluò	v.; n.	12
contradiction	矛盾		máodùn	n.	3
control remotely; remote control	遥控		yáokòng	v.; n	8
conventional (things), conventionality	老一套		lǎoyítào	n.	1
cook, cooking; culinary art	烹饪	烹飪	pēngrèn	v.; n.	5
correct, right, proper	正确	正確	zhèngquè	adj.	2
count, compute; statistics, census	统计	統計	tǒngjì	v.; n.	20
cover up, conceal; dissimulation	掩饰	掩飾	yǎnshì	v.; n.	1
cover, encounter, suffer	蒙		méng	v.	15
cradle, origin	发祥地	發祥地	fāxiángdì	n.	15
create, produce	创造	創造	chuàngzào	v.	5
create, produce; work of literature or art	创作	創作	chuàngzuò	v.; n.	3
cross; horizontal	横	橫	héng	v.; adj.	1
cucurbit flute (or hulusi)	葫芦丝	葫蘆絲	húlusī	n.	3
culinary skill	厨艺	廚藝	chúyì	n.	5
curriculum	课程	課程	kèchéng	n.	16
customers come first	顾客至上	顧客至上	gùkèzhìshàng	成语	17
cut off	剪掉		jiǎndiào	v.	3
cut, sever	割裂		gēliè	v.	12
damage, ruin	毁掉		huǐdiào	v.	11
dare to	敢于	敢於	gǎnyú	adv.	6
dare, have courage to (do things)	敢		gǎn	v.	2
data	数据	數據	shùjù	n.	6
database	数据库	數據庫	shùjùkù	n.	6
dazzle; dazzling	耀眼		yàoyǎn	n.; adj.	15
decision-making authority	决策权	決策權	juécèquán	n.	16
deep pool, pond	潭		tán	n.	11
deep, profound	深刻		shēnkè	adj.	19
delay, hold up	耽误	耽誤	dānwù	v.	7
delete	删除	刪除	shānchú	v.	10
deposit slip, certificate of deposit	存款单	存款單	cúnkuǎndān	n.	19

depressed, downhearted	苦闷	苦悶	kǔmèn	adj.	7
describe	形容		xíngróng	v.	10
desert	沙漠		shāmò	n.	15
desilt, desilting	清淤	清淤	qīngyū	vo.	19
diagnose; diagnosis	诊断	診斷	zhěnduàn	v.; n.	2
diet	节食	節食	jiéshí	v.; n.	5
differentiate, distinguish	辨别	辨別	biànbié	v.	12
dignify, add to the prestige of	增光		zēngguāng	v.	3
diligent, hard working	勤快		qínkuài	adj.	19
disappear, vanish, dissolve	消失		xiāoshī	v.	18
discard, abandon	摒弃	摒棄	bìngqì	v.	10
disconsolate, melancholy	惆怅	惆悵	chóuchàng	adj.	18
discount, subsidized interest	贴息	貼息	tiēxī	v.; n.	20
Disney, Disneyland	迪士尼		díshìní	pn.	13
disparage, derogate	贬损	貶損	biǎnsǔn	v.	13
display, show; exhibition	展览	展覽	zhǎnlǎn	v.; n.	9
distant, remote, faraway	遥远	遙遠	yáoyuǎn	adj.	16
distribute; distribution	分布		fēnbù	v.; n.	20
disturb residents	扰民	擾民	rǎomín	vo.	3
ditch, waterway	沟	溝	gōu	n.	19
ditty, tune, minor (for music)	小调	小調	xiǎodiào	n.	19
do concurrently	兼		jiān	v.; adv.	10
do with high proficiency, handy	得心应手	得心應手	déxīnyìngshǒu	成语	10
dominate, govern; control, domination	支配		zhīpèi	v.; n.	16
double; simultaneously, concurrently	兼		jiān	v.; adv.	3
dragon robe, imperial robe	龙袍	龍袍	lóngpáo	n.	11
draw, pull, retrieve	挽		wǎn	v.	1
dream, dreamland	梦境	夢境	mèngjìng	n.	18
dress up, attire, decorate	装扮		zhuāngbàn	v.	8
drive, pilot, sail	驶	駛	shǐ	v.	15
drum set	架子鼓		jiàzigǔ	n.	3
dub; dubbing (a film, etc.)	配音		pèiyīn	vo.; n.	8
duty, obligation, responsibility	职责	職責	zhízé	n.	7
each other, one another	彼此		bǐcǐ	pr.	6
eagle	鹰	鷹	yīng	n.	11
ecology, habits, way of life	生态	生態	shēngtài	n.	20
economize, save	节省	節省	jiéshěng	v.	19

emerge in a large number, spring up	涌现	涌現	yǒngxiàn	v.	9
emotion, feeling, mood	情绪	情緒	qíngxù	n.	7
employ, hire	雇佣	雇傭	gùyōng	v.	8
empower, authorize, license	授权		shòuquán	v.	8
enchanting, attractive, fascinating	迷人		mírén	adj.	15
endure, put up with	熬		áo	v.	14
enjoy (rights, benefits, etc.); pleasure	享受		xiǎngshòu	v.; n.	16
enormous changes	翻天覆地		fāntiānfùdì	成语	19
enrich; rich, abundant	充实	充實	chōngshí	v.; adj.	12
enterprise, company	企业	企業	qǐyè	n.	7
equipment, facilities	设备	設備	shèbèi	n.	20
escape, flee, run away	逃		táo	v.	11
ethnic group, nation	民族		mínzú	n.	9
eve, on the eve of	前夕		qiánxī	n.	8
eventually, in the end, after all	终归	終歸	zhōngguī	adv.	12
excellent, outstanding	优秀	優秀	yōuxiù	adj.	1
excited and indignant	激昂		jī'áng	adj.	1
exclaim with admiration, marvel at	惊叹	驚嘆	jīngtàn	v.	2
exhale, cry out, call	呼		hū	v.	1
exhort; exhortation	叮嘱	叮囑	dīngzhǔ	v.; n.	9
eye socket, rim of the eye	眼眶		yǎnkuàng	n.	13
fall behind; out of date	落伍		luòwǔ	vo.; adj.	3
fall in love at first sight	一见钟情	一見鐘情	yíjiànzhōngqíng	成语	10
fans	粉丝	粉絲	fěnsī	n.	8
farewell to the old year and welcome to the new	辞旧迎新	辭舊迎新	cíjiùyíngxīn	成语	9
farming, agriculture	农耕	農耕	nónggēng	n.	20
fascinated by, crazy about	迷上		míshàng	v.	3
fascinated, longing	神往		shénwǎng	v.	15
fashion, vogue	时尚	時尚	shíshàng	n.	14
fat	脂肪		zhīfáng	n.	5
fatigued by a long journey	舟车劳顿		zhōuchēláodùn	成语	8
feel; experience	感受		gǎnshòu	v.; n.	19
feel (take) somebody's pulse	把脉	把脈	bǎmài	vo.	2
feeling, emotion, affection	感情		gǎnqíng	n.	10
feeling as if in paradise, "in heaven"	飘飘欲仙	飄飄欲仙	piāopiāoyùxiān	成语	4

field of vision, perspective	视野	視野	shìyě	n.	16
filled with	充满	充滿	chōngmǎn	v.	3
film, movie	片子		piànzi	n.	2
filter	筛选	篩選	shāixuǎn	v.	10
Financial Times	金融时报	金融時報	jīnróng shíbào	pn.	6
find one another congenial, hit it off perfectly	情投意合		qíngtóuyìhé	成语	10
fish; fishing	垂钓	垂釣	chuídiào	v.; n.	4
fix; regular, fixed	固定		gùdìng	v.; adj.	17
fog, mist	雾气	霧氣	wùqì	n.	15
folk custom	民俗		mínsú	n.	9
follow (an issue) closely, pay close attention to; concern	关注	關注	guānzhù	v.; n.	18
follow, pursue, admire	追捧		zhuīpěng	v.	13
following upon	随之而来	隨之而來	suízhīérlái	phr.	19
force somebody to do something; reluctant; reluctantly	勉强	勉強	miǎnqiǎng	v.; adj.; adv.	10
foreign country	异国他乡	異國他鄉	yìguótāxiāng	成语	6
foreign nationality, non-local residents	外籍		wàijí	n.	1
foreigner	老外		lǎowài	n.	19
forum, tribune, place to express oneself in public	论坛		lùntán	n.	8
foster, raise, bring up	抚养	撫養	fǔyǎng	v.; n.	19
fry and deep fry (cooking method)	煎炸		jiānzhá	v.	5
full time	全职	全職	quánzhí	n.; adj.	4
fungus	菌类	菌類	jūnlèi	n.	5
garbage, junk, trash	垃圾		lājī	n.	19
gather sb/sth round	扎堆		zhāduī	vo.	1
general reference	泛指		fànzhǐ	v.; n.	16
geography	地理		dìlǐ	n.	11
get along well with others; gregarious	合群		héqún	vo.; adj.	1
girl, daughter	闺女	閨女	guīnü	n.	19
give aid to, support, hold up	扶持		fúchí	v.; n.	20
glance	侧目	側目	cèmù	vo.	3
globalize; globalization	全球化		quánqiúhuà	v.; n.	1
go as planned regardless of the weather	风雨无阻	風雨無阻	fēngyǔwúzǔ	成语	4
go far gradually, get apart gradually	渐行渐远	漸行漸遠	jiànxíngjiànyuǎn	成语	10
go over, travel across	走遍		zǒubiàn	v.	20

go to, attend	赴		fù	v.	13
grant a loan, provide a loan; loan, credit	贷款	貸款	dàikuǎn	v.; n.	20
grasp; mastery	掌握		zhǎngwò	v.; n.	5
guide, coach; guidance, coaching	辅导	輔導	fǔdǎo	v; n.	3
guilty feeling	罪恶感	罪惡感	zuì'ègǎn	n.	10
handle, deal with; disposal	处理	處理	chǔlǐ	v.; n.	6
happiness, blessedness; happy, blessed	幸福		xìngfú	n.; adj.	17
harden, stiffen	硬质化	硬質化	yìngzhìhuà	v.; adj.	19
harvest	丰收	豐收	fēngshōu	n.	11
have a leisure time activity; leisure	休闲	休閑	xiūxián	v.; adj.	4
have an antique flavor, classic beauty	古色古香		gǔsègǔxiāng	成语	14
have an interview with; interview	采访	採訪	cǎifǎng	v.; n.	9
having low self-esteem	自卑		zìbēi	adj.	4
head, chief, leader; first, foremost, first of all	首		shǒu	n.; adj.	14
height above sea level, elevation	海拔		hǎibá	n.	15
help, support; assistance	援助		yuánzhù	v.; n.	12
hepatitis	肝炎		gānyán	n.	2
hide, avoid	躲避		duǒbì	v.	11
hide, conceal, keep out of sight	隐藏	隱藏	yǐncáng	v.	10
hide, conceal, store away	藏		cáng	v.	13
high buildings and large mansions	高楼大厦	高樓大廈	gāolóudàshà	成语	18
hills, mounds	丘陵		qiūlíng	n.	15
hinder, hamper, obstruct	妨碍	妨礙	fáng'ài	v.; n.	18
hold a memorial ceremony for	祭奠		jìdiàn	v.; n.	9
hold up, sustain, support	支撑	支撐	zhīchēng	v.	13
honest and pure	纯朴	純樸	chúnpǔ	adj.	20
honor, glory; honorable, glorious	光荣	光榮	guāngróng	n.; adj.	9
human feelings, human kindness	人情味		rénqíngwèi	n.	14
human resources department	人力资源部	人力資源部	rénlìzīyuánbù	n.	7
hunt, go hunting; hunt, hunting	狩猎	狩獵	shòuliè	v.; n.	20

idea	理念		lǐniàn	n.	5
ignore, neglect	忽略		hūlüè	v.	6
ignore, neglect, overlook	忽视	忽視	hūshì	v.	15
image	形象		xíngxiàng	n.	11
immediate (family members)	直系		zhíxì	adj.	12
imperceptibly influence, influence unconsciously	潜移默化	潛移默化	qiányímòhuà	成语	13
imposing manner; dignified	气派	氣派	qìpài	n.; adj.	2
improvement, sign of recovery	起色		qǐsè	n.	10
in a flash, a very short time, in the twinkling of an eye	一刹那	一刹那	yíchànà	phr.	13
in groups, in crowds	成群结队	成群結隊	chéngqúnjiéduì	成语	14
in succession, one after another	相继	相繼	xiāngjì	adv.	20
in tune	搭调	搭調	dādiào	adj.	17
incomplete (with parts missing)	残缺	殘缺	cánquē	v.	3
individuality	个体	個體	gètǐ	n.	1
induction, response, reaction	感应	感應	gǎnyìng	n.	17
industry, estate, property	产业	產業	chǎnyè	n.	18
inevitability; inevitably	必然		bìrán	n.; adv.	3
injure, damage; incomplete	残	殘	cán	v.; adj.	20
inland, interior	内地	內地	nèidì	n.	20
inn, tavern	客栈	客棧	kèzhàn	n.	15
integrate; integration	一体化	一體化	yìtǐhuà	v.; n.	16
international corporation	跨国公司	跨國公司	kuàguógōngsī	n.	7
interviewer	面试官	面試官	miànshìguān	n.	7
intricate, precise about details	细致	細緻	xìzhì	adj.	2
introduce to	导入	導入	dǎorù	vc.	1
intrude into, suddenly get in	闯进	闖進	chuǎngjìn	v.	4
invitation card, written invitation	请柬	請柬	qǐngjiǎn	n.	13
invite (someone to a banquet)	宴请	宴請	yànqǐng	v.	9
invite applications, give public notice of vacancies to be filled	招聘		zhāopìn	v.	7
(it) is not so; otherwise	不然		bùrán	v.; conj.	12

issue, distribute	发行	發行	fāxíng	v.	20
it goes without saying, it is self-evident	不言而喻		bùyán'éryù	成语	13
job applicant	应聘者	應聘者	yìngpìnzhě	n.	7
judging by; basis	依据	依據	yījù	v.; n.	6
just as before, in the past or as always	一如既往		yírújìwǎng	成语	12
just right, just enough, happen to	正好		zhènghǎo	adv.	12
keep in good health, care for life	养生	養生	yǎngshēng	v.	5
keep off, block off	挡	擋	dǎng	v.	14
keep to the house, stay home	足不出户		zúbùchūhù	成语	10
Kennedy (Harvard John F. Kennedy School of Government)	肯尼迪		Kěnnídí	pn.	18
Kentucky Fried Chicken	肯德基		Kěndéjī	pn.	17
key	钥匙	鑰匙	yàoshi	n.	15
key point, crucial importance	关键	關鍵	guānjiàn	n.	11
killed, die in an accident	遇难	遇難	yùnàn	vo.	11
kind, pattern, type	款		kuǎn	m.	17
kind, sort, for counting occurrences	番		fān	m.	7
kindergarten, nursery	幼儿园	幼兒園	yòuéryuán	n.	1
kiss, give a kiss	接吻		jiēwěn	vo.	1
kite	风筝	風箏	fēngzhēng	n.	9
knit, weave	织	織	zhī	v.	13
known to all	众所周知	眾所周知	zhòngsuǒzhōuzhī	成语	4
lane, alley, bystreet	胡同	衚衕	hútòng	n.	18
late at night	半夜三更		bànyèsāngēng	成语	13
latent capability, potential, potentiality	潜力	潛力	qiánlì	n.	17
lay off employees	裁员	裁員	cáiyuán	vo.	7
lead along	牵	牽	qiān	v.	13
leave comments, leave a message; message	留言		liúyán	vo.; n.	8
leave home to make a living	闯荡	闖蕩	chuǎngdàng	v.	13
legacy, inheritance, heritage	遗产	遺產	yíchǎn	n.	20
level (of knowledge); levels	层次	層次	céngcì	n.	19
lift, raise	抬		tái	v.	13

lift, surge	掀起		xiānqǐ	v.	3
limpid, crystal clear	清澈		qīngchè	adj.	19
line up, form into lines	列队	列隊	lièduì	vo.	1
listen attentively to	倾听	傾聽	qīngtīng	v.	17
located, situated	位于	位於	wèiyú	vc.	15
long, deep-fried, twisted dough sticks	油条	油條	yóutiáo	n.	17
look at carefully, examine	审视	審視	shěnshì	v.	6
lose a battle or war, be defeated	战败	戰敗	zhànbài	v.	11
lose; loss	损失	損失	sǔnshī	v.; n.	17
love and respect like before	恩爱如初	恩愛如初	ēn'àirúchū	成语	10
magical	神奇		shénqí	adj.	2
mahjong	麻将	麻將	májiàng	n.	4
maintain, keep, support	维持	維持	wéichí	v.	10
make a sudden attack, make a concentrated effort	突击	突擊	tūjī	v.	3
make policy; policy decision	决策	決策	juécè	v.; n.	6
make up one's mind	下决心	下決心	xiàjuéxīn	vo.	10
make a wry smile; forced smile	苦笑		kǔxiào	v.; n.	2
manage, run; operation	经营	經營	jīngyíng	v.; n.	4
mark, print	印迹	印跡	yìnjì	n.	18
marketing	营销	營銷	yíngxiāo	n.	7
marriage is arranged	婚姻包办	婚姻包辦	hūnyīnbāobàn	phr.	10
(a man) marry to (a woman), take a wife	娶		qǔ	v.	19
(a woman) marry to (a man)	嫁		jià	v.	19
massage	按摩		ànmó	v.; n.	4
master and apprentice	师徒	師徒	shītú	n.	15
mean; meaning	意味		yìwèi	v.; n.	5
means, method	手段		shǒuduàn	n.	4
measure word (for building, houses)	栋	棟	dòng	m.	20
mediate, reconcile	排解		páijiě	v.; n.	14
meet	相遇		xiāngyù	v.	10
methods to gain money	生财之道	生財之道	shēngcáizhīdào	成语	20
microblog	微博		wēibó	n.	8
Ming and Qing Dynasties	明清		míngqīng	n.	15
missionary	传教士	傳教士	chuánjiàoshì	n.	11
mist; misty	迷蒙	迷濛	míméng	n.; adj.	15

misunderstand; misunderstanding	误会	誤會	wùhuì	v.; n.	5
mix together, fuse, merge	融合		rónghé	v.; n.	11
model, pattern	模式		móshì	n.	18
monologize; monolog	独白		dúbái	v.; n.	8
morning sunlight, first rays of the morning sun	晨曦		chénxī	n.	15
(computer) mouse	鼠标	鼠標	shǔbiāo	n.	16
moving, charming	动人	動人	dòngrén	adj.	10
muddled	懵		měng	adj.	5
music instrument company	琴行		qínháng	n.	3
namely	即		jí	adv.	18
nationality, class or group of things or people with common features	族		zú	n.	8
negate; negation	否定		fǒudìng	v.; n.	16
negative, passive, dispirited	消极	消極	xiāojí	adj.	7
nervous, intense	紧张	緊張	jǐnzhāng	adj.	7
network	网络	網絡	wǎngluò	n.	8
never seen or heard again (like a stone dropped into the sea)	石沉大海		shíchéndàhǎi	成语	7
new and developing, rising, newly developing	新兴	新興	xīnxīng	adj.	20
news media	媒体	媒體	méitǐ	n.	13
no other choice	别无选择	別無選擇	biéwúxuǎnzé	成语	13
notice, find out, discover; discovery	发现	發現	fāxiàn	v.; n.	1
nutrition	营养	營養	yíngyǎng	n.	5
objective, target, goal	目标	目標	mùbiāo	n.	16
obstacle, obstruction, barrier	障碍	障礙	zhàng'ài	n.	16
obtain, acquire	获得	獲得	huòdé	v.	11
occupy, take	占	佔	zhàn	v.	16
offer sacrifice to gods, worship	祭神		jìshén	vo.; n.	11
official, of the government	官方		guānfāng	n.	20
old, outdated, old fashioned	陈旧	陳舊	chénjiù	adj.	12
one can well imagine	可想而知		kěxiǎng'érzhī	成语	10

one-tenth, percentage	成		chéng	m	16
original, firsthand, primitive	原始		yuánshǐ	adj.	20
originate; origin, source	来源	來源	láiyuán	v.; n.	5
orthopedics	骨科		gǔkē	n.	2
outcome; actually, after all	究竟		jiūjìng	n.; adv.	12
overjoyed, happy beyond expectations	喜出望外		xǐchūwàngwài	成语	2
pack	打包		dǎbāo	v.	13
packed to capacity, full house	座无虚席	座無虛席	zuòwúxūxí	成语	4
palm leaf fan	芭蕉扇		bājiāoshàn	n.	15
participate in, take part in, be a part of	参与	參與	cānyù	v.	16
pass a test or examination; a pass grade	及格		jígé	v.; n.	1
pass from mouth to mouth; legend	传说	傳說	chuánshuō	v.; n.	11
pass out; dizzy	晕	暈	yūn	v.; adj.	2
pass through; by means of	通过	通過	tōngguò	v.; prep.	8
pedal	花瓣		huābàn	n.	9
People's Democratic Republic of Algeria	阿尔及利亚	阿爾及利亞	Āěrjílìyà	pn.	6
permeate, infiltrate; infiltration	渗透	滲透	shèntòu	v.; n.	13
persist in; persistence	坚持	堅持	jiānchí	v.; n.	4
personal (experience/ understanding)	切身		qièshēn	adj.	19
photographer, cameraman	摄影师	攝影師	shèyǐngshī	n.	15
pick, choose, select	挑选	挑選	tiāoxuǎn	v.	1
pickled vegetables	咸菜	鹹菜	xiáncài	n.	13
pile up; pile	堆		duī	v.; m. n.	13
place (one's hope, feeling, etc.) on	寄托	寄託	jìtuō	v.	9
play mahjong or cards	打牌		dǎpái	vo.	12
play, play with	耍		shuǎ	v.; n.	4
plot, plan	策划		cèhuà	v.	8
pocket money	零花钱	零花錢	línghuāqián	n.	16
pool, pond	塘		táng	n.	19
pool money	凑钱	湊錢	còuqián	vo.	3
popularity, fame	知名度		zhīmíngdù	n.	13
(website) portals	门户网站	門戶網站	ménhùwǎngzhàn	pn.	16
portrait	肖像		xiāoxiàng	n.	3

post (a thread, message, advertisement)	发帖		fātiě	vo.	8
post, position	岗位	崗位	gǎngwèi	n.	7
poster	海报	海報	hǎibào	n.	3
postpone, put off, delay, extension	延期		yánqī	v.	13
potato	土豆		tǔdòu	n.	20
pound, assault, impact, affect	冲击	衝擊	chōngjī	v.; n.	14
pre-examine; initial inspection	预检	預檢	yùjiǎn	v.; n.	2
prefecture and county system	郡县	郡縣	jùnxiàn	n.	15
prepare, arrange, plan	筹备		chóubèi	v.	8
prescription	处方	處方	chǔfāng	n.	2
press (with the hand); according to, in accordance with	按		àn	v.; prep.	2
prestige, credit, reputation	信誉	信譽	xìnyù	n.	13
primeval ecology	原生态		yuánshēngtài	n.	20
professional killer, hitman	杀手	殺手	shāshǒu	n.	5
progress in proper order; sequencially	依次		yīcì	v.; adv.	1
prohibit	禁止		jìnzhǐ	v.	5
prohibit by explicit order	明令禁止		mínglìngjìnzhǐ	成语	1
propagate, broadcast	传播	傳播	chuánbō	v.	17
propagate, disseminate; propaganda	宣传		xuānchuán	v.; n.	8
propose, suggest; suggestion	建议	建議	jiànyì	v.; n.	9
protect (life, property, rights, etc.) from damage or violation; guarantee	保障		bǎozhàng	v.; n.	19
protein	蛋白质	蛋白質	dànbáizhì	n.	5
Provence (France)	普罗旺斯	普羅旺斯	Pǔluówàngsī	pn.	15
prudent, careful, cautious	谨慎	謹慎	jǐnshèn	adj.	16
pull out, dig	掏		tāo	v.	4
pulse	脉	脈	mài	n.	11
Pumi minority	普米族		Pǔmǐzú	pn.	11
pure, genuine	纯正	純正	chúnzhèng	adj.	16
pure; purely	纯	純	chún	adj.; adv.	9
put, place	摆	擺	bǎi	v.	4
Qin dynasty (221–206 BC)	秦		qín	n.	15
questionnaire, survey	调查问卷	調查問卷	diàocháwènjuàn	n.	17

quick, sharp (eyes), acute (sense)	敏锐	敏銳	mǐnruì	adj.	20
radio play	广播剧		guǎngbōjù	n.	8
rapid, prompt	迅速		xùnsù	adj.	3
reach, attain, amount to	达	達	dá	v.	20
react, respond; reaction	反应	反應	fǎnyìng	v.; n.	7
read, look up	查阅	查閱	cháyuè	v.	9
real estate	房地产	房地產	fángdìchǎn	n.	18
realize suddenly, be enlightened	醍醐灌顶	醍醐灌頂	tíhúguàndǐng	成语	12
recommend; recommendation	推荐	推薦	tuījiàn	v.; n.	1
recover, restore	恢复	恢復	huīfù	v.	6
reddish brown	赭红		zhěhóng	n.	15
reexamine; reexamining	复查	復查	fùchá	v.; n.	2
reflect	反映		fǎnyìng	v.	4
refuse; rejection	拒绝	拒絕	jùjué	v.; n.	9
register at a hospital	挂号	掛號	guàhào	vo.	2
reject, exclude	排斥		páichì	v.	4
related, interrelated	相关	相關	xiāngguān	adj.	6
relatives, kinship	亲属	親屬	qīnshǔ	n.	12
religion	宗教		zōngjiào	n.	12
rely on, depend on	凭	憑	píng	v.	10
remain married until old age	白头偕老	白頭偕老	báitóuxiélǎo	成语	10
renowned, famous	驰名	馳名	chímíng	adj.	4
report (an offender), lodge an accusation against	告发	告發	gàofā	v.	3
respect, honor; honorable	尊敬		zūnjìng	v.; adj.	16
retire	退休		tuìxiū	v.	4
return from oversea; returnees	海归	海歸	hǎiguī	v.; n.	6
return to original place; regression	回归	回歸	huíguī	v.; n.	3
revolt against; rebel	叛逆		pànnì	v.; n.	16
rhythm	节奏	節奏	jiézòu	n.	3
rich and thick, rich and generous	丰厚	豐厚	fēnghòu	adj.	15
rich and varied, rich and colorful	丰富多彩	豐富多彩	fēngfùduōcǎi	成语	17
rich, greasy	肥腻	肥膩	féinì	adj.	5
ride, going out for a drive	兜风	兜風	dōufēng	v.; n.	13
ridge (of a mountain or hill)	山梁		shānliáng	n.	11
rights and interests	权益	權益	quányì	n.	17
rigorous, strict, precise	严谨	嚴謹	yánjǐn	adj.	7

rise abruptly, rise as a political force	崛起		juéqǐ	v.	18
rise and fall; rising and falling	起伏		qǐfú	v.; adj.	11
risk, danger	风险	風險	fēngxiǎn	n.	6
roar, growl, shout	吼		hǒu	v.	3
rock and roll music	摇滚乐	搖滾樂	yáogǔnyuè	pn.	3
romantic	浪漫		làngmàn	adj.	10
rooted in	扎根		zhāgēn	vo.	13
rotate, do sth in turn, take turns, alternate	轮流	輪流	lúnliú	v.	19
rules, regulations	纪律	紀律	jìlǜ	n.	4
run into, bump into	碰到		pèngdào	v.	3
satisfy; satisfaction	满意	滿意	mǎnyì	v.; n.	2
say as an aside; aside (in a play)	旁白		pángbái	v.; n.	8
say to each other, greet each other	互道		hùdào	v.	20
scale new heights, attain a yet higher goal	更上一层楼	更上一層樓	gèngshàngyìcénglóu	成语	17
scared, frighten	吓坏	嚇壞	xiàhuài	v.	5
school district	学区	學區	xuéqū	n.	1
screen	屏幕		píngmù	n.	16
screen wall	影壁		yǐngbì	n.	18
search engine	搜索引擎		sōusuǒyǐnqíng	pn.	16
seat cushion	座垫	座墊	zuòdiàn	n.	4
secret (of success)	秘诀	秘訣	mìjué	n.	10
section, part	段		duàn	m. n.	12
seemingly, as if	仿佛	仿佛	fǎngfú	adv.	15
seize, grasp, take (into one's arms)	揽	攬	lǎn	v.	4
self-agreement, self-identification	自我认同	自我認同	zìwǒrèntóng	成语	16
self-run, self-support	自营	自營	zìyíng	v.	18
senior	资深	資深	zīshēn	adj.	3
sense of satiety	饱腹感	飽腹感	bǎofùgǎn	n.	5
separate oneself from, away from, out of	脱离	脫離	tuōlí	v.	12
separate, cut off, impede, be at a distance from	隔		gé	v.	16
shadow	阴影	陰影	yīnyǐng	n.	7
shake (the air), shock	震天		zhèntiān	vo.	11
shake, shock, vibrate	震动	震動	zhèndòng	v.	17
shaman, monk	僧人		sēngrén	n.	9
shape of a face, face	脸庞	臉龐	liǎnpáng	n.	15
share	分享		fēnxiǎng	v.	8

share the same ideals and thoughts	志同道合		zhìtóngdàohé	成语	15
show forebearing; tolerant	宽容	寬容	kuānróng	v.; adj.	10
shut up, blot out	遮住		zhēzhù	v.	1
silly things	傻事		shǎshì	n.	13
sink into, get caught up in	陷入		xiànrù	v.	4
sit-ups	仰卧起坐	仰臥起坐	yǎngwòqǐzuò	phr.	4
skyscraper	摩天大楼	摩天大樓	mótiāndàlóu	n.	18
slope	斜坡		xiépō	n.	13
snow capped	白雪皑皑	白雪皚皚	báixuě áiái	phr.	15
soak, immerse	泡		pào	v.	4
social contact, social life	社交		shèjiāo	n.	8
socialize with; social engagement	应酬	應酬	yìngchou	v.; n.	13
soon, upcoming	即将	即將	jíjiāng	adv.	12
sorrow; sad, sorrowful	悲伤	悲傷	bēishāng	n.; adj.	9
sorry, regret	抱歉		bàoqiàn	n.	7
source of happiness	幸福之源		xìngfúzhīyuán	phr.	10
soymilk	豆浆	豆漿	dòujiāng	n.	17
spare one's life	饶命	饒命	ráomìng	vo.	2
spareribs, steak, rib	排骨		páigǔ	n.	20
special, particular, exceptional	特殊		tèshū	adj.	6
spectacular sight, wonderful and mighty panorama	气象万千	氣象萬千	qìxiàngwànqiān	成语	15
spin, rotate	打转	打轉	dǎzhuàn	v.	13
spiritual outlook	精神面貌		jīngshénmiànmào	phr.	19
stage, phase, period	阶段	階段	jiēduàn	n.	6
staircase, steps	台阶	臺階	táijiē	n.	18
stand by anxiously	干瞪眼		gāndèngyǎn	ci	3
standard, norm, criteria	标准	標準	biāozhǔn	n.	4
Starbucks	星巴克		Xīngbākè	pn.	17
stare at, glare with displeasure	瞪		dèng	v.	13
stew slowly, braise	炖	燉	dùn	v.	20
still, as before	依然		yīrán	adv.	4
still, yet	仍然		réngrán	adv.	3
stone lions	石狮	石獅	shíshī	n.	18
stop work for the day	收工		shōugōng	vo.	13
street stall	地摊	地攤	dìtān	n.	13
strictly enforce; serious (attitude), solemn	严肃	嚴肅	yánsù	v.; adj.	7
string (of a musical instrument)	弦		xián	n.	3
strong, powerful, intense	强烈	強烈	qiángliè	adj.	10

structure	结构	結構	jiégòu	n.	2
style and features, manner	风貌	風貌	fēngmào	n.	18
suburb, outskirts	郊区	郊區	jiāoqū	n.	4
suddenly enlightened	茅塞顿开	茅塞頓開	máosèdùnkāi	成语	7
sum of people participating, visitor count	人次		réncì	cm.	20
sun	太阳	太陽	tàiyáng	n.	15
sunglasses	墨镜	墨鏡	mòjìng	n.	13
superior, advantageous	优越	優越	yōuyuè	adj.	16
supersede; alternately	交替		jiāotì	v.; adv.	1
supervisor, superintendent	监督员	監督員	jiāndūyuán	n.	17
support gently by the hand or arm	搀扶	攙扶	chānfú	v.	2
supporting pillow	靠枕		kàozhěn	n.	4
surrounding feeling, atmosphere	气氛		qìfēn	n.	8
sweep a grave, pay respect to the dead people	扫墓	掃墓	sǎomù	vo.	9
sweethearts, lovers	情侣	情侣	qínglǚ	n.	1
swing	秋千	鞦韆	qiūqiān	n.	9
symbolize, indicate; sign, mark, symbol	标志	標誌	biāozhì	v.; n.	14
symbolize, signify, stand for; symbol	象征		xiàngzhēng	v.; n.	8
synthesize; synthesis	综合	綜合	zōnghé	v.; n.	11
system, organization	体制	體制	tǐzhì	n.	1
tacit understanding	默契		mòqì	n.	10
take (an X-ray examination)	拍		pāi	v.	2
take disciplinary action against, punish; punishment	处分	處分	chǔfèn	v.; n	1
take for granted; it goes without saying	理所当然	理所當然	lǐsuǒdāngrán	成语	1
take medicine	服药	服藥	fúyào	vo.	2
take pride in oneself	自豪		zìháo	v.	8
take the same action or view without prior consultation	不约而同	不約而同	bùyuē'értóng	成语	2
take turns; round	轮	輪	lún	v.; m.; n.	2
taste, try	尝	嘗	cháng	v.	3
test; testing	测试	測試	cèshì	v.; n.	7
this life	这辈子	這輩子	zhèbèizi	n.	10
thought, idea, intention	念头	念頭	niàntou	n.	10

thousands of families and households	千家万户	千家萬戶	qiānjiāwànhù	成语	8
through the night, overnight	通宵		tōngxiāo	n.	14
Tibetan minority group	藏族		Zàngzú	pn.	20
tide, current, trend	潮		cháo	n.	6
time, beat, tempo	节拍	節拍	jiépāi	n.	1
topple over, greatly admire	倾倒	傾倒	qīngdǎo	v.	16
totem	图腾	圖騰	túténg	n.	11
tragedy	悲剧	悲劇	bēijù	n.	13
train; training	培训	培訓	péixùn	v.; n.	20
travel to hunt; hunting trip	游猎	游獵	yóuliè	v.; n.	20
treat coldly; deserted, desolate	冷落		lěngluò	v.; adj.	17
tree shade	林荫	林蔭	línyīn	n.	4
tremble, shiver	打哆嗦		dǎduōsuō	vo.	15
tribe	部落		bùluò	n.	11
tug-of-war (a Chinese sports game)	拔河		báhé	v.; n.	9
Turfan Basin in Xinjiang Province, China	吐鲁番	吐魯番	Tǔlǔfān	pn.	15
turn round, twist, sprain	扭		niǔ	v.	2
turtleneck, pullover	套头	套頭	tàotóu	adj.	13
twinkle, brilliant, shiny	闪亮	閃亮	shǎnliàng	adj.	10
ultimate, final	最终	最終	zuìzhōng	n.	7
unchanged, unchangeable	一成不变	一成不變	yìchéngbúbiàn	成语	16
undertake	承担	承擔	chéngdān	v.	16
unemployed person	失业者	失業者	shīyèzhě	n.	7
unexpectedly, to one's surprise	竟然		jìngrán	adv.	2
unexpectedly, to one's surprise	居然		jūrán	adv.	5
unimpeded, unblocked	畅通	暢通	chàngtōng	adj.	16
uninterruptedly, continuously, constantly	不断	不斷	búduàn	adv.	1
universal, general	普遍		pǔbiàn	adj.	4
University of Nottingham	诺丁汉大学	諾丁漢大學	Nuòdīnghàndàxué	pn.	6
unobstructed, easy and smooth	通畅	通暢	tōngchàng	adj.	19
unreasoning passion; be infatuated	痴情		chīqíng	n.; adj.	13
uphold, advocate	崇尚		chóngshàng	v.	12

vacillate, wave, shake	动摇	動搖	dòngyáo	v.	10
values	价值观	價值觀	jiàzhíguān	n.	6
varied and colorful	多姿多彩		duōzīduōcǎi	成语	14
vary with each individual, different from person to person	因人而异	因人而異	yīnrén'éryì	成语	5
vast territory with rich resources	地大物博		dìdàwùbó	成语	15
veil	面纱	面紗	miànshā	n.	15
very long	已久		yǐjiǔ	adj.	15
video	视频	視頻	shìpín	n.	9
vigorous, exuberant, robust	旺盛		wàngshèng	adj.	16
village committee	村委会	村委會	cūnwěihuì	n.	18
village official	村官		cūnguān	n.	19
village, town	村落		cūnluò	n.	15
village, town	庄	莊	zhuāng	n.	18
virtual, fictitious	虚拟	虛擬	xūnǐ	adj.	8
vocabulary entry, lexical item	词条	詞條	cítiáo	n.	20
volunteer to do something; wish, will	志愿	志願	zhìyuàn	v.; n.	1
walk about, (of relatives and friends) visit each other	走动	走動	zǒudòng	v.	12
wallpaper	墙纸		qiángzhǐ	n.	8
Wal-Mart	沃尔玛		Wòěrmǎ	pn.	17
wander, scatter, drift	流散		liúsàn	v.	20
war	战争	戰爭	zhànzhēng	n.	11
warm, cozy	温馨	溫馨	wēnxīn	adj.	14
warn; warning	警告		jǐnggào	v.; n.	1
weaken; weak, feeble, young	弱		ruò	v.; adj.	20
well	井		jǐng	n.	11
well-to-do, be comfortably off, plenty	宽裕	寬裕	kuānyù	adj.	19
well-to-do, well off, rich and prosperous	富裕		fùyù	adj.	19
western regions in ancient China	西域		xīyù	n.	15
wet mud	泥		ní	n.	19
Wharton School of the University of Pennsylvania	沃顿商学院	沃頓商學院	Wòdùnshāng xuéyuàn	pn.	6
whether or not, is it so or not	是否		shìfǒu	adv.	13
white collar	白领		báilǐng	n.	8
wipe out, scrub off	擦掉		cādiào	v.	12

wisdom comes from extensive observation	见多识广	見多識廣	jiànduōshíguǎng	成语	20
with tears, in tears	含泪	含淚	hánlèi	vo.	12
wonder, spectacle, spectacular sight	奇观	奇觀	qíguān	n.	15
wonton	馄饨	餛飩	húntun	n.	4
work from nine to five every day	朝九晚五		zhāojiǔwǎnwǔ	成语	13
worry, concern; anxiety	忧虑	憂慮	yōulù	v.; n.	15
worry; sorrow	愁		chóu	v.; n.	19
worship	崇拜		chóngbài	v.; n.	11
wound; injury; wounded	伤	傷	shāng	v.; n.; adj.	20
wrap up; bag, sack	兜		dōu	v.; n.	13
wrinkle, furrow, lines (facial)	皱纹	皺紋	zhòuwén	n.	20
write a play; playwright, screenwriter	编剧		biānjù	vo.; n.	8
Xinjiang Province, China	新疆		Xīnjiāng	pn.	15
yoga	瑜伽		yújiā	n.	4
Zhengzhou (capital of Henan Province, China)	郑州	鄭州	Zhèngzhōu	pn.	6